Introduction to
MATHEMATICAL TECHNIQUES
IN PATTERN RECOGNITION

Introduction to
MATHEMATICAL TECHNIQUES IN PATTERN RECOGNITION

Harry C. Andrews
Department of Electrical Engineering
University of Southern California
Los Angeles, California

WILEY-INTERSCIENCE
a division of John Wiley & Sons, Inc.
New York   London   Sydney   Toronto

Library of Congress Cataloging in Publication Data
Andrews, Harry C.

Introduction to mathematical techniques in pattern recognition.

Includes bibliographies.
1. Pattern perception. I. Title.

Q327.A54   001.53'4   72-772
ISBN 0-471-03172-0

Printed in the United States of America

10 9 8 7 6 5 4 3 2 1

TO MY WIFE AND TO MY MOTHER

PREFACE

This textbook is an introductory subject into the application of mathematical techniques to pattern recognition problems. The world is full of pattern recognition experts (every human being), but few if any can accurately describe the processes by which they successfully classify patterns. Worse still, little is known about phenomena which occur but which are too grandiose or too complex for even a human to perceive and untangle. The art of pattern recognition has evolved over many centuries, the science of pattern recognition is still in its infancy. During the past 20 years researchers have attempted to shed light on that science with varying degrees of success. The results of their research can be loosely cataloged into three classes: heuristic, structural or linguistic, and mathematical. This text is concerned with the latter phase of pattern recognition, that of utilizing the vehicle of mathematics in an attempt at quantifying certain aspects of an art which has proven exceedingly complex to unravel. It is important to emphasize that no claims to new material or research results are made here but considerable appreciation must be expressed to those authors whose works are represented here. However, the virtue in not presenting new research results lies in the potential for objective evaluation of others' work, which is so important in an introductory text.

The text is designed as an introductory book to mathematical pattern recognition. Thus some background in vector spaces or higher dimensional geometry, probability theory, and undergraduate mathematics is assumed. The text is intended for a senior level or first year graduate course in the curriculums of computer science, mathematics, and engineering departments, and is the outgrowth of a one-year sequence of two semester courses taught in the first year graduate program of a computer science-engineering series.

vii

The author feels that the "science" of mathematical pattern recognition has evolved to a point where such a course is justified. Unfortunately, while the literature is full of reports on the subject, nowhere does there seem to be a complete and unified description of the variety of mathematical techniques available. In fact notational differences and a wide spectrum of levels of presentation make it quite difficult for the beginning student of pattern recognition to understand the literature. Therefore it is the intention of this text to provide a means of introduction to the subject so that those interested readers can then pursue further literature investigations with a minimal of wasted effort.

The text is outlined into six chapters: mathematical pattern recognition, feature extraction, distribution free classification, statistical classification, nonsupervised learning, and sequential learning. The author has used the material of Chapters 1, 3, and 4 in the first semester and Chapters 2, 5, and 6 in the second. It will be noted that this sequence leaves Chapter 2, feature extraction, in an unusual position. This is because the major breakthroughs necessary in mathematical pattern recognition must occur in feature extraction which currently is still in its embryonic stage. However, by placing Chapter 2 in its present position a more complete concept of the pattern recognition task is developed.

The structure of each chapter is such that a minimal of surveying and referencing to other material is made in order that continuity is preserved. However, at the end of each chapter there is included an extensive list of related bibliography for that particular subject matter for the interested reader. In addition, at the chapter's end problems are included for testing comprehension of the material and they range from quite elementary to those that require computer solution. The problems are designed to emphasize basic concepts rather than obscure notions.

I am indebted to many people for their help and encouragement throughout the development of this text. Particular acknowledgment must go to Dr. William S. Meisel who initially interested me in this subject and with whom I have had numerous fruitful discussions. I would like to thank Dr. Zorhab Kaprielian, Dr. Jack Munushian, and Dr. George Bekey for providing a university atmosphere in which such a project could be undertaken and for their particular encouragement of my research interests. A great deal of appreciation must be given those students who so painfully suffered through the genesis and smoothing of both the text and problems and whose solutions future readers can be thankful for. Of course it goes without stating that all such projects would come to a rapid halt without the expert technical typing support provided by the technical typing pool and especially Mrs. Kristin Behnke within the Electrical Engineering Department. Finally, I owe a tremendous debt of appreciation to my wife, Beth, without whose patience, support, and motivation this project would never have been undertaken, much less completed.

Los Angeles   *Harry C. Andrews*

CONTENTS

APPENDICES

A   MULTIDIMENSIONAL ROTATIONS IN FEATURE SELECTION 211

B   A RATE DISTORTION CRITERION FOR FEATURE SELECTION . . . 225

MATHEMATICAL PATTERN RECOGNITION

1.0 Introduction

The subject of pattern recognition has a controversial background possibly perpetuated by the expectation of the development of machines with human-like performance due to the advent of high speed digital computers. Initially the subject of pattern recognition included any attempt at developing descriptions (models) of phenomena which in some way mimicked man. This included research in the areas of artificial intelligence, interactive graphic computers, computer aided design, psychological and biological pattern recognition, linguistic and structural pattern recognition, and a variety of other research topics. While this is not the place to describe the results of this research, let it suffice to state that the subject of mathematical pattern recognition has evolved by contributions from all of these fields. However, more importantly, through the vehicle of mathematics, the results of research in one area of pattern recognition can be related to other areas. Unfortunately this is not true for nonmathematical pattern recognition. Thus the heuristic computer algorithm which feature selects chromosomal abnormalities according to a physician's experience will have little use for the selection of wheat fields from a photointerpretation viewpoint. However, had some mathematical principle been utilized to find pertinent chromosome features, that same principle could possibly be attempted in the wheat field problem. An alternative approach, that of developing a structural or linguistic approach to pattern recognition, provides a context-free environment where primitive elements or building blocks can be described as elementary particles which make up a pattern. Thus a tree structure develops which can then be stored and compared with unknowns for future recognition. Unfortunately, the linguistic or structural technique often suffers from noise, a phenomenon in whose presence man has effectively learned to live. Figure 1.1 presents an example of this particular failing where the letter "H" is described as two vertical lines connected at their midpoints by a horizontal line. However, the "H" in Figure 1.1b would not be recognized because of the lack

(a) A context free "H"

(b)   An unrecognizable "H"

FIGURE I.I.   Structural pattern recognition.

of connections at the endpoints of the horizontal line. Thus it seems logical that some combination of a structural algorithm with mathematical or higher dimensional geometry pattern recognition will lead to useful results. Again because of space limitations only the mathematical aspect of the pattern recognition problem will be treated here.

What is desired is a unifying theory which will allow the partial generalized solutions of some problems to be carried over to other areas. Thus, the results in one application area can or should somehow be related to those results and problems in other areas. Mathematics gives us the tools for the development of that theory. However, when the criterion is to be compared with human experience, the machine is wrong by definition. Mathematical pattern recognition is the study of mathematical techniques to build machines to aid human experience. The forte of the computer is in the area of large masses of numerical data, a weakness of man. Towards the utilization of that power it is convenient to conceptualize the pattern recognition problem in three stages or spaces, the pattern space, the feature space, and the classification space. Figure 1.2 illustrates the concept. The physical world is sensed by some transducer system which inputs its data into the pattern space. The physical world can be represented by a continuum of parameters and is essentially infinite in dimensionality. The transducers describe a representation of that world and will be described by R scalar values where R is typically quite large. This, then, becomes the dimensionality of the pattern space. Because R is large and because the transducers are often defined by economic rather than pattern recognition specifications, it is desirable to reduce the dimensionality of R while still maintaining the discriminatory power for classification purposes

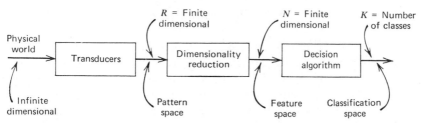

FIGURE 1.2. The conceptualized pattern recognition problem.

which is inherently in the data. Thus a feature space is postulated of dimensionality N (which is much smaller than R) and in which classification rules can be computed in reasonable amounts of time. The classification space then, simply is the decision space in which one of K classes has been selected, and therefore is of dimensionality K. As an example consider the transducer to be the raster scanning of a two-variable field of view of the numerals. If the field of view is quantized into 100 by 100 or 10,000 elements and input into the pattern space then $R = 10,000$. If we decide that only the 500 center points are important, then those points define the feature space and $N = 500$. Finally we may choose to classify the numerals into one of 11 classes (the numerals zero through nine and "undecidable"); and then the classification space will have dimensionality $K = 11$. Conceptually then the pattern recognition problem can be described as a transformation from the pattern space, P, to the feature space F, and finally to the classification space C.

$$P \to F \to C$$

Chances are these transformations will be highly nonlinear and noninvertible, and the only objective is to maintain classification discrimination throughout. As a means toward describing these transformations use of a variety of applied mathematical theories will be undertaken. Some of these include the results from statistical decision theory, sequential probability ratio testing, linear algebra and finite dimensional vector spaces, probability theory, information theory, threshold logic, dynamic programming, and a variety of other specialty areas. Towards that direction, then, let's investigate more closely the three somewhat artificial spaces briefly described above.

1.1   Pattern Space

The pattern space is essentially that domain which is defined by the discretization of sensor data observing the real world. Its dimensions must necessarily reflect that fact and thus, in a linear algebra sense, its axes will represent sampled values of data in units of the real world. Its dimensionality will be denoted by the value R whether each axis is one sample of a time waveform or if all axes represent different units of real world data (apples and oranges). A column vector **x** in the pattern space will have scalar elements

$$\mathbf{x} = (x_1, x_2, \ldots, x_r, \ldots, x_R)^t \tag{1.1}$$

where each x_r represents the particular value associated with the rth dimension. Here r will index the dimensions of the pattern space and the "t" in equation (1.1) signifies "transpose." Examples of x_r might be gross national product, a sample in time, a color, or any other measurable quantity. Thus the vector **x** is comprised of the scalar values descriptive of a set of R measurements which the designer has determined will define the pattern space. Note that we can interpret the vector **x** as a point in R space with coordinate values x_r.

In the context of supervised learning, to be described briefly, we will be interested in data vectors for which we have a priori knowledge as to their correct classification. These vectors will be referred to as prototypes, and denoted by the column vector $\mathbf{y}_m^{(k)}$ where k indexes the particular class and m indicates the mth prototype of class S_k. Thus

$$\mathbf{y}_m^{(k)} = (y_{1m}^{(k)}, \ldots, y_{rm}^{(k)}, \ldots, y_{Rm}^{(k)})^t \tag{1.2}$$

and it will be assumed that there may be M_k prototypes which are descriptive of the kth class S_k. Consequently r ranges from one to R, m ranges from one to M_k, and k ranges from one to K. As an example consider the two-dimensional ($R = 2$) problem illustrated in Figure 1.3. In two space the prototypes can be represented as points on the plane. A similar analogy exists for 3 and higher dimensions where prototypes become points in R dimensional space.

The classification problem is now simply one of finding separating surfaces in R dimensions which correctly classify the known prototypes and which, according to some criterion, affords some degree of confidence in correctly classifying unknown patterns. In order that such a task may successfully be carried out, it becomes necessary to define similarity measures between points in our R dimensional pattern space and often the use of such a metric presupposes that the pattern space forms a metric space, an assumption which is often invalid in certain social science data (see Chapter 5). However, given that the pattern space does form a metric space, the necessary

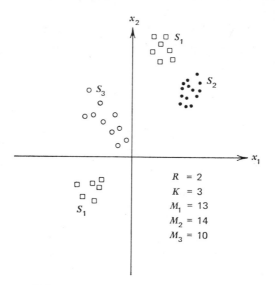

FIGURE 1.3.   Pattern space example.

metric must then satisfy the following conditions with relation to these points $(\mathbf{x}, \mathbf{y}, \mathbf{z})$ in the space.

(a) $d(\mathbf{x}, \mathbf{y}) = d(\mathbf{y}, \mathbf{x})$

(b) $d(\mathbf{x}, \mathbf{y}) \leq d(\mathbf{y}, \mathbf{z}) + d(\mathbf{x}, \mathbf{z})$

(c) $d(\mathbf{x}, \mathbf{y}) \geq 0$

(d) $d(\mathbf{x}, \mathbf{y}) = 0$ iff $\mathbf{y} = \mathbf{x}$

Such a metric is often referred to as a distance function of which there are a large variety. Thus it is conceivably possible now to describe the similarity of a point $\mathbf{x}$ with the kth class S_k as [1]

$$S(\mathbf{x}, \{\mathbf{y}_m^{(k)}\}) = \frac{1}{M_k} \sum_{m=1}^{M_k} d^2(\mathbf{x}, \mathbf{y}_m^{(k)}) \qquad (1.3)$$

Such a similarity simply is an average of the squared distance between the point $\mathbf{x}$ and the set of prototypes $\mathbf{y}_m^{(k)}$ defining the kth class and may be useful in some decision process later on. However, even if the pattern space is a metric space in the sense that each dimension or axis is a quantitative measurement of some physical phenomenon, it is still important to realize that we must not make the error of comparing "apples with oranges." Thus one axis may represent the gross national product while another measures federal discount rate. In one case the units may be millions of dollars while in the other percentage units are utilized. Thus each dimension may be a measure of unrelated parameters and must itself be normalized before being combined with other dimensions, as in a distance calculation. This has been referred to as "squaring up the pattern space" [2] or normalization in order to force the dynamic ranges of various axes to be somewhat well behaved. Various normalization techniques exist and should be selected according to their respective applicability to a given pattern recognition problem. One example is simply extremal value normalization such that the rth dimension becomes

$$x'_r = x_r/a_r \tag{1.4}$$

where

$$a_r = \max_{m,k}\{y_{rm}^{(k)}\} - \min_{m,k}\{y_{rm}^{(k)}\} \tag{1.5}$$

Another example is to use a variance normalization within a dimension, which could be less sensitive to extremal noise values. Thus

$$x'_r = x_r/\sigma_r \tag{1.6}$$

where

$$\sigma_r^2 = \left(\sum_{k=1}^{K} M_k\right)^{-1} \sum_{k=1}^{K} \sum_{m=1}^{M_k} (y_{rm}^{(k)} - \bar{y}_r)^2 \tag{1.7}$$

and for this example

$$\bar{y}_r = \left(\sum_{k=1}^{K} M_k\right)^{-1} \sum_{k=1}^{K} \sum_{m=1}^{M_k} y_{rm}^{(k)} \tag{1.8}$$

Thus equation (1.7) represents a type of variance of the rth dimension defined by the prototypes. Of course various other techniques for normalization may be developed but the point will not be pursued further.

1.2   Feature Space

It was indicated earlier that the feature space was an intermediate domain between the data gathering space and the classification process. One may be tempted to question the need for such a space in the pattern recognition process, and yet it is this author's contention that the greatest advances in pattern recognition, which have yet to be made, will occur when a meaningful pattern to feature space transformation is defined. Let us observe two distinct reasons why there exists a need for such a domain.

First, the pattern space is defined by sensor data which itself may be defined by convenience rather than classification discriminatory power. Thus it does not seem unreasonable to conjecture that there may be linear or highly nonlinear combinations of the "convenient" dimensions of the pattern space which afford meaningful classification power which otherwise would not be exploited. A case in point is the Fourier frequency analysis (a linear pattern to feature space transformation) of the R sample (dimensional) time waveform for specific signature recognition. In addition it is intuitively satisfying that the dimensions which successfully help discriminate the letter "A" from "H" could possibly be useless in discriminating "A" from "O." Thus the feature space must be defined by the inherent discriminatory power of data present in the pattern space but optimized for specific class problems.

The second need for a feature space lies in the pragmatic requirement of a space in which classification algorithms can be efficiently implemented. Typically the dimensionality of the pattern space can be quite high ($R = 10^6$ is not uncommon). Unfortunately even the simplest classification algorithms are quite time-consuming on large scale modern digital computers, and it is therefore desirable to do some "preprocessing" to reduce the dimensionality of the space in which classification algorithms must be computed. Besides, man does not require 10^6 independent pieces of information to do successful pattern recognition. Thus it is desirable that the dimension of the feature space, N, be much smaller than R. Consequently in the feature space

$$\mathbf{x} = (x_1, x_2, \ldots, x_n, \ldots, x_N)^t \qquad (1.9)$$

While the objective in defining the feature space is to reduce the dimensionality of the pattern space yet maintaining discriminatory power for classification purposes, successful transformations along these lines still seem to be in their infancy. There exist a variety of linear techniques as well as some nonlinear methods which are developing particular appeal but the real frontiers of pattern recognition research still lie ahead in developing a viable feature selection transformation that undoes the redundant data gathering inherent in the definition of the pattern space.

1.3   Classification Space

This space is the easiest to describe in the sense that it is K dimensional and simply contains the decisions implemented by the classification algorithms. The simplest such space may be two-dimensional where we only have a two-class problem, S_1 and S_2, or for example it may be 26-dimensional for alphabet recognition. Typically the classification algorithms which define the space partition the N dimensional feature space into disjoint regions, each region associated with only one class. Figure 1.4 illustrates such a partition for the data of Figure 1.3. The separating surfaces are often referred to as hyperplanes and are $N - 1$ in dimension. Thus the hyperplane separating data on the real line ($N = 1$) is a point (0 dimensionality), on the plane ($N = 2$) is a line (1-dimensional), in the volume ($N = 3$) is a plane (2-dimensional), etc. The easiest partition is a linear partition and requires on the order of N computations. However, quite often nonlinear surfaces are necessary as it is highly unlikely that the data which has been selected from natural phenomena is itself linearly separable. The classification algorithms are usually designed to implement some optimal criterion utilizing various branches of applied mathematics. These partitions may be defined by deterministic criteria, statistical criteria, information theoretic criteria, etc., the result always being the segmentation of the N dimensional feature space. It is then an easy task to classify unknowns simply by observing their location in the partitioned space.

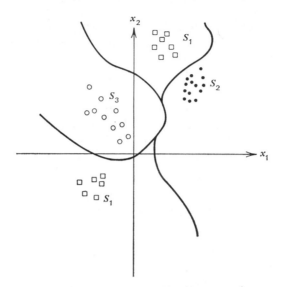

FIGURE 1.4. A possible partition.

1.4 Text Outline

The text is divided into two appendices and six chapters, the last five of which represent particular phases or aspects of approaches to the mathematical solution of pattern recognition problems. The first chapter simply serves as an introduction to concepts and notation, the latter being half the battle in understanding results reported in the literature. Thus it is hoped that the common notation throughout the text will serve as an aid in that direction.

Chapter 2 is devoted entirely to the important but still ill-defined task of feature selection. A variety of selection techniques are surveyed but the chapter is not to be considered a catalog of existing feature selection procedures. Rather, the material is presented in transformation terminology beginning with the simplest diagonal transform and working up to highly complex nonlinear transformations. The chapter is quite lengthy and represents an area where further research is necessary but where present knowledge should be made available.

The next chapter (3), is devoted to the topic of distribution free classification theory, a subject which involves the partitioning of the data space, be it pattern or feature, into a set of mutually exclusive regions according to nonstatistical criteria. The concept of a discriminant function and its use for all classification purposes is introduced, followed by the topic of linearly separable training algorithms [3]. Piecewise linear machines are next developed followed by the topic of potential functions, a subject which will recur in the context of statistical classification algorithms.

Chapter 4 is devoted to the use of statistical classification theory in the classification process of the pattern recognition problem. Classical techniques are introduced, in the pattern recognition context, as a basis for studying parametric classification theory, probably the most restrictive of the classification techniques with respect to a priori assumptions on the prototype and unknown data. These restrictive assumptions are relaxed in the nonparametric classification procedures to be discussed next by avoiding the assumption of a functional form on various probability densities.

The fifth chapter gives a few simple examples of nonsupervised learning. Thus our prototypes will not be known as to their correct classification and the subject of clustering and distribution free nonsupervised learning is developed. Mode estimation and statistical nonsupervised learning [4] are next discussed with emphasis on relatively simple concepts and techniques. Minimum spanning trees are introduced as clustering aids and a thorough discussion on intrinsic dimensionality is presented.

Chapter 6, sequential learning [5], attempts to present a relatively new subject, in the context of a pattern recognition environment. Specifically, sequential feature selection is suggested and the sequential probability ratio test is introduced. Modifications of that test are then developed from both a deterministic and stochastic stopping boundary criterion. Again both parametric and unparametric statistical viewpoints are developed in a sequential environment and a brief diversion to nonsupervised sequential pattern recognition is presented. The chapter ends in a similar fashion to the previous ones with problems, references, and related bibliography.

The two appendices are included to help clarify dimensionality concepts, multidimensional rotations (Appendix A), and to suggest a possible criterion for future feature selection work (Appendix B). In Appendix A an experimental comparison is made between the usefulness of various multidimensional rotations for feature selection purposes in a classic numeral character recognition experiment. In Appendix B the rate distortion concept, borrowed from Information Theory, is introduced as a possible tool in the feature selection task. The ideas are purely conjectural but appear well founded in the Information Theoretic context.

Due to the limitation of scope and presentation of the text, several other approaches for pattern recognition cannot be discussed. The author apologizes for these omissions and has attempted to reconcile the problem by including rather extensive related bibliographies for the interested reader. The author would also like to take this opportunity to apologize to those authors whose work has been included but possibly not treated with due justice. Such offenses are the author's own responsibility and for which he hopes no one is too deeply offended.

1.5   References

1. Sebestyen, G. S., *Decision Making Processes in Pattern Recognition*, Macmillan, New York, 1962.
2. Meisel, W. S., *Computer-Oriented Approaches to Pattern Recognition*, Academic Press, New York, N.Y., 1972
3. Nilsson, N. J., *Learning Machines*, McGraw-Hill, New York, 1965.
4. Mendel, J. M. and K. S. Fu, *Adaptive, Learning and Pattern Recognition Systems*, Academic Press, New York, 1970.
5. Fu, K. S., *Sequential Methods in Pattern Recognition and Machine Learning*, Academic Press, New York, 1968.

1.6   Related Bibliography

Blackwell, D. and M. A. Girshick, *Theory of Games and Statistical Decisions*, Wiley, New York, 1954.

Bongard, N., *Pattern Recognition*, Spartan-Macmillan, New York, 1970.

Cheng et al., *Pictorial Pattern Recognition*, Thompson Book Co., Washington, D.C., 1968.

Fu, K. S., *Sequential Methods in Pattern Recognition and Machine Learning*, Academic Press, New York, 1968.

Kanal, L. N., *Pattern Recognition*, Thompson Book Co., Washington, D.C., 1968.

Kolers, P. A. and M. Eden, *Recognizing Patterns, Studies in Living and Automatic Systems*, MIT Press, Cambridge, Mass., 1968.

Meisel, W. S., *Computer-Oriented Approaches to Pattern Recognition*, Academic Press, New York, 1972.

Mendel, J. M. and K. S. Fu, *Adaptive, Learning and Pattern Recognition Systems: Theory and Applications*, Academic Press, 1970.

Minsky, M. and S. Papert, *Perceptrons*, MIT Press, Cambridge, Mass., 1969.

Nilsson, N. J., *Learning Machines*, McGraw-Hill, New York, 1965.

Palgen, J. J., *International Bibliography of Pictoral Pattern Recognition*, Allied Research Associates, Inc., Concord, Mass., April 1970.

Sebestyen, G. S., *Decision Making Processes in Pattern Recognition*, Macmillan, New York, 1962.

Uhr, L., *Pattern Recognition*, Wiley, New York, 1966.

Watanabe, S., *Methodologies of Pattern Recognition*, Academic Press, New York, 1969.

FEATURE
SELECTION

2.0 Introduction

Probably the most important aspect of pattern recognition is that of feature selection. With proper and efficient feature selection, both simple and sophisticated classification algorithms can be implemented owing to the large dimensionality reduction provided by the feature extraction process. In addition the selected features in the reduced space may cluster better than in the pattern space and possibly will allow simpler decision surfaces (linear versus higher order discriminant functions). With improper or ineffective feature extraction the classification algorithms will necessarily be less efficient and classification errors will increase. Feature selection is usually presented in the context of supervised pattern recognition because a priori knowledge of prototype classification is often used for defining intra versus inter class considerations as well as for comparing the feature selection results. However, many of the principles described here can just as well apply to nonsupervised tasks of clustering, mode selection, and subset generation.

To attempt formal mathematical modeling of the feature extraction process is a formidable task because comparison is inevitably made with man (an efficient but still Gestalt feature extractor). Human "pre-processing" or feature selection is a highly complex and apparently nonlinear operation which has not, as yet, been duplicated through mathematical formalism. In fact when a human is used to replace the feature selector in a pattern recognition machine, he evinces a heuristic feature selection based upon his past experience, and the selection process is difficult if not impossible to describe as he himself often cannot explain upon what specific attributes he based his decision. While research into the area of modeling how the human accomplishes feature extraction (or dimensionality reduction) is active, this is not the place to describe such results. Note also that man's utility for feature selection is limited to two- or three-dimensional problems, as he has difficulty visualizing higher order spaces. The mathematical techniques which will be described here are not subject to this limitation, and indeed will increase in effectiveness as the pattern space dimensionality increases.

What then can we say about the task of feature selection and dimensionality reduction which provides a sound mathematical basis upon which to build efficient recognition devices? Perhaps the greatest justification for research into this area of mathematically defined feature selection is that successful techniques based on mathematical principles are readily machine implementable regardless of how they correctly or even remotely model human thought processes. Thus the topics to which this chapter is addressed fall into the category of mathematically defined feature selection techniques derived from any biological, physical, chemical, statistical, or other system model found useful for this purpose. The context of the development which follows will be purely mathematical and will be in the form of an R dimensional vector space where R is defined by the maximum number of samples in a given prototype. It will be assumed that the R dimensions in the pattern space have been suitably "squared up" or normalized to meaningful comparisons. Unfortunately, the pattern space is usually of high dimensionality due to the fact than man traditionally doesn't know what specific features he desires and therefore the "if a little data is good, a lot of data is better" philosophy seems to dominate his data acquisition system accordingly. The objective of feature selection is to retain the salient features necessary for the recognition process and reduce the dimensionality so that classification can be implemented on a vastly reduced feature space. Again the dimensionality of the feature space will be N where N is much smaller than R.

The underlying philosophy of any feature selection mechanism should be the retention of class discriminatory information and the reduction of class commonality information. Thus, discovering the properties of patterns of one class which discriminate those from another class should maintain recognition capability but in a reduced dimensionality feature space. Feature selection, then, should be the optimal retention of a minimum number of dimensions (variables) while maintaining and/or maximizing probability of correct classification. Unfortunately, such a fidelity criterion is difficult to evaluate and often recourse is made to other criteria which provide suboptimal but analytically tractable feature selection. Therefore it will become necessary to investigate a variety of feature selection techniques in order to get a flavor for the analytic tools which are presently available.

The following material is presented in six sections each of which is based upon a particular philosophy or set of assumptions concerning the pattern recognition environment and specific feature selection objective. The first two approaches refer to simple diagonal transformations and rotational transformations of the pattern space in the definition of the feature space. Other linear transformations are then discussed followed by a section on two-class Gaussian statistic assumptions utilizing the concepts of divergence and Bhattacharyya distance. A discussion of nonlinear transformation for feature selection follows and finally the last section discusses the relevance of feature selection in the sequential and system environment of contextual class knowledge and feedback mechanisms.

2.1 Diagonal Transformations

One technique for increasing the similarity, commonness, or cluster-ing of prototypes in the same class is through a minimization of a metric between the points defining the class. Such an intraclass measure has been defined by Sebestyen [1] and is based on a Euclidean square metric. The technique could be considered a clustering one because of the tendency to cluster the prototypes defining a given class. For the kth class, S_k, we have a total of M_k prototypes $\mathbf{y}_m^{(k)}$ (column vector) indexed by $m = 1, \ldots, M_k$. Each prototype is a point in R dimensional space and let the metric be defined as

$$d^2(\mathbf{x}, \mathbf{y}_m^{(k)}) = \sum_{r=1}^{R} (x_r - y_{rm}^{(k)})^2 \qquad (2.1a)$$

or

$$d^2(\mathbf{x}, \mathbf{y}_m^{(k)}) = (\mathbf{x} - \mathbf{y}_m^{(k)})^t(\mathbf{x} - \mathbf{y}_m^{(k)}) \qquad (2.1b)$$

Then the mean square intraset distance for class, S_k, assuming equally likely generation of each prototype defining the class, is

$$D_k^2 = \frac{1}{M_k(M_k - 1)} \sum_{p=1}^{M_k} \sum_{m=1}^{M_k} d^2(\mathbf{y}_p^{(k)}, \mathbf{y}_m^{(k)}) \qquad (2.2)$$

where we have summed the $M_k(M_k - 1)$ nonzero pairs of all the points defining the kth class. In order to minimize D_k^2 a variable weighting, w_r, for each dimension in the pattern space will be provided. This is equivalent to multiplication of the pattern space by a diagonal matrix $[W_k]$ and thus the name of this section. The mean square intraset distance for minimization now becomes

$$D_k^2 = \frac{1}{M_k(M_k - 1)} \sum_{p=1}^{M_k} \sum_{m=1}^{M_k} \sum_{r=1}^{R} w_r^2(y_{rp}^{(k)} - y_{rm}^{(k)})^2 \qquad (2.3)$$

and the w_r must now be determined. Note that w_r must be greater than zero for D_k^2 to remain a valid metric. To avoid nontrivial solutions some additional constraint must be applied to the w_r.

Two standard constraints which are often invoked are

$$\sum_{r=1}^{R} w_r = 1 \tag{2.4a}$$

or

$$\prod_{r=1}^{R} w_r = 1 \tag{2.4b}$$

The first constraint implies that the rth feature dimension is weighted in arithmetic proportion to the other features according to a constant sum. The second constraint implies a constant volume weighting and is related to the norm of the pattern space. Using the method of Lagrange multipliers, the minimization process for the constant sum constraint results in

$$w_r = \frac{\left(\sum_{s=1}^{R} \frac{1}{\sigma_s^2} \right)^{-1}}{\sigma_r^2} \tag{2.5a}$$

where σ_r^2 is the variance for the rth dimension. Thus the rth coordinate dimension is directly proportional to a constant, $(\sum_{s=1}^{R} 1/\sigma_s^2)^{-1}$, and inversely proportional to the variance of the rth dimension. The solution can be interpreted as stating that small relative weight is to be given those coordinates with large variance because these particular coordinates have little in common over the prototypes of the kth class. Note that for those dimensions with near constant values the variance will be small which will imply large weighting and a fairly important feature.

For the case of a constant volume constraint on the coordinate weights, w_r, a somewhat similar solution results.

$$w_r = \frac{\left(\prod_{s=1}^{R} \sigma_s \right)^{1/R}}{\sigma_r} \tag{2.5b}$$

Thus, under the constant volume constraint the rth coordinate weight is directly proportional to a constant, $(\prod_{s=1}^{R} \sigma_s)^{1/R}$, and inversely proportional to the standard deviation of the data in that dimension. Again the intuitive conclusions suggested earlier hold here with the exception that standard deviation rather than variance is the proportionality parameter. Unfortunately both constraint solutions are particularly sensitive to those dimensions which conceivably could have no variation, an example of which might be the corners in the raster scan of handwritten characters. Numerous other examples of near zero or zero variance coordinates can easily be envisioned.

While the above results were developed for the minimization of the mean square intraset distance of the kth class, the feature selection task is hardly complete. By ordering the weights, w_r, in monotonically decreasing order and noting that the diagonal matrix $[W_k]$ will be defined by the ordered weights, the feature selection task for the kth class then becomes an ordering permutation matrix operation on the pattern space of R dimensions followed by a diagonal matrix transformation where the resulting feature space can be defined by the N largest weights where $N \ll R$. The dimensionality reduction factor becomes R/N and a possible measure of fidelity, γ, for determining N could be $\gamma = \sum_{r=1}^{N} w_r$ or $\gamma = \sum_{r=1}^{N} w_r / \sum_{r=1}^{R} w_r$ for the constant sum and constant volume constraint solutions respectively. Figure 2.1 indicates a typical example in 2-space.

Unfortunately the technique outlined above must be repeated for all K classes resulting in K diagonal matrices $[W_k]$. This can be an inordinate task for large K and the resulting selected features are only defined on an intraclass basis. In other words, no consideration has been given to interclass interaction and separation. Just as we searched for a measure of similarity for intraclass feature selection, so might we consider searching for maximization of dissimilarity between classes.

From a statistical point of view the results of the above analysis are based only on second order properties (variances and standard deviations) and it would be gratifying if all order statistics were used if possible. This, of course, can be done when probability distribution functions are known. In addition, it would be desirable to relate the statistics to interclass rather than only intraclass phenomena and the use of a concept known as entropy, borrowed from information theory, allows us to do just that. While the results of this analysis

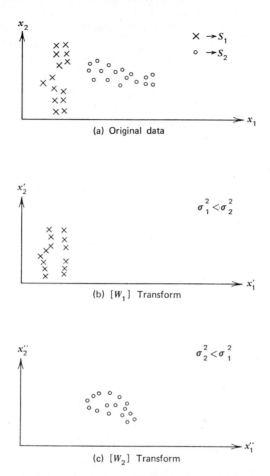

(a) Original data

(b) $[W_1]$ Transform

(c) $[W_2]$ Transform

FIGURE 2.1. Diagonal transformation weightings.

will again be equivalent to a diagonal transformation, the analogy to entropy can be pursued further in searching rotational transformations.

We will consider a source of classes S_k such that the source provides prototypes from one of k classes sequentially. (See Abramson [2] for a thorough treatment of entropy sources.) If the source is considered zero memory, then the class described by a prototype subscripted by k is independent of the class described the prototype subscripted by $k + 1$. This implies that contextual information between classes is being ignored because interclass dependencies are assumed to be zero. For inclusion of contextual information, higher order sources are examined and Markov assumptions are usually involved. Assuming a zero memory source let $P(S_k)$ describe the distribution of the kth class comprising the source. We then have the K distributions $P(S_1), P(S_2), \ldots, P(S_K)$ describing the source statistics and each distribution will be known as the a priori distribution for the kth class.

In order to define the entropy of the source it will be necessary to define an information unit to be

$$I(S_k) = \log \frac{1}{P(S_k)} \tag{2.6}$$

where the base of the logarithm describes the units of measurements; i.e., base 2 implies bits, base e implies nats, base 10 implies Hartleys, etc. Thus if the class S_k is described by the output of the source, we say that we have obtained $-\log P(S_k)$ units of information. The average amount of information provided by the source is known as entropy, $H(S)$, and is defined as:

$$H(S) = \sum_{k=1}^{K} P(S_k) I(S_k) \tag{2.7a}$$

or

$$H(S) = -\sum_{k=1}^{K} P(S_k) \log P(S_k) \tag{2.7b}$$

which becomes the source entropy. Note that $H(S)$ will always be non-negative and it can be shown that $H(S)$ will be maximized when $P(S_k) = 1/K$ for all k. This implies that we learn the most by observing the output of a uniformly distributed source which is equivalent to stating that we have the greatest uncertainty about such a distributed source because every class is as equally likely to come up as any other class.

We assume that the rth dimension or axis of our R dimensional pattern space has been quantized to a total of L_r quantum levels $q_r(l)$ indexed by $l = 1, \ldots, L_r$. We want a measure, based on quantitative information, to select the most important or "best" feature based on the above model. The concept of mutual information provides such a measure. Consider what we have learned about the kth class, S_k, given that we are told what quantum value, $q_r(l)$, the rth dimension takes on. This implies the need for a conditional probability $P(S_k | q_r(l))$ with an associated unit of information $-\log P(S_k | q_r(l))$. Thus the entropy of the source given an observed feature value becomes

$$H(S \mid q_r) = -\sum_{k=1}^{K} \sum_{l=1}^{Lr} P(S_k, q_r(l)) \log P(S_k \mid q_r(l)) \qquad (2.8)$$

$H(S \mid q_r)$ is known as the equivocation of the source given $q_r(l)$ and is equal to the entropy of the source given that we are allowed to observe the rth dimension. In the pattern recognition environment we are interested in learning as much about the classes by observing the fewest (but most information-bearing) dimensions in order to achieve a meaningful feature selection. The amount of information gained by observing a given dimension must be

$$I(S, q_r) = H(S) - H(S \mid q_r) \qquad (2.9a)$$

which is the same as saying that the uncertainty of the source has been reduced by the amount of the equivocation. The quantity $I(S, q_r)$ is known as mutual information and can be represented as

$$I(S, q_r) = \sum_{k=1}^{K} \sum_{l=1}^{Lr} P(S_k, q_r(l)) \log\{P(S_k \mid q_r(l))/P(S_k)\} \quad (2.9b)$$

Thus the mutual information of the rth dimension taking on the value $q_r(l)$ becomes the criterion of "goodness" of that particular coordinate. By ordering the coordinate dimensions such that $I(S, q_1) \geq I(S, q_2) \geq \cdots \geq I(S, q_R)$ and retaining only the N largest such dimensions, the pattern space will be reduced to the feature space by the ratio R/N and the criterion for reduction is now based on complete distributions rather than on only second order statistics. Other properties of the mutual information which will be useful are:

(a) $I(S, q_r) \geq 0$
There can be no negative learning.

   (b) $I(S, q_r) = 0$ iff $P(S_k, q_r(l)) = P(S_k)P(q_r(l))$
       We will learn nothing only when all classes are
       statistically independent of the rth dimension.

   (c) $I(S, q_r) = I(q_r, S)$
       A symmetry exists such that knowledge of classes also
       implies knowledge of dimensions.

   (d) $I(S, q_r)$ is convex.

The entropy criterion for feature selection presented above has taken into account interclass information and has resulted in a permutation and a diagonal transform $[W]$ which has elements defined as $w_r = I(S, q_r)$. While only one transformation results from this technique, as compared to K diagonal transforms for the minimum mean square intraclass distance criteria earlier, both techniques result in feature selection only in the original pattern space. Essentially we have only admitted to stretching and shrinking of the original dimensions of the pattern space. Yet restricting our attention to the space selected for transducer sensing of the outside environment would only coincidentally be optimum for measuring commonality within classes and dissimilarities between classes. In fact, chances are that the pattern space defined by the transducers is the result of convenience developed by the evolution of hardware equipment. Thus it becomes necessary to look further than simply coordinate scale changes in the original pattern space for a dimensionality reduction coupled with feature selection.

2.2   Rotational Transformations

As suggested above, other than scale changes in the original pattern space ought to be considered as techniques for feature selection. One approach that immediately suggests itself is the linear transformation described by an orthogonal matrix. Such a transformation is equivalent to a rotation of the original pattern space to a new set of coordinate vectors which are also orthogonal and which hopefully provide a domain for easier feature identification, dimensionality reduction, and which is more amenable to simpler classification algorithms. There are a variety of conditions which result in selection of an orthogonal transformation for feature selection but most of the techniques utilize a covariance matrix. Again for intraclass prototypes the covariance matrix can be defined as

$$[\Phi_k] = \mathscr{E}_p\{\mathbf{z}_m^{(k)}\mathbf{z}_m^{(k)t}\} \tag{2.10a}$$

where

$$\mathbf{z}_m^{(k)} = \mathbf{y}_m^{(k)} - \mathscr{E}_p\{\mathbf{y}_m^{(k)}\} \tag{2.10b}$$

is the zero mean vector where the expectation operator is taken over the kth intraclass prototypes. If there is a known probability density p describing the set of prototypes, then expectation should be taken with respect to that density. Thus

$$[\Phi_k] = \overline{(\mathbf{y}_m^{(k)} - \overline{\mathbf{y}}_m^{(k)})\,(\mathbf{y}_m^{(k)} - \overline{\mathbf{y}}_m^{(k)})^t} \tag{2.10c}$$

where the upper bar indicates an expectation mean, and for the entries on the diagonal, the elements are equal to σ_r^2 the variance of the rth dimension. If the prototypes of class S_k are real then $[\Phi_k]$ is real positive definite and symmetric and will have all its eigenvalues greater than zero.

From an estimation viewpoint (Tou and Heydorn [3, 4]) the "best" features are those which approximate the original prototypes with the fewest dimension in a mean square error sense. Let the features be expanded in a set of vectors $\{\mathbf{e}_n : n = 1, \ldots, N < R\}$ which are orthonormal and are elements of the family of all complete orthonormal bases in the pattern space. Let $\mathbf{z}_m^{(k)}$ be the mean zero prototype as defined in equation (2.10b) and expand $\mathbf{z}_m^{(k)}$ into the set of N basis vectors $\mathbf{e}_n$ with coefficients a_{mn}. Thus by minimizing the error due to this expansion we will have obtained the "best" feature coordinates $\mathbf{e}_n$. This error can be expressed as

$$E_N^{(k)} = \mathscr{E}_p\left\{\left|\mathbf{z}_m^{(k)} - \sum_{n=1}^{N} a_{mn}\mathbf{e}_n\right|^2\right\} \tag{2.11}$$

where $\mathscr{E}_p\{\cdot\}$ again integrates over the prototypes according to their distribution p, if known. But

$$\mathbf{z}_m^{(k)} = \sum_{r=1}^{R} a_{mr}\mathbf{e}_r \tag{2.12a}$$

for any complete set of orthonormal basis vectors $\{\mathbf{e}_r\}$. Premultiplying equation (2.12a) by $\mathbf{e}_i^t$ yields

$$\mathbf{e}_i^t \mathbf{z}_m^{(k)} = \sum_{r=1}^{R} a_{mr} \mathbf{e}_i^t \mathbf{e}_r \tag{2.12b}$$

but due to the orthonormal conditions

$$\mathbf{e}_i^t \mathbf{z}_m^{(k)} = a_{mi} \tag{2.12c}$$

or

$$a_{mi} = \mathbf{z}_m^{(k)^t} \mathbf{e}_i \tag{2.12d}$$

Thus the error becomes

$$E_N^{(k)} = \mathscr{E}_p \left\{ \left| \sum_{r=N+1}^{R} a_{mr} \mathbf{e}_r \right|^2 \right\} \tag{2.13a}$$

or using equation (2.12d)

$$E_N^{(k)} = \mathscr{E}_p \left\{ \left| \sum_{r=N+1}^{R} (\mathbf{z}_m^{(k)^t} \mathbf{e}_r) \mathbf{e}_r \right|^2 \right\} \tag{2.13b}$$

Expanding the square

$$E_N^{(k)} = \mathscr{E}_p \left\{ \sum_{r=N+1}^{R} \mathbf{e}_r^t \mathbf{z}_m^{(k)} \mathbf{z}_m^{(k)^t} \mathbf{e}_r \right\} \tag{2.13c}$$

and finally

$$E_N^{(k)} = \sum_{r=N+1}^{R} \mathbf{e}_r^t [\Phi_k] \mathbf{e}_r \tag{2.13d}$$

Because $\mathbf{e}_r^t [\Phi_k] \mathbf{e}_r$ is positive definite we can minimize equation (2.13d) by minimizing each term of the result, $\mathbf{e}_r^t [\Phi_k] \mathbf{e}_r$. Again using the method of Lagrange multipliers and utilizing the orthonormality constraint we have

$$E_N^{(k)} = \sum_{r=N+1}^{R} \mathbf{e}_r^t [\Phi_k] \mathbf{e}_r - \lambda_r \mathbf{e}_r^t \mathbf{e}_r + \lambda_r \tag{2.13e}$$

and taking partial derivatives with respect to $\mathbf{e}_r^t$ we obtain

$$\frac{\partial E_N^{(k)}}{\partial \mathbf{e}_r^t} = 0 = [\Phi_k] \mathbf{e}_r - \lambda_r \mathbf{e}_r \tag{2.14a}$$

and finally

$$[\Phi_k] \mathbf{e}_r = \lambda_r \mathbf{e}_r \tag{2.14b}$$

Equation (2.14b) implies that e_r is an eigenvector of the covariance matrix $[\Phi_k]$ and λ_r is the rth corresponding eigenvalue. The minimum estimation error, $E_N^{(k)}$, then becomes

$$E_N^{(k)} = \sum_{r=N+1}^{R} e_r^t \lambda_r e_r \qquad (2.15a)$$

and

$$E_N^{(k)} = \sum_{r=N+1}^{R} \lambda_r \qquad (2.15b)$$

where λ_r, $r = N + 1, \ldots, R$, are the eigenvalues associated with those eigenvectors not included in the expansion of equation (2.12a). Thus $E_N^{(k)}$ will be minimum if the first N feature eigenvectors are chosen to correspond to the largest eigenvalues. The problem of minimizing $E_N^{(k)}$ is essentially a factor or principal component analysis problem and falls under the class of Karhunen-Loève expansions. Figure 2.2 illustrates the utility of such rotations as described above.

So far we have obtained the optimum transformation for a given dimensionality reduction R/N, resulting in selecting those N features which are the eigenvectors corresponding to the N largest eigenvalues of the covariance matrix defined by the prototypes in the kth class, S_k. This, then, defines $[T_k]$. However, the "best" features are based upon a mean square error criterion of approximating the original prototypes with N features and it is important to realize that a mean square error is not necessarily the best criterion to be used. Therefore, we can say that for mean square error or reproducibility of the original prototype, choose those features corresponding to the eigenvectors associated with the N largest eigenvalues to achieve a dimensionality reduction of R/N. The transformation is then a rotation of the R dimensional pattern space to a feature space where the maximal amount of energy lines up on the fewest, N, axes and the $R-N$ coordinate dimensions in the feature space are ignored.

Until now we have restricted our attention only to rotational transformations which are optimal according to some criteria (minimum estimation error) independent of any consideration as to interclass relationships. Thus the set of K rotational transforms, one for each class, may provide little if any improvement for classification due to the nonexistence of any relationship between the K

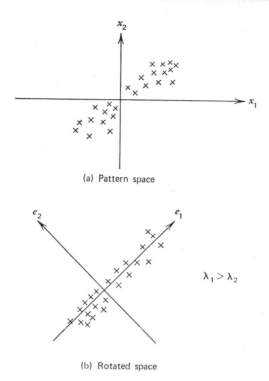

(a) Pattern space

(b) Rotated space

FIGURE 2.2.   A two-dimensional rotation example.

transforms. Consequently, one single interclass rotation should be obtained for feature selection based on inter as well as intra class measures. Thus, one would like to emphasize the similarities of prototypes within a class and the dissimilarities between classes. One technique which provides a rotation based on interclass information is that developed by the Karhunen-Loève expansion [5, 6]. The Karhunen-Loève expansion has been generalized to multiclass problems [7, 8] such that an overall covariance matrix, [Φ], in the discrete case, is defined which is descriptive of the entire pattern recognition problem and not restricted to a given intraclass set of prototypes. The generalization suggests that there are K stationary stochastic processes, one for each class, S_k, and each process is known at least to second order statistics [Φ_k]. The distribution of the K processes is given by the a priori class probabilities, $P(S_1) \cdots P(S_K)$, and the total covariance matrix is then just an average of the individual class covariance matrices:

$$[\Phi] = \sum_{k=1}^{K} P(S_k)[\Phi_k] \qquad (2.16)$$

The N eigenvectors $\{e_n : n = 1, \ldots, N\}$ form an orthonormal set and if they are selected according to the N largest eigenvalues then this particular rotation provides the best approximation, in a mean square error sense, to the data in the original pattern space. The eigenvalues can be shown to be the variances of the transformed coefficient. Note that an equivalent feature ordering has been effected by the eigenvalue ordering and Fu [8] presents some experimental results on ordered versus unordered classification errors based on the Karhunen-Loève rotation. By working with unity normalized variance data, an entropy analogy can be developed showing that this rotation minimizes a pseudo-entropy function. Watanabe [9] has suggested the use of the Karhunen-Loève transform in various pattern recognition environs including clustering [10] and has contributed to reports of the results of such expansions (rotations) [11, 12].

Often it is desirable to obtain a measure of fidelity of the retained coordinates in the feature space and if we let γ represent such a measure then

$$\gamma = \left(\sum_{n=1}^{N} \lambda_n \right) \bigg/ \left(\sum_{r=1}^{R} \lambda_r \right) \qquad (2.17)$$

could be a likely candidate. Note that $0 \leq \gamma \leq 1$ and is essentially measuring the ratio of the retained energy (or variances) to total energy (or variance). While such a measure is useful, it often is desirable to select the truncation error value, $E_N = \sum_{r=N+1}^{R} \lambda_r$, a priori. Thus the question may be asked as to what linear transformation is obtained for a fixed truncation, error E_N, rather than fixed dimensionality reduction, N. When z_m (any prototype) is expanded into any set of orthonormal function vectors $\{e_r\}$ we obtain

$$z_m = \sum_{r=1}^{R} a_{mr} e_r \qquad (2.18)$$

and for a fixed truncation error

$$E_N = \mathscr{E}_p \left\{ \left| \sum_{r=N+1}^{R} a_{mr} \mathbf{e}_r \right|^2 \right\} \tag{2.19}$$

The question of minimizing the expected value of N over the choice of orthonormal vectors $\{\mathbf{e}_r\}$ is a function of the distribution of the original prototypes and not simply of the second order statistics of those prototypes. However, Algazi and Sakrison [13] have reported a solution for the Gaussian distributed process whose sufficient statistics are second order moments. Their results indicate that again the Karhunen-Loève expansion is optimum under the criterion of minimizing the expected dimensionality of the feature space, N, for a given truncation error E_N.

There are a variety of drawbacks to the use of the rotational transform techniques presented above mainly due to the fact that coordinate rotations are still often not sufficient to properly separate classes. The transformation matrix, $[T]$, which is $N \times R$ dimensions and consists of ordered eigenvectors $\mathbf{e}_1, \ldots, \mathbf{e}_N$ for its rows can be defined as

$$[T] = \begin{bmatrix} \mathbf{e}_1^t \\ \mathbf{e}_2^t \\ \cdot \\ \cdot \\ \cdot \\ \mathbf{e}_N^t \end{bmatrix} \tag{2.20a}$$

Actually the complete $R \times R$ transform can be defined by appending the remaining eigenvectors.

$$[T] = \begin{bmatrix} \mathbf{e}_1^t \\ \cdot \\ \cdot \\ \cdot \\ \mathbf{e}_R^t \end{bmatrix} \tag{2.20b}$$

This defines an orthogonal transformation or rotation of the pattern space, and then feature selection results by ignoring certain coordinates in the transformed space. From a computer implementation viewpoint, however, defining the eigenvectors which make up

[T] can be a near computationally impossible task. This is because the $R \times R$ covariance matrix [Φ] must first be calculated. For high dimensionality data and a large number of prototypes such a calculation in itself can be monumental. [However, this calculation must be made only once if the prototypes are stationary with time.] Even if the covariance matrix is available through a model or other technique, it still must be diagonalized which computationally is again infeasible for large R. Finally, implementation of the rotation of the pattern space will take NR or R^2 operations depending on equation (2.20a) or (2.20b), respectively.

Because of the computational tasks described in the above paragraph and because often other than Karhunen-Loève rotations are useful in providing orthogonal transform domains for feature selection, a brief comment will be made on the possible application of generalized spectral analysis to the feature selection task [14]. In finite dimensional space any orthogonal transform could be considered a valid candidate for obtaining a feature selection domain. In fact the eigenvector approach can be pursued by noting that the eigenvectors defined by certain physical systems might be perfectly valid elements in defining a feature selection rotation matrix. Thus the eigenvectors describing the all pass linear system are the complex trigonometric waveforms thereby defining a Fourier transform [15]. For the ideal low pass linear system the prolate spheroidal waveform transform would result [16]. For a system defined by a dyadic correlation, the Walsh transform would result [17]. Of course the space of orthogonal transforms is infinite but certain rotations although suboptimal in a Karhunen-Loève sense, may provide a valuable domain for feature selection. Two of the transforms mentioned above, Fourier and Walsh, were suggested because they are two of a class of transformations which have a very rapid implementation algorithm [18]. In fact both the Fourier and Walsh transforms can be factored into a product of matrices, each of dimension $R \times R$ and with a low number of nonzero entries, such that rotation of the pattern space can be accomplished in $R \log R$ rather than R^2 computer operations. This has come to be known as the fast Fourier and fast Walsh transform algorithms [19, 20]. In addition to a desirable rapid implementation, an information theoretic justification using rate distortion theory has been suggested and appears in Appendix B.

Pattern recognition results using the fast Fourier transform as a means of feature selection have been reported with large dimensionality reductions for handwritten character recognition [21] and the work is being extended to the Walsh domain [22, 23]. Appendix A presents an example of the use of a few fast orthogonal transformations as feature selectors in a pattern recognition experiment.

2.3 Other Linear Transforms

When looking at the results of the rotation transforms for interclass interaction it is not all together clear that the classes themselves have been optimally separated for further classification. In fact the interclass rotations discussed thus far have all been based on an energy or variance criteria. Ideally, it is desired to extract features which represent differences between pattern classes and would thereby tend to suppress commonly shared important features with correspondingly large eigenvalues but with no separability capability. Efforts under the assumption of a two-class problem for separability using the Karhunen-Loève expansion have been reported by Fukunaga and Koontz [24]. For the two-class case the generalized covariance matrix can be represented as

$$[\Phi] = [C_1] + [C_2] \tag{2.21}$$

where

$$[C_1] = P(S_1)[\Phi_1] \tag{2.22a}$$

and

$$[C_2] = P(S_2)[\Phi_2] \tag{2.22b}$$

Let $[E]$ be the matrix made up of the eigenvectors which diagonalize $[\Phi]$, equation (2.21). The existence of $[E]$ is known because $[\Phi]$ is a generalized covariance matrix (therefore generalized Karhunen-Loève expansions).

Therefore

$$[E]^t[\Phi][E] = [I] \tag{2.23}$$

where $[I]$ is the identity matrix and the eigenvalues have been normalized into the eigenvectors. Thus the matrix $[E]$ defines the generalized Karhunen-Loève expansion discussed in the last section but restricted to a two-class problem. Therefore the $[E]$ transformation (dimension $R \times R$) maps the pattern space into the feature space. The feature space representation of the a priori weighted intraclass covariance matrices can then be expressed as

$$[\Phi_1^E] = [E]^t[C_1][E] \qquad (2.24a)$$

$$[\Phi_2^E] = [E]^t[C_2][E] \qquad (2.24b)$$

where the $[C_k]$ matrices are obtained from equation (2.22). The transformed covariance matrices in the feature space defined by $[E]$ will not necessarily be diagonal but will satisfy the following property:

$$[\Phi_1^E] + [\Phi_2^E] = [I] \qquad (2.25)$$

as can be seen from equations (2.21) and (2.23). Thus an effective normalization has been provided by the rotation $[E]$. The eigenvalues and eigenvectors of the component classes are defined as

$$[\Phi_1^E]e_r^{(1)} = \lambda_r^{(1)}e_r^{(1)} \qquad (2.26a)$$

and

$$[\Phi_2^E]e_r^{(2)} = \lambda_r^{(2)}e_r^{(2)} \qquad (2.26b)$$

Assuming that the eigenvalues of class S_1 are in monotonic decreasing order, and combining equations (2.25) and (2.26b)

$$[\Phi_2^E]e_r^{(2)} = ([I] - [\Phi_1^E])e_r^{(2)} = \lambda_r^{(2)}e_r^{(2)} \qquad (2.27a)$$

Rearranging terms

$$[\Phi_1^E]e_r^{(2)} = (1 - \lambda_r^{(2)})e_r^{(2)} \qquad (2.27b)$$

which is an eigenvector equation for $[\Phi_1^E]$ in terms of the eigenvectors of $[\Phi_2^E]$. Therefore

$$e_r^{(1)} = e_r^{(2)} \qquad (2.28a)$$

and

$$\lambda_r^{(1)} = 1 - \lambda_r^{(2)} \qquad (2.28b)$$

Note that equation (2.27) does not imply that $[\Phi_1^E]$ must equal $[\Phi_2^E]$. On the contrary, due to the normalization rotation provided by $[E]$, the eigenvectors of the two rotated covariance matrices become identical but their eigenvalues are related componentwise by

$$\lambda_r^{(1)} + \lambda_r^{(2)} = 1 \qquad r = 1, \dots, R \qquad (2.28c)$$

This result is equivalent to stating that the eigenvector for the largest feature (and eigenvalue) for class S_1 represents the smallest feature (and eigenvalue) for class S_2. Because the $\lambda_r^{(1)}$ were ordered monotonically decreasing, the $\lambda_r^{(2)}$ are ordered monotonically increasing. Thus due to the prenormalization transform $[E]$ the important features of class S_1 are the least important features of class S_2 and vice versa. Therefore selection of the ultimate transformation matrix $[T]$ becomes construction of a composite transform $[E^{(1,2)}]$ of dimension $N \times R$ following the normalization transform $[E]$ of dimension $R \times R$

$$[T] = [E^{(1,2)}]^t [E]^t \tag{2.29}$$

where the rows of $[E^{(1,2)}]^t$ are the first N_1 eigenvectors $e_r^{(1)}$ for class S_1 and the last N_2 eigenvectors for class S_2.

While the above results are indeed encouraging for the two class problem there are schools of thought which suggest some basic changes are necessary in the premises upon which many of the techniques presented so far have been based. For instance it is suggested that a Euclidean metric (which is philosophically equivalent to an energy criterion and second order statistics) is a poor measure upon which to base class separations. It is argued that large distances are weighted too heavily due to the quadratic nature of the measure thus overpowering smaller but possible equally important distances for classification and clustering. Other arguments which strike at the Karhunen-Loève expansion work are that the techniques are based only upon second order statistics and it is not difficult to develop quite different density functions exhibiting the same covariance matrix [25]. Thus it is due to the search for a new metric and more complete statistics that has resulted in work reported by Patrick and Fischer [26] in which the two class pattern recognition problem is analyzed based on density function estimates. Parzen [27] (see the method of potential functions and Chapter 4) estimates of the multivariate class distributions, $\hat{p}(\mathbf{x}/S_1)$ and $\hat{p}(\mathbf{x}/S_2)$, are formed from the respective class prototypes $\mathbf{y}_m^{(k)}$, $k = 1, 2, \ldots$. A distance function is defined to be the squared difference between the two a priori weighted estimated distribution such that:

$$d(S_1, S_2) = d(P(S_1)\hat{p}(\mathbf{x}/S_1), P(S_2)\hat{p}(\mathbf{x}/S_2)) \tag{2.30a}$$

and

$$d(S_1, S_2) = \left\{ \int_{-\infty}^{\infty} (P(S_1)\hat{p}(\mathbf{x}/S_1) - P(S_2)\hat{p}(\mathbf{x}/S_2))^2 \, d\mathbf{x} \right\}^{\frac{1}{2}} \quad (2.30b)$$

where we note that $d(a, a) = 0$ and if the correlation of the two estimates, $\int_{-\infty}^{\infty} \hat{p}(\mathbf{x}/S_1)\hat{p}(\mathbf{x}/S_2) \, d\mathbf{x}$, decreases the metric increases and we can equate correlation as a measure of separability. Therefore, if the distance function increases due to a decrease in correlation of estimates the classes are more separated and maximization of the metric will be a chief objective. The distribution estimates essentially use a potential function method where each prototype is represented by a Gaussian kernel and the distribution is the superposition of the kernels of all prototypes [28],

$$\hat{p}(\mathbf{x}/S_k) = \frac{1}{M_k(h(M_k))^N} \sum_{m=1}^{M} (2\pi\sigma^2)^{-N/2} \exp\left\{ -\frac{1}{2\sigma^2} \|\mathbf{x}\|^2 \right\} \quad (2.31)$$

for $k = 1, 2$. When the kernel has certain properties [27, 28] then the estimates in equation (2.31) approach the true distributions with probability one. The objective of the technique is to find a linear transformation, $[T]$, from the pattern to the feature space, of dimensionality $N \times R$ such that the metric defined in the feature space is maximum. Therefore the density estimates and distances will become a function of the linear transformation $[T]$ and the distance function becomes

$$\begin{aligned}
d([T]) = \Bigg\{ &\left(\frac{P(S_1)}{M_1} \right)^2 \left(\frac{1}{2\pi\sigma^2} \right)^N \sum_{m=1}^{M_1} \sum_{p=1}^{M_1} \exp\left\{ -\frac{1}{4\sigma^2} ([T](\mathbf{y}_m^{(1)} - \mathbf{y}_p^{(1)}))^t \right. \\
&\left. \cdot ([T](\mathbf{y}_m^{(1)} - \mathbf{y}_p^{(1)})) \right\} + \left(\frac{P(S_2)}{M_2} \right)^2 \left(\frac{1}{2\pi\sigma^2} \right)^N \\
&\cdot \sum_{m=1}^{M_2} \sum_{p=1}^{M_2} \exp\left\{ -\frac{1}{4\sigma^2} ([T](\mathbf{y}_m^{(2)} - \mathbf{y}_p^{(2)}))^t \right. \\
&\left. \cdot ([T](\mathbf{y}_m^{(2)} - \mathbf{y}_p^{(2)})) \right\} - \frac{2P(S_1)P(S_2)}{M_1 M_2} \left(\frac{1}{2\pi\sigma^2} \right)^N \\
&\cdot \sum_{m=1}^{M_1} \sum_{p=1}^{M_2} \exp\left\{ -\frac{1}{4\sigma^2} ([T](\mathbf{y}_m^{(1)} - \mathbf{y}_p^{(2)}))^t \right. \\
&\left. \cdot ([T](\mathbf{y}_m^{(1)} - \mathbf{y}_p^{(2)})) \right\} \Bigg\}^{\frac{1}{2}}
\end{aligned} \quad (2.32a)$$

The first and second terms can be considered as a type of intraclass measure which is essentially the sum of the norm of the transformed densities. The third term is the interclass measure and was discussed as a correlation earlier. The best $[T]$ for a given N and kernel then is the one which maximizes $d([T])$ and becomes the best linear transformation from the pattern to the feature space. Unfortunately maximizing $d([T])$ with respect to the elements of the transformation matrix $[T]$ requires a gradient or hill climbing approach due to the nonlinear relation of the elements of $[T]$ and the metric. This particular metric exhibits the property that samples separated by a Euclidean distance of more than 3σ are essentially the same "distance" using the new metric. A graphical representation of such an effect, is presented in Figure 2.3. To investigate the effect of the smoothing function, σ, we can fix all other variables and let σ take on limiting values. As $\sigma \to \infty$, it is clear that $d([T]) \to 0$ and a two-term Taylor series expansion results in

$$d([T]) \cong \left(\frac{1}{2\pi\sigma^2}\right)^{N/2} \left\{ \left(\frac{P(S_1)}{M_1}\right)^2 + \left(\frac{P(S_2)}{M_2}\right)^2 - 2\frac{P(S_1)P(S_2)}{M_1 M_2} \right.$$

$$+ 2\sum_{m=1}^{M_1}\sum_{p=1}^{M_2} ([T](\mathbf{y}_m^{(1)} - \mathbf{y}_p^{(2)}))^t([T](\mathbf{y}_m^{(1)} - \mathbf{y}_p^{(2)}))$$

$$\left. - \sum_{k=1}^{2}\sum_{m=1}^{M_k}\sum_{p=1}^{M_k} ([T](\mathbf{y}_m^{(k)} - \mathbf{y}_p^{(k)}))^t([T](\mathbf{y}_m^{(k)} - \mathbf{y}_p^{(k)})) \right\}^{1/2} \quad (2.32b)$$

Note that the first summation is a Euclidean interclass distance and

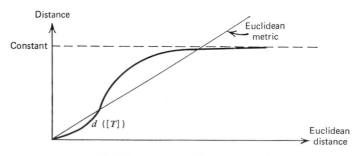

FIGURE 2.3.   Patrick and Fischer metric.

the second summation is the Euclidean intraclass distance. Therefore for large σ the metric becomes the interclass minus intraclass Euclidean distances. However as $\sigma \to 0$, Patrick and Fischer have shown that the optimum transform $[T]$ maximizes the minimum interclass Euclidean distance while minimizing the minimum intraclass distance. This, of course, would be expected of a metric which tends to ignore large Euclidean distances as is graphically demonstrated in Figure 2.3.

2.4 Divergence and Bhattacharyya Transforms

One of the main objections to many of the approaches for feature selection presented so far is the fact that often second order statistics and covariance matrices are all that the resulting transforms are based upon. It is particularly appealing to be able to assume Gaussian distributions because, then, second order statistics are a sufficient statistic for complete definition of the density functions. In addition the Gaussian distribution has the appealing property that linear transformations from the pattern space to the feature space leave the functional forms of the distributions invariant, (i.e., Gaussian). Only the means and variances are changed and recalculation of those quantities will completely define the feature space distributions. Thus if the prototype samples or model can safely be assumed to exemplify a Gaussian process, then such an assumption becomes particularly useful. There has been considerable work in the analyses of feature selection techniques based on the assumption of Gaussian statistics, and two measures become particularly useful, divergence and the related Bhattacharyya distance [29–32]. Again for a two-class problem, these measures are related to the probabilistic distribution of the two classes as

$$J(S_1, S_2) = \int_{-\infty}^{\infty} [p(\mathbf{x} \mid S_1) - p(\mathbf{x} \mid S_2)] \log\left\{\frac{p(\mathbf{x} \mid S_1)}{p(\mathbf{x} \mid S_2)}\right\} dx \quad (2.33a)$$

$$B(S_1, S_2) = -\log\left\{\int_{-\infty}^{\infty} (p(\mathbf{x} \mid S_1)p(\mathbf{x} \mid S_2))^{1/2} dx\right\} \quad (2.34)$$

respectively. Note the relation of the Bhattacharyya distance, equation (2.34), and the cross product correlation term used in the definition of the distance function in equation (2.30). The divergence can be interpreted with respect to a likelihood ratio measure. Let $\lambda = \log\{p(\mathbf{x} \mid S_1)/p(\mathbf{x} \mid S_2)\}$. Then

$$J(S_1, S_2) = \int_{-\infty}^{\infty} \lambda p(\mathbf{x} \mid S_1) \, d\mathbf{x} - \int_{-\infty}^{\infty} \lambda p(\mathbf{x} \mid S_2) \, d\mathbf{x} \qquad (2.33b)$$

which is equivalent to stating that the divergence is the difference in the means of the likelihood ratios conditioned on their respective classes. In other words [8]

$$J(S_1, S_2) = \mathscr{E}\{\lambda \mid S_1\} - \mathscr{E}\{\lambda \mid S_2\} \qquad (2.33c)$$

The divergence measure and Bhattacharyya distance are not true metrics (violation of the triangle inequality) but they still remain quite useful for optimization purposes. In fact it is desirable to choose a linear transformation which will minimize the probability of error, P_e, of classification over all linear transformations. However such a criterion is difficult to evaluate and consequently suboptimal solutions provided by the maximization of the above measures, equations (2.33) and (2.34), will cause the distributions to tend to be separated in the transform space. (Recall that this was the objective in the Patrick and Fischer work [26].) Indeed, let $\chi = \{x: P(S_1)p(\mathbf{x} \mid S_1) \leq P(S_2)p(\mathbf{x} \mid S_2)\}$ and let $\bar{\chi}$ be the complement space. Then

$$P_e = P(S_1) \int_{\chi} p(\mathbf{x} \mid S_1) \, d\mathbf{x} + P(S_2) \int_{\bar{\chi}} p(\mathbf{x} \mid S_2) \, d\mathbf{x} \qquad (2.35a)$$

$$= \int_{-\infty}^{\infty} \min\{P(S_1)p(\mathbf{x} \mid S_1), \, P(S_2)p(\mathbf{x} \mid S_2)\} \, d\mathbf{x} \qquad (2.35b)$$

$$\leq \int_{-\infty}^{\infty} \{P(S_1)P(S_2)p(\mathbf{x} \mid S_1)p(\mathbf{x} \mid S_2)\}^{\frac{1}{2}} \, d\mathbf{x} \qquad (2.35c)$$

$$= (P(S_1)P(S_2))^{\frac{1}{2}} \int_{-\infty}^{\infty} \{p(\mathbf{x} \mid S_1)p(\mathbf{x} \mid S_2)\}^{\frac{1}{2}} \, d\mathbf{x} \qquad (2.35d)$$

$$= (P(S_1)P(S_2))^{\frac{1}{2}} \exp\{-B(S_1, S_2)\} \qquad (2.35e)$$

While the bound given in equation (2.35e) is for general distributions, the bound can be replaced by

$$P_e \leq (P(S_1)P(S_2))^{1/2}\left\{\frac{J(S_1, S_2)}{4}\right\}^{-1/4} \tag{2.35f}$$

for Gaussian distributions [31, 32]. Thus by maximizing $B(S_1, S_2)$ or $J(S_1, S_2)$ by linear transformations into the feature space, the error bound will become tighter. Under the Gaussian assumption

$$p(\mathbf{x} \mid S_k) = \frac{1}{(2\pi)^{R/2}|[\Phi_k]|^{1/2}}$$

$$\times \exp\{-\tfrac{1}{2}(\mathbf{x} - m_k)^t[\Phi_k]^{-1}(\mathbf{x} - m_k)\} \tag{2.36a}$$

$$= N(m_k, [\Phi_k]) \tag{2.36b}$$

where $[\Phi_k]$ is the covariance matrix, and m_k is the mean vector, of the kth class $\{\mathbf{y}_m^{(k)}\}$, for $k = 1, 2$; and the absolute bars around a matrix imply the determinant of that matrix. However, the divergence and Bhattacharyya distance are to be optimized over all linear transformations $[T]$, of dimension $N \times R$, which implies Gaussian distributions in the transformed space as well:

$$p(\mathbf{x} \mid S_k, [T]) = N(\boldsymbol{\mu}_k, [\Phi_k^T]) \tag{2.37}$$

where

$$\boldsymbol{\mu}_k = [T]\mathbf{m}_k$$

and

$$[\Phi_k^T] = [T]^t[\Phi_k][T]$$

Therefore the divergence and Bhattacharyya distance now become functions of the transformation and will be denoted as $J([T])$ and $B([T])$ respectively. It now remains to optimize the above measures with respect to $[T]$ remembering that the feature space is of dimension $N \ll R$. The two measures can be further expressed as [3, 33]

$$J([T]) = \tfrac{1}{2}\,\mathrm{tr}[[\Phi_2^T]^{-1}[\Phi_1^T] + [\Phi_1^T]^{-1}[\Phi_2^T] - 2[I]]$$

$$+ \tfrac{1}{2}\,\mathrm{tr}[[[\Phi_1^T]^{-1} + [\Phi_2^T]^{-1}][(\boldsymbol{\mu}_1 - \boldsymbol{\mu}_2)(\boldsymbol{\mu}_1 - \boldsymbol{\mu}_2)^t]] \tag{2.38}$$

$$B([T]) = \tfrac{1}{8}\,\mathrm{tr}[[[\Phi_1^T] + [\Phi_2^T]]^{-1}[(\boldsymbol{\mu}_1 - \boldsymbol{\mu}_2)(\boldsymbol{\mu}_1 - \boldsymbol{\mu}_2)^t]]$$

$$+ \tfrac{1}{4}\log\{|[[\Phi_2^T]^{-1}[\Phi_1^T] + [\Phi_1^T]^{-1}[\Phi_2^T] + 2[I]]|\,\tfrac{1}{4}\} \tag{2.39}$$

But since the trace of a matrix is equal to the sum of its eigenvalues and the determinant of a matrix equals the product of its eigenvalues, the above results can be simplified. Let the various eigenvalues and eigenvectors be determined by

$$[\Phi_2^T]^{-1}[\Phi_1^T]\mathbf{e}_n = \lambda_n \mathbf{e}_n \qquad (2.40a)$$

Therefore

$$[\Phi_1^T]\mathbf{e}_n = \lambda_n[\Phi_2^T]\mathbf{e}_n \qquad (2.40b)$$

which, in terms of the pattern space covariances, becomes

$$[T]^t[\Phi_1][T]\mathbf{e}_n = \lambda_n[T]^t[\Phi_2][T]\mathbf{e}_n \qquad (2.40c)$$

Note that the eigenvector solution to equation (2.40) is often referred to as a double orthogonal expansion and, in terms of continuous parameters, can be represented as

$$\int_a^b \Phi_1(\tau, \tau')e_s(\tau)\, d\tau = \lambda_s \int_a^b \Phi_2(\tau, \tau')e_s(\tau)\, d\tau \qquad (2.40d)$$

and is to be contrasted to the single orthogonal expansion usually encountered in the Karhunen-Loève literature. Returning to the expressions for $J([T])$ and $B([T])$, it will be necessary to define further eigenvectors for the mean difference matrices. Because equation (2.40) defines N eigenvalues, let λ_J and λ_B be reserved for

$$[[\Phi_2^T]^{-1} + [\Phi_1^T]^{-1}][(\mu_1 - \mu_2)(\mu_1 - \mu_2)^t]\mathbf{e}_J = \lambda_J \mathbf{e}_J \quad (2.41a)$$

$$[[\Phi_1^T] + [\Phi_2^T]]^{-1}[(\mu_1 - \mu_2)(\mu_1 - \mu_2)^t]\mathbf{e}_B = \lambda_B \mathbf{e}_B \quad (2.41b)$$

Note that equations (2.41a) and (2.41b) have only one nonzero eigenvalue apiece due to the degrees of freedom restriction in the definition of those matrices (i.e., $(\mu_1 - \mu_2)(\mu_1 - \mu_2)^t$). It is now possible to represent $J([T])$ and $B([T])$ in nonmatrix form

$$J([T]) = \lambda_J - N + \frac{1}{2}\sum_{n=1}^N \left(\lambda_n + \frac{1}{\lambda_n}\right) \qquad (2.42)$$

$$B([T]) = \frac{1}{8}\lambda_B + \frac{1}{4}\log \prod_{n=1}^N \frac{1}{4}\left(\lambda_n + \frac{1}{\lambda_n} + 2\right) \qquad (2.43a)$$

or

$$B([T]) = \frac{1}{8}\lambda_B + \frac{1}{4}\sum_{n=1}^N \log\left\{\left(\frac{1}{4}\left(\lambda_n + \frac{1}{\lambda_n} + 2\right)\right)\right\} \qquad (2.43b)$$

Necessary conditions for the two measures to be a maximum have been established [3, 33] but are extremely complex to interpret. Gradient techniques and iterative convergence solutions are necessary for solution of the general case, (i.e., $[\Phi_1] \neq [\Phi_2]$ and $m_1 \neq m_2$). Tou and Heydorn [3], Caprihan and de Figueiredo [33], and Fukunaga and Koontz [24], all present computer simulations for this case. Henderson and Lainiotis [34] present a compromise solution for computer implementation. While the general case solution requires gradient and iterative techniques, for certain simplifying assumptions the results of equations (2.42) and (2.43) become meaningful.

CASE I: $m_1 = m_2$, $[\Phi_1] \neq [\Phi_2]$

In this case with common mean vectors and different covariances equation (2.41) becomes zero implying $\lambda_J = \lambda_B = 0$ and the divergence and Bhattacharyya distance become respectively:

$$J([T]) = \frac{1}{2} \sum_{n=1}^{N} \left(\lambda_n + \frac{1}{\lambda_n} \right) - N \qquad (2.44)$$

and

$$B([T]) = \frac{1}{4} \sum_{n=1}^{N} \log \left\{ \frac{1}{4} \left(\lambda_n + \frac{1}{\lambda_n} + 2 \right) \right\} \qquad (2.45)$$

Therefore if we order the eigenvalues according to $\lambda_1 + 1/\lambda_1 \geq \lambda_2 + 1/\lambda_2 \geq \cdots \geq \lambda_N + 1/\lambda_N$ and choose the corresponding eigenvectors, then both $J([T])$ and $B([T])$ will be maximized and a sufficient solution to the maximization problem is therefore available. Thus the eigenvector-eigenvalue solution to the double orthogonal expansion of the covariance matrices given by equation (2.40) provides a sufficient solution to the equal mean case. Lainiotis and Henderson [35] have suggested an efficient computer algorithm for computing the eigensolutions of equation (2.40) using the concepts of state space. It is interesting to note that the optimal solution for the constant mean case is the same whether using the divergence or Bhattacharyya distance as the criterion for maximization.

CASE II: $m_1 \neq m_2$, $[\Phi_1] = [\Phi_2]$

For the common covariance case the eigenvalues determined by the double orthogonal expansion of equation (2.40) become all equal to unity, as seen below:

$$[\Phi_2^T]^{-1}[\Phi_1^T]\mathbf{e}_n = \lambda_n \mathbf{e}_n$$

$$[\Phi_1^T]^{-1}[\Phi_1^T]\mathbf{e}_n = \lambda_n \mathbf{e}_n$$

$$\mathbf{e}_n = \lambda_n \mathbf{e}_n$$

Therefore

$$\lambda_n = 1 \qquad n = 1, \ldots, N$$

Consequently the divergence and Bhattacharyya distance determined by equations (2.42) and (2.43) simplify to

$$J([T]) = \lambda_J - N + \frac{1}{2}\sum_{n=1}^{N}\left(1 + \frac{1}{1}\right) \qquad (2.46a)$$

$$= \lambda_J \qquad (2.46b)$$

$$B([T]) = \tfrac{1}{8}\lambda_B + \tfrac{1}{4}\sum_{n=1}^{N}\log \tfrac{1}{4}(1 + \tfrac{1}{1} + 2) \qquad (2.47a)$$

$$= \tfrac{1}{8}\lambda_B \qquad (2.47b)$$

and by observing equations (2.41a) and (2.41b) which define the eigenvalues λ_J and λ_B respectively, it becomes evident that $\lambda_J = 4\lambda_B$. The optimal solution then, for the case with unequal means and constant covariances will be a feature space of one dimension, $N = 1$, determined by the largest eigenvalue (in this case the only nonzero eigenvalue) and corresponding eigenvector which satisfies the solution to

$$[\Phi_1^T]^{-1}[(\boldsymbol{\mu}_1 - \boldsymbol{\mu}_2)(\boldsymbol{\mu}_1 - \boldsymbol{\mu}_2)^t]\,\mathbf{e} = \lambda_1 \mathbf{e} \qquad (2.48)$$

to within a multiplicative constant. Again the optimal solution is the same whether maximization is performed over $J([T])$ or $B([T])$. Note that in this particular case no information is lost by going to one dimension (because all other eigenvalues are zero). The particular dimension which provides the maximum separation of the two classes is that axis which perpendicularly bisects the vector connecting the means of the two classes in the pattern space. In two dimensions this is simply illustrated as in Figure 2.4.

Of course some of the major drawbacks of the use of either divergence or Bhattacharyya distance transforms is the fact that both assumptions of Gaussian statistics and two-class problems are

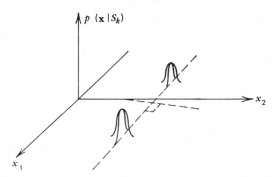

FIGURE 2.4. Common covariance separating plane ($R = 2$).

often quite restrictive. There have been a variety of researchers who have suggested that the average of the pairwise divergence or Bhattacharyya distance might provide a measure for optimization for the multiclass problem [8, 36, 37]. Thus for K classes the measure becomes

$$J = \sum_{i=1}^{K} \sum_{k=1}^{K} P(S_k)P(S_i)J(S_i, S_k) \qquad (2.49)$$

or

$$B = \sum_{i=1}^{K} \sum_{k=1}^{K} P(S_k)P(S_i)B(S_i, S_k) \qquad (2.50)$$

In fact a simple extension of the results of equation (2.35) will provide upper bounds on the total misclassification error for a Gaussian assumption for divergence and any distribution for the Bhattacharyya distance (see Chapter 4). Fu [8] pursues the analysis for the common covariance case and the divergence measure, and Lainiotis [36] uses the Bhattacharyya distance (actually a derivation of the distance) to establish the upper bound for any distribution; and using a normal Parzen [27] estimator, he defines the upper bound more completely.

2.5 Nonlinear Transformations

One of the major disadvantages with linear techniques is that they often will not separate prototypes of classes that are clearly separable (nonoverlapping) but which do not separate due to rotations, scaling or other linear operations. In fact, if it is known a priori that the K classes $S_1, \ldots, S_K$ are linearly separable, then a feature space of K dimensions will be sufficient for classification. Kharkevich [38] has shown that sufficient features for a set of K linearly separable classes are the normals to the hyperplanes separating each pair of classes. This is simply the use of dichotomies for discriminant function generation in distribution free classification (see Nilsson [39] Chapter 2). However just as convex nonoverlapping classes can be separated by linear hyperplanes so it is hoped that nonconvex nonoverlapping classes can be made linearly separable first by unfolding and then by using linear hyperplanes. Figure 2.5 graphically illustrates the situation for nonoverlapping convex classes (linearly separable) as well as the desired nonlinear transformation for the nonconvex nonoverlapping nonlinearly separable case. The nonlinear transformation, T, should transform the pattern space into a feature space so that nonlinearly separable classes become linearly separable. Hopefully the transformation will retain local structure at the expense of global properties. Such a transformation is equivalent to finding nonlinear features or finding Φ functions in the context of Nilsson [39]. Thus if $\mathbf{y}_m$ is a prototype in the pattern space then $\mathbf{v}_m$ will denote the same prototype projected into the feature space. When the transformation $[T]$, is linear then

$$\mathbf{v}_m = [T]\mathbf{y}_m \tag{2.51a}$$

or

$$v_{nm} = \sum_{r=1}^{R} t_{nr} y_{rm} \tag{2.51b}$$

and when nonlinear

$$\mathbf{v}_m = T(\mathbf{y}_m) \tag{2.52}$$

Examples of nonlinear transformations might be zero crossing counts, random line intersections, sign function generators (ideal hard limiters or thresholding devices), and a variety of other well defined operations. Again we face the problem of developing intraclass versus interclass transformations and the majority of work to date has been concentrated on the simplest problem, that of intraclass nonlinear transforms, T_k. The usual objective of the intraclass transformation is the learning of some underlying structure

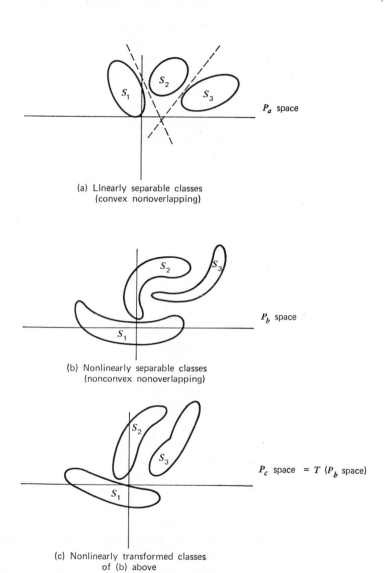

(a) Linearly separable classes
(convex nonoverlapping)

P_a space

(b) Nonlinearly separable classes
(nonconvex nonoverlapping)

P_b space

(c) Nonlinearly transformed classes
of (b) above

P_c space $= T (P_b$ space)

FIGURE 2.5.   Some ideal nonlinear transformations.

of nonlinearly related independent parameters which appear to be at the heart of the generation of the intraclass prototypes. Thus, the concept of intrinsic dimensionality emerges as a criterion or objective for the transformation definition. Often iteratively defined transformations result, adding additional difficulty in explicit representations. However, before developing the intrinsic dimensionality concepts in Chapter 5 it is useful to investigate a variety of explicitly defined nonlinear transformations for the feature selection process. When the nonlinear transformation is restricted to the class of polynomials, the components of the vector prototype $\mathbf{v}_m$ in the feature space (equation (2.52)) become

$$v_{nm} = \sum_{l=0}^{L} a_{ln} \left(\sum_{r=1}^{R} T_{nr} y_{rm} \right)^{l} \qquad (2.53a)$$

where an Lth order polynomial has been assumed with coefficients a_{ln}. Such a transformation can be related to Φ functions for distribution free classification. For simple pattern space coordinates transformed by polynomial functions, the cross product terms of equation (2.53a) become zero. In other words without a linear transformation, prior to the nonlinear operation, the components of the prototypes become

$$v_{rm} = \sum_{l=1}^{L} a_{lr} y_{rm}^{l} \qquad (2.53b)$$

This transformation maps the origin into itself and Sebestyen [1] has used it for clustering as well as two-class separation procedures.

The nonlinear transforms described by equations (2.53a) or (2.53b) are a priori defined to be polynomial expansions which may or may not conveniently fit a nonlinear transformation obtainable from a particular error criterion. Thus iteratively defined transformations will not be constrained to fit a polynomial structure and will simply be described by equation (2.52).

A simple example of a nonlinear transformation which is iteratively defined and which can be used to achieve a fixed dimensionality reduction independent of intrinsic dimensionality considerations is that given by Sammon [40]. The nonlinearly transformed feature space will be of dimension N and the prototype vectors for the kth class, S_k, will be described by $\mathbf{v}_m^{(k)}$

$$\mathbf{v}_m^{(k)} = T_k(\mathbf{y}_m^{(k)}) \tag{2.54}$$

The squared Euclidean distance between points in the pattern space is given by

$$d^2(\mathbf{y}_p^{(k)}, \mathbf{y}_m^{(k)}) = \sum_{r=1}^{R} (y_{rp}^{(k)} - y_{rm}^{(k)})^2 \tag{2.55a}$$

In the transform space the squared Euclidean distance between points becomes

$$d^2(\mathbf{v}_p^{(k)}, \mathbf{v}_m^{(k)}) = \sum_{n=1}^{N} (v_{np}^{(k)} - v_{nm}^{(k)})^2 \tag{2.55b}$$

The nonlinear transform will be defined to be that transformation which minimizes the error, E, defined to be

$$E = \sum_{p=1}^{M_k} \sum_{m=1}^{M_k} (d(\mathbf{y}_p^{(k)}, \mathbf{y}_m^{(k)}) - d(\mathbf{v}_p^{(k)}, \mathbf{v}_m^{(k)}))^2 \tag{2.56a}$$

The error is a function of the $(N)(M_k)$ variables v_{nm} $n = 1, \ldots, N$, and $m = 1, \ldots, M_k$. Therefore an iteratively defined steepest descent procedure can be used to search for a minimum of E over the $(N)(M_k)$ variable v_{nm}.

Thus expanding E

$$E = \sum_{p=1}^{M_k} \sum_{m=1}^{M_k} \left\{ \left(\sum_{r=1}^{R} (y_{rp}^{(k)} - y_{rm}^{(k)})^2 \right)^{1/2} - \left(\sum_{n=1}^{N} (v_{np}^{(k)} - v_{nm}^{(k)})^2 \right)^{1/2} \right\}^2 \tag{2.56b}$$

and taking partials results in

$$\frac{\partial E}{\partial v_{nm}} = \sum_{p=1}^{M_k} -2(v_{np}^{(k)} - v_{nm}^{(k)}) + \frac{2}{2} \left(\sum_{n=1}^{N} (v_{np}^{(k)} - v_{nm}^{(k)})^2 \right)^{-1/2}$$

$$\times 2(v_{np}^{(k)} - v_{nm}^{(k)}) \cdot \left(\sum_{r=1}^{R} (y_{rp}^{(k)} - y_{rm}^{(k)})^2 \right)^{1/2} \tag{2.57a}$$

or,

$$\frac{\partial E}{\partial v_{nm}} = 2 \sum_{\substack{p=1 \\ p \neq m}}^{M_k} (v_{np}^{(k)} - v_{nm}^{(k)}) \left\{ \frac{d(\mathbf{y}_p^{(k)}, \mathbf{y}_m^{(k)}) - d(\mathbf{v}_p^{(k)}, \mathbf{v}_m^{(k)})}{d(\mathbf{v}_p^{(k)}, \mathbf{v}_m^{(k)})} \right\} \tag{2.57b}$$

In an iterative environment the error will become a function of the iteration, $E(i)$, as will the variables, $v_{nm}(i)$. Thus at each stage the new points in the feature space will be updated according to

$$v_{nm}(i + 1) = v_{nm}(i) - b\Delta_{nm}(i) \qquad (2.58)$$

where b is a rate of convergence constant and $\Delta_{nm}(i)$ is a function of the partial derivatives of first and higher order depending on the gradient technique used for steepest descent. The resulting nonlinear transformation is a prototype to prototype (one to one) mapping and a many to few dimensionality mapping. Under worst case conditions all $(N)(M_k)$ mappings would need to be defined to be able to explicitly describe T_k.

One of the major drawbacks of the method described above is the need for a priori definition of the dimension of the feature space N. Thus no consideration has been given to investigating E over N as well as over v_{nm}. Consequently inherent structure has been ignored in the sense that certain feature space dimensionalities may provide far superior error results than others. However one instance where a priori feature spaces are known is in an interactive computer mode in which two- and three-dimensional feature spaces are desirable due to graphic display technology and human visualization processes [40, 41].

In order to avoid the need for a priori definition of the feature space dimension and to learn more about the intrinsic structure of the processes generating the prototypes it becomes useful to study proximity analysis and rank preservation transformations. The underlying motivation for the study is the intuitive belief that the coordinates of the pattern space have little to do with the intrinsic structure describing prototype generation for given classes. Results utilizing this approach will be deferred until Chapter 5 where the environment of nonsupervised learning provides a better background for discussion.

2.6 Systems Feature Selection

Until now we have divorced the feature selection task form the classification procedure in the pattern recognition problem. However the ultimate goal is correct classification and the intermediate step of feature selection and dimensionality reduction is, in a sense, subservient to that goal and is not an end in itself. It therefore seems logical that a "Gestalt" or systems approach to feature selection, based on classification considerations, should be developed. Appendix B suggests an Information Theoretic approach to that problem. In addition to systems considerations for feature selection criteria [42], it would be desirable to be able to adapt the feature selector to follow contextual considerations where applicable. Thus if the classifier has selected class S_k then there may be a priori knowledge that the next pattern will have a high probability of being a certain other class. A good case example is the recognition of English text: the reception of a "q" gives a good indication of a "u" to follow. Thus it is desirable to utilize as much external or contextual information as possible in both the feature selection and classification task. Possibly a block diagram of the following form could be applicable to this task:

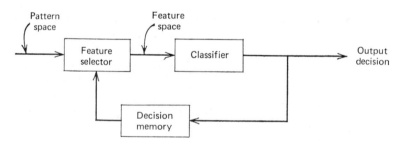

Heuristic approaches to the context problem often result in the use of tables of "confidence" entries indicating the degree of confidence of obtaining any other class following the given class [43]. Often such systems can be successfully modeled by a finite order Markov process in which case Markov statistics can be applied. Under such an assumption a tth order ergodic source can be assumed such that the source outputs samples from class S_k with probability determined by the t previous classes. Following the entropy analogy in section 2.1 we can define a unit of information from the tth order source to be

$$I(S_k \mid S_{jt} \cdots S_{j1}) = -\log P(S_k \mid S_{jt} \cdots S_{j1}) \qquad (2.59)$$

The conditional source entropy can be found by averaging over the information defined above. Thus

$$H(S \mid S_{jt} \cdots S_{j1}) = \sum_{k=1}^{K} P(S_k \mid S_{jt} \cdots S_{j1}) I(S_k \mid S_{jt} \cdots S_{j1}) \quad (2.60)$$

The entropy of the tth order source then becomes the average of the conditional entropies:

$$H(S) = \sum_{S(t)} P(S_{jt} \cdots S_{j1}) H(S \mid S_{jt} \cdots S_{j1}) \quad (2.61)$$

where the summation is over the set $S(t) = \{K^t \text{ possible combin-}$ ations of occurrences of K classes taken t at a time$\}$. This summation is essentially integrating out each S_{ji} for all $i = 1, \ldots, t$ which is the same as exhausting all possible orderings of the t previous classes. Thus the entropy becomes

$$H(S) = - \sum_{S(t+1)} P(S_k, S_{jt} \cdots S_{j1}) \log P(S_k \mid S_{jt} \cdots S_{j1}) \quad (2.62)$$

where Bayes law has been applied, (i.e., $p(x, y) = p(x \mid y)p(y)$). Notice that for $t = 0$ the entropy reduces to that of equation (2.7b). Again, as in the previous work, we assume that the rth dimension of the pattern space has been quantized to a total of L_r levels, $q_r(l)$, indexed by $l = 1, \ldots, L_r$. The entropy of the source given knowledge of the t past classifications as well as the observation of the rth dimension now becomes $H(S \mid q_r)$ with a corresponding mutual information

$$I(S, q_r) = H(S) - H(S \mid q_r) \quad (2.63)$$

which then becomes the feature selecting parameter.

The above described classification–feedback–feature selection technique has been investigated in the context of a sequential decision problem with a finite memory by Chien [44] for the situation of known classification correctness. This assumption is valid for the training phase of the algorithm. A subset of features of reduced dimensionality are selected. Let the subsets be described by F_i $i = 1, \ldots, I$ and for each F_i there exists a probability p_i of correct classification assuming F_i is the only subset of features used in the classifier. The objective of the feedback feature selection loop, then, is to select that subset F_i which maximizes the long run proportion of correct classification. Equivalently it is desired that

$$\text{Lim}_{n \to \infty}(N_c/n) = \max_i(p_i) \tag{2.64}$$

where N_c is the number of correct classifications in n successive prototype samples. However because of the desire to maintain a finite feedback memory a tth order selection strategy will be imposed. This will imply that the feature subset selection will be a function of only the t previous classification decisions, equivalent to the tth order Markov process assumption. In such a case it is possible to show that

$$\text{Lim}_{n \to \infty}(N_c/n) = \left(\sum_{i=1}^{I} p_i \prod_{\substack{j=1 \\ j \neq i}}^{I} (1 - p_j)^t\right) \left(\sum_{i=1}^{I} \prod_{\substack{j=1 \\ j \neq i}}^{I} (1 - p_j)^t\right)^{-1} \tag{2.65}$$

with probability one. Note that as $t \to \infty$ (infinite memory source) the right hand side of the equation becomes $\max_i(p_i)$ in the limit. The selection strategy which results in the equation (2.64) is to cycle consecutively though the feature subsets until at least one corrected classification followed by t incorrect classifications occur at which point the cycling resumes. Thus such a selection strategy, in the long run, will maximize the probability of correct classification with better performance for increased history retention (t). Note that no assumption of a priori knowledge of the p_i is necessary. However one major unanswered question is the definition of the subset of features themselves. Conceivably feature subsets defined by linear and nonlinear transformations could be used to define the F_i. The question still remains as to this definition process, but once a set of such feature subsets are defined, the above selection process can be used to maximize over such a set.

2.7 Conclusions

This chapter has been devoted to the subject of feature selection, the motivation of which will become readily apparent after the next two chapters. The objective is to reduce the number of features, dimensions, or coordinates necessary to discriminate successfully between classes. The need for dimensionality reduction is to simplify computational algorithms necessary for classification. We have described a set of techniques, here, where certain features can be ignored in the subsequent classification process. Beginning with the simplest technique, dimensions are weighted according to their variance in the original pattern space. However, this is simply a stretching or shrinking technique and a bit more appealing is the algorithm which also includes multidimensional rotations. The use of orthogonal expansions (rotation) may be practical if one finds a rapid implementation technique and a rotated space in which effective feature selection can be developed. When more statistical knowledge is available, techniques based upon that information become relevant. Again, however, linear transformations are not necessarily sufficient for effective feature selection and attempts at nonlinear techniques are made. Unfortunately the state of the art in this field is quite limited and much remains to be done. Of course feature selection is not a goal in itself but must be coupled with effective classification techniques. This then implies some sort of classification decision feedback mechanism to modify or adapt the feature selector. Unfortunately research in this area is still quite limited.

This chapter should not be construed to encompass all feature selection techniques. In fact, we have only touched upon a few which may provide the reader with a feel for some existing approaches which in certain circumstances have been quite successful. It should be evident from the references and related bibliography that considerable work is being developed in the feature selection task and space limitations prohibit us from exploring all such approaches.

2.8 Problems

1. (a) Find the eigenvalues and eigenvectors of the following matrix:

$$[\phi] = \begin{bmatrix} 1.00 & .90 & .81 \\ .90 & 1.00 & .90 \\ .81 & .90 & 1.00 \end{bmatrix}$$

(b) Is the resulting matrix comprised of the eigenvectors of [φ] suitable for a rotation of a three-dimensional pattern space?

(c) Given the following matrix:

$$
A = \begin{bmatrix} 1 & 1 & 1 \\ 1 & \exp\left(\dfrac{2\pi i}{3}\right) & \exp\left(\dfrac{4\pi i}{3}\right) \\ 1 & \exp\left(\dfrac{4\pi i}{3}\right) & \exp\left(\dfrac{2\pi i}{3}\right) \end{bmatrix}
$$

Is this matrix suitable for use as a rotation transformation? Do you recognize the matrix?

2. Given three prototype vectors:

$$
\mathbf{y}_1 = \{1, 1, 1, 1\}
$$
$$
\mathbf{y}_2 = \{1, -1, 1, -1\}
$$
$$
\mathbf{y}_3 = \{1, -1, -1, 1\}
$$

Find a coordinate rotation (transformation) which maximally separates the prototypes and reduces the necessary features for classification by 25%.

3. Given that the Karhunen-Loève (K-L) expansion is optimum in a mean square sense, define a metric for selection of a given number of features, N, between the K-L rotation and an arbitrary (but realistically implementable) rotation (expansion) and show that your metric is a function of only the difference in the square of the remaining $\infty - N$ coefficients of expansion.

4. You have judiciously decided upon the Karhunen-Loève expansion as a means for feature extraction in the following pattern recognition problem.

Prototypes for class S_1

$$
\mathbf{y}_1^{(1)} = (1, 2, 4)
$$
$$
\mathbf{y}_2^{(1)} = (1.2, 3, 2)
$$
$$
\mathbf{y}_3^{(1)} = (.9, 4, 3)
$$

Prototypes for class S_2

$$\mathbf{y}_1^{(2)} = (2, 3, 4)$$
$$\mathbf{y}_2^{(2)} = (3, 3.2, 3)$$
$$\mathbf{y}_3^{(2)} = (4, 2.8, 2)$$

Prototypes for class S_3

$$\mathbf{y}_1^{(3)} = (2, 4, 4)$$
$$\mathbf{y}_2^{(3)} = (2.2, 4.1, 3)$$
$$\mathbf{y}_3^{(3)} = (2.1, 3.9, 2)$$

Prototypes for class S_4

$$\mathbf{y}_1^{(4)} = (2, 4, 4)$$
$$\mathbf{y}_2^{(4)} = (3, 3, 4.1)$$
$$\mathbf{y}_3^{(4)} = (1, 1, 4.2)$$

With a priori probabilities

$$P(S_1) = 1/4 \qquad P(S_3) = 1/6$$
$$P(S_2) = 1/6 \qquad P(S_4) = 5/12$$

(a) Find the eigenvalues and the eigenvectors of the "cumu-lative" covariance matrix.
(b) Describe the first prototype of each class in the transformed pattern space.
(c) Using a Euclidean distance function, classify the unknown pattern

$$\mathbf{x} = \{3.1, 3.2, 3\}$$

as "closest" to the mean of each class in the two dimensions defined by the two largest eigenvalues.
(d) List the 4 distances you calculated in (c).

5. You have a feature selection task in which all the probability statistics are known quite accurately. Therefore, you decide to use an entropy criterion as a basis for feature selection and mutual information seems suitable. The following data is available to you. There are three classes of interest and three features or dimensions in the pattern space. Each feature can

take on one of four values. The transition matrices are:

$$
\begin{array}{c}
\quad\quad\ f_1(1)\ \ f_1(2)\ \ f_1(3)\ \ f_1(4) \\
\begin{array}{c} S_1 \\ S_2 \\ S_3 \end{array}
\left[
\begin{array}{cccc}
.5 & .25 & .25 & 0 \\
.25 & .25 & .25 & .25 \\
.125 & .25 & .125 & .5
\end{array}
\right] \leftarrow P(f_1(l)/S_i)
\end{array}
$$

$$
\begin{array}{c}
\quad\quad\ f_2(1)\ \ f_2(2)\ \ f_2(3)\ \ f_2(4) \\
\begin{array}{c} S_1 \\ S_2 \\ S_3 \end{array}
\left[
\begin{array}{cccc}
.25 & .25 & .5 & 0 \\
.125 & .125 & .5 & .25 \\
.25 & .125 & .125 & .5
\end{array}
\right] \leftarrow P(f_2(l)/S_i)
\end{array}
$$

$$
\begin{array}{c}
\quad\quad\ f_3(1)\ \ f_3(2)\ \ f_3(3)\ \ f_3(4) \\
\begin{array}{c} S_1 \\ S_2 \\ S_3 \end{array}
\left[
\begin{array}{cccc}
.25 & 0 & .5 & .25 \\
.25 & .25 & .25 & .25 \\
.25 & .25 & 0 & .5
\end{array}
\right] \leftarrow P(f_3(l)/S_i)
\end{array}
$$

and the a priori class probabilities are:

$$P(S_1) = 1/3 = P(S_2) = P(S_3)$$

Find the necessary mutual informations and order the three features in decreasing order of importance.

6. (a) Under what circumstances will the mutual information technique for feature extraction be useless even though all distributions are accurately known?

(b) Given that the dimensions in the pattern space take on variance $\sigma_r^2 = r^{-2}$, what is the optimum scalar weighting w_r, to minimize the Euclidean distance between prototypes of a given class subject to a constant sum constraint $\sum_{r=1}^{R} w_r = 1$.

(c) Given the variances of (b), find the scalar weightings subject to a constant volume constraint.

(d) For a 4-dimensional problem describe the diagonal matrices for (b) and (c) with entries ordered according to increasing significance.

7. Again you have decided to use mutual information as a criterion for feature extraction. You have variable feature-valued-dimensions $q_r(l)$ where $l = 1, 2, \ldots, v_r$ and $v_r = r + 2$. The conditional distributions of the feature values given class S_1 are uniform:

$$p(q_r(l)/S_1) = \frac{1}{r + 2} \qquad l = 1, \ldots, v_r$$

given class S_2 are: $p(q_r(l)/S_2) = \frac{1}{2}\delta(l - r) + \frac{1}{2}\delta(l - 3)$
given class S_3 are: $p(q_r(l)/S_3) = \frac{1}{2}\delta(l - 2) + \frac{1}{2}\delta(l - 3)$

    For a 4-dimensional pattern space and a three-class problem, find the mutual information

$$I(S, q_r), \quad r = 1, \ldots, 4 \quad \text{when} \quad P(S_1) = \tfrac{1}{2}, \ P(S_2) = \tfrac{1}{4} = P(S_3).$$

8. (a) You have diagonalized the kth class covariance matrix. Given an estimation criterion (mean square error) what eigenvector do you retain in a dimensionality reduction?

    (b) Repeat part (a) for a minimum mean square intraclass distance criterion.

    (c) What is the major drawback (theoretical and not computational) for using the Karhunen-Loève rotation for feature selection based on intraclass information?

9. (a) Define divergence.

    (b) Define Bhattacharyya distance.

    (c) Which parts, (a) and (b); provides an upper bound on probability of error of misclassification independent of assumed probability distributions?

10. (a) Prove that the Bhattacharyya distance is not a distance for the complete definition of a distance function (metric).

    (b) Prove that the divergence is not a true distance.

11. Consider the generalized K-L expansion as a prenormalization processor for a K-class problem. Determine the relationships between the K eigenvector sets $\{e_r^{(k)}\}$ and eigenvalues $\{\lambda_r^{(k)}\}$ similar to the two-class problem. Define the ultimate linear transformation given by your analysis.

12. Derive the results of equation (2.9b), $I(s, q_r)$, from the definition of entropy, equation (2.7), and equivocation, equation (2.8).

13. Using the method of Lagrange multipliers and the notation of equations (2.1) through (2.4), derive the weights necessary for minimum average intraclass distance subject to the constant sum and constant volume constraints (see equations (2.5a) and (2.5b)).

14. Show that it is possible to normalize the eigenvalues into the eigenvectors such that equation (2.23) is valid.

$$[E]^t[\Phi][E] = [I]$$

15. Fill in the details between equations (2.13b) and (2.13c).

2.9 References

1. Sebestyen, G. S., *Decision Making Processes in Pattern Recognition*, Macmillan, New York, 1962.

2. Abramson, N., *Information Theory and Coding*, McGraw-Hill, New York, 1963.

3. Tou, J. T., and R. P. Heydorn, "Some Approaches to Optimum Feature Extraction," in *Computers and Information Sciences—II*, ed. by J. Tou, Academic Press, New York, 1967.

4. Tou, J. T., "Feature Extraction in Pattern Recognition," *Pattern Recognition* (Pergamon Press) Vol. 1, pp. 3–11, 1968.

5. Loève, M., *Probability Theory*, Van Nostrand, Princeton, N.J., 1955.

6. Davenport, W. B., Jr., and W. L. Root, *An Introduction to the Theory of Random Signals and Noise*, McGraw-Hill, New York, 1958.

7. Chien, Y. T., and K. S. Fu, "On the Generalized Karhunen-Loève Expansion," *IEEE PGIT*, Vol. IT-13, July 1967, pp. 518–520.

8. Fu, K. S., *Sequential Methods in Pattern Recognition and Machine Learning*, Academic Press, New York, 1968.

9. Watanabe, S., "Karhunen-Loève Expansion and Factor Analysis, Theoretical Remarks and Applications," *Proc. of 4th Prague Conference on Info. Theory*, 1965.

10. Kaminuma, T., T. Takekawa, and S. Watanabe, "Reduction of Clustering Problem to Pattern Recognition," *Pattern Recognition*, Vol. 1, No. 3, March 1969, pp. 195–206.

11. Watanabe, S., "Automatic Feature Extraction in Pattern Recognition," Chapter 5 in *Automatic Interpretation and Classification of Images*, ed. by A. Grasselli, Academic Press, New York, 1969.

12. Watanabe, S., et al., "Evaluation and Selection of Variables in Pattern Recognition," in *Computers and Information Sciences—II*, ed. by J. Tou, Academic Press, New York, 1967.

13. Algazi, V. R., and D. J. Sakrison, "On the Optimality of the Karhunen-Loève Expansion," *IEEE Transactions on Information Theory*, March 1969, pp. 319–321.

14. Andrews, H. C., and K. L. Caspari, "A Generalized Technique for Spectral Analysis," *IEEE Trans. on Computers*, Vol. C-19, No. 1, January 1970, pp. 16–25.

15. Papoulis, A., *The Fourier Integral and its Applications*, McGraw-Hill, New York, 1962.

16. Slepian, D., and H. O. Pollak, "Prolate Spheroidal Wave Functions, Fourier Analysis and Uncertainty—I," *BSTJ*, January 1961, pp. 43–63.

17. Pichler, F., "Walsh Functions and Linear System Theory," *Proceedings of Symp. and Workshop Applications of Walsh Functions*. Wash D.C. (April, 1970)

18. Andrews, H. C., *Computer Techniques in Image Processing*, Chapter 5, Academic Press, New York, 1970.

19. Cooley, J. W., and J. W. Tukey, "An Algorithm for the Machine Calculation of Complex Fourier Series," *Mathematics of Computation*, Vol. 19, No. 90, 1956, pp. 297–301.

20. Whelchel, J. E., Jr., and E. F. Guinn, "The Fast Fourier-Hadamard Transform and its Use in Signal Representation and Classification," from *Eascon '68 Record*, Electronic

and Aerospace Systems Convention held at the Sheraton-Park Hotel, Washington, D.C., September 9–11, 1968, published by IEEE Transactions on Aerospace and Electronic Systems.

21. Tallman, O. H., Lt. Col. USAF, "The Classification of Visual Images by Spatial Filtering," Air Force Institute of Technology, School of Engineering, dissertation, June 1969.

22. Carl, J. W., Capt., USAF, "Generalized Harmonic Analysis for Pattern Recognition: a Biologically Derived Model," Air Force Institute of Technology, School of Engineering, thesis, August 1968.

23. Boulton, P. I. P., "Smearing Techniques in Pattern Identification," Ph.D. dissertation, University of Toronto, 1966.

24. Fukunaga, K., and W. L. G. Koontz, "Application of the Karhunen-Loève Expansion to Feature Selection and Ordering," *IEEE Trans. on Computers*, Vol. C-19, No. 4, April 1970, pp. 311–318.

25. Ball, G. H., "Data Analysis in the Social Sciences: What About the Details?", *Proc. Fall JCC*, December 1965, pp. 533–559.

26. Patrick, E. A., and F. P. Fischer, "Non Parametric Feature, Selection," *IEEE Trans. Info. Theory*, Vol. IT-15, No. 5, September 1969, pp. 577–584.

27. Parzen, E., "On Estimation of a Probability Density Function and Mode," *Annals of Mathematical Statistics*, Vol. 33, 1962, pp. 1065–1076.

28. Specht, D. F., "Generation of Polynomial Discriminant Functions for Pattern Recognition," *IEEE Trans. Electronic Computers*, Vol. 16, No. 3, June 1967, pp. 308–319.

29. Marill, T., and D. M. Green, "On the Effectiveness of Receptors in Recognition Systems," *IEEE Trans. on Info. Theory*, Vol. IT-9 1963, pp. 11–17.

30. Kullback, S., *Information Theory and Statistics*, Wiley, New York, 1959.

31. Kadota, T. T., and L. A. Shepp, "On the Best Set of Linear

Observables for Discriminating Two Gaussian Signals," *IEEE PGIT*, Vol. IT-13, April 1967, pp. 278–284.

32. Kailath, T., "The Divergence and Bhattacharyya Distance Measures in Signal Detection," *IEEE Trans. on Commun. Tech.*, Vol. 15, No. 1, 1967, pp. 52–60.

33. Caprihan, A., and R. J. P. de Figueiredo, "On the Extraction of Pattern Features from Continuous Measurements," *IEEE Symposium on Adaptive Processes*, 1969, pp. 3-e-1 to 3-e-5.

34. Henderson, T. L., and D. G. Lainiotis, "Comments on Linear Feature Extraction," *IEEE Trans. PGIT*, Vol. IT-15, No. 6, November 1969, pp. 728–730.

35. Lainiotis, D. G., and T. L. Henderson, "Application of State Variable Techniques to Optimal Feature Extraction," *Proc. IEEE (Letters)*, Vol. 56, December 1968, pp. 2175–2176.

36. Lainiotis, D. G., "A Class of Upper Bounds on Probability of Error for Multihypotheses Pattern Recognition," *IEEE PGIT*, Vol. IT-15, No. 6, November 1969, pp. 730–731.

37. Grettenberg, T. L., "Signal Selection in Communication and Radar Systems," *IEEE PGIT*, Vol. IT-9, 1963, pp. 265–275.

38. Kharkevich, A. A., "The Choice of Identifying Features for Recognition Machines," *Engineering Cybernetics* (English Translation), No. 2, March–April 1963, pp. 1–7.

39. Nilsson, N. J., *Learning Machines*, McGraw-Hill, New York, 1965.

40. Sammon, J. W., Jr., "A Nonlinear Mapping for Data Structure Analysis," *IEEE Trans. on Computers*, Vol. C-18, No. 5 May 1969, pp. 401–409.

41. Sammon, J. W., "On-Line Pattern Analysis and Recognition System (OLPARS)," Technical Report #RADC-TR-68-263, August 1968.

42. Wee, W. G., "On Feature Selection in a Class of Distribution-Free Pattern Classifiers," *IEEE Trans. PGIT*, Vol. IT-16, No. 1, January 1970, pp. 47–55.

43. Duda, R. O., and P. E. Hart, "Experiments in the Recognition

of Hand-Printed Text: Part II—Context Analysis," *Proc. FJCC*, San Francisco, California, 1968, Thompson Book Co., Washington, D.C., 1968.

44. Chien, Y. T., "Adaptive Strategies of Selecting Feature Subsets in Pattern Recognition," *Proceedings of 1969 Symposium Adaptive Processes*, p. 3-f-1 through 3-f-7.

2.10 Related Bibliography

Alexandridis, N. A., "The Hadamard Transform in Template Matching Pattern Recognition," *Proc. 3rd Hawaii Inter. Conf. Syst. Science*, pp. 127–130 (January 1960).

Andrews, H. C., "Multidimensional Rotations in Feature Selection," *IEEE Trans. on Computers*, Vol. C-20, No. 9, pp. 1045–1051 (September, 1971).

Bakke, F. I. and G. J. McMurtry, "A Pattern Recognition Algorithm Using the Concept of Intrinsic Dimensionality," *Symp. on Information Processing, Vol. II*, pp. 446–452, Purdue University, April 1969.

Bremermann, H. J., "Pattern Recognition, Functionals, and Entropy," *IEEE Trans. on Bio-Medical Engineering*, pp. 201–207 (July 1968).

Calvert, T. W., "Nonorthogonal Projections for Feature Extraction in Pattern Recognition," *IEEE Trans. on Computers*, vol. C-19, no. 5, pp. 447–452 (May 1970).

Carl, J. W., "An Application of Walsh Functions to Image Classification," *Proc. Appl. of Walsh Functions*, NRL, Washington, D.C. (April 1970).

Chien, Y. T. and K. S. Fu, "Selection and Ordering of Feature Observations in a Pattern Recognition System," *Information and Control*, vol. 12, pp. 394–415 (1968).

Chuang, P. C., "Recognition of Handprinted Numerals by Two-Stage Feature Extraction," *IEEE Trans. on SSC*, vol. SSC-6, no. 2, pp. 153–154 (April 1970).

Deutsch, S., "A Technique for Feature Extraction in Visual Pattern

Recognition," presented at *Symposium on Pertinent Concepts in Computer Graphics*, Urbana, Illinois, March 31, 1969.

Donaldson, R. W. and G. T. Toussaint, "Use of Contextual Constraints in Recognition of Contour-Traced Handprinted Characters," *IEEE Trans. Comp.* (Short Notes) vol. C-19, pp. 1096–1099 (November, 1970).

Fu, K. S., P. J. Min and T. J. Li, "Feature Selection in Pattern Recognition," *IEEE Trans. System Science and Cybernetics*, vol. SSC-6, no. 1, pp. 33–40 (January 1960).

Fukunaga, K. and W. L. G. Koontz, "Representation of Random Processes Using the Finite Karhunen-Loève Expansion," *Information and Control*, vol. 16, pp. 85–101, (March 1970).

Fukunaga, K. and D. R. Olson, "An Algorithm for Finding Intrinsic Dimensionality of Data," *IEEE Trans. on Computers*, vol. C-20, no. 2, pp. 176–183 (February 1971).

Fukushima, K., "Visual Feature Extraction by a Multilayered Network of Analog Threshold Elements," *IEEE Trans. SSC*, vol. SSC-5, no. 4, pp. 332–334 (October 1969).

Gulliksen, H. and S. Messick, *Psychological Scaling: Theory and Method*, Wiley, New York, 1960.

Henderson, T. L. and D. G. Lainiotis, "Application of State-Variable Techniques to Optimal Feature Extraction—Multichannel Analog Data," *IEEE Trans. Information Theory*, vol. IT-16, no. 4, pp. 396–406 (July 1970).

Henderson, T. L. and D. G. Lainiotis, "Optimum Techniques for Linear Feature Extraction," University of Texas at Austin, Tech. Report No. 73, December 1, 1969, AFOSR-69-2759.

Hong, J. P., "Pattern Recognition: Invariant Stochastic Feature Extraction and Statistical Classification," *JPL Space Programs Summary* 37–58, vol. III, pp. 80–84.

IEEE Conference Record of the Symposium on Feature Extraction and Selection in Pattern Recognition (October 5–7, 1970) Argonne National Laboratories.

IEEE Transactions on Computers, Special Issue on Feature Extraction, vol. C-20, no. 9 (September 1971).

Jerman, W. H., "Redundancy in Deterministic Sequences," *IEEE Trans. SSC*, vol. SSC-6, no. 4, pp. 358–360 (October 1970).

Lainiotis, D. G., "Optimal Feature Extraction in Pattern Recognition," *Proc 1967 Inter. Symp. on Information Theory.*

Levine, M. D., "Feature Extraction: A Survey," *Proc. IEEE*, vol. 57, no. 8, pp. 1391 (August 1969).

McClure, D. E., "Feature Selection for the Analysis of Live Patterns," Ph.D. dissertation, Division of Applied Mathematics, Center for Computer and Information Sciences, Brown University, Providence, R.I., May 1970.

Nagy, G., "Feature Extraction on Binary Patterns," *IEEE Trans. on System Science and Cybernetics*, vol. SSC-5, pp. 273–278 (October 1969).

Nelson, G. D. and D. M. Levy, "Selection of Pattern Features by Mathematical Programming Algorithms," *IEEE Trans. Systems Science and Cybernetics*, vol. SSC-6, no. 1, pp. 20–25 (January 1970).

Patrick, E. A., D. R. Anderson and F. K. Bechtel, "Mapping Multidimensional Space to One Dimension for Computer Output Display," *Proc. 23rd Nat'l. Conf. JACM*, Princeton, New Jersey, Braden/Systems Press, pp. 511–515, 1968.

Rao, C. R., "The Use and Interpretation of Principal Components Analysis in Applied Research," *Sankhya, Indian J. Stat. Ser.*, A 26, pp. 329–359 (1964).

Raviv, J., "Decision Making in Markov Chains Applied to the Problem of Pattern Recognition," *IEEE PGIT*, 13, no. 4, pp. 536–551 (1967).

Schweppe, F. C., "On the Bhattacharyya Distance and the Divergence between Gaussian Processes," *Information and Control*, vol. 11, pp. 373–395 (1967).

Schweppe, F. C., "State Space Evaluation of the Bhattacharyya Distance between Two Gaussian Processes," *Information and Control*, vol. II, pp. 352–372 (1967).

Tomita, S. S. Soguchi, and J. Oizumi, "On Evaluation of Handwritten Characters by Karhunen-Loève Orthonormal System,"

Third Hawaii International Conf. on Syst. Science, Part I, pp. 501–504 (1970).

Trunk, G. V., "Statistical Estimation of the Intrinsic Dimensionality of Data Collections," *Information and Control*, vol. 12, pp. 508–525 (1968).

Wong, E. and J. A. Steppe, "Invariant Recognition of Geometric Shapes," *Methodologies of Pattern Recognition* (S. Watanabe ed.) p. 535, Academic Press, New York, 1969.

DISTRIBUTION
FREE
CLASSIFICATION

3.0 Introduction

The topic of classification theory in the context of mathematical pattern recognition is one which has evolved to a higher state of refinement than that of feature selection. Aided by the tools of statistics, probability, information and automata theory, as well as other branches of applied mathematics, classification techniques have been developed which provide a fairly sound basis upon which decision algorithms can be implemented. Communication theory has provided a wealth of statistical classification algorithms originally developed for detection theory in early radar and communication systems. On the other side of classification theory lies an approach completely independent of statistical knowledge or assumptions, often referred to as distribution free or nonparametric classification. Unfortunately, nomenclature evolving as it has, some people strongly differ on the validity of discriminating between classification algorithms based on statistics versus nonstatistics using titles such as "parametric," "nonparametric," and "distribution free." In fact, in terms of discriminant function analysis, all classification algorithms can be reduced to partitions (fixed or varying) of pattern or feature spaces; and the description of the hyperplane boundaries may or may not be defined in the context of statistical distributions. Without becoming overly sensitive or critical of nomenclature, let it suffice to say that this chapter is devoted to those classification algorithms which can be described without reference to probability distributions. The following chapter is devoted to the statistically defined discriminant functions.

This chapter develops the concept of discriminant function with emphasis on linear, piecewise linear, quadratic, polynomial, and potential function-defined separating surfaces. A variety of linear discriminant function training algorithms are then developed. Some specific classification algorithms are discussed with their various convergence properties and classification capabilities.

Before developing the distribution free classification material, a brief comment on dimensionality is in order. The previous chapter was devoted to the topic of feature selection in which an attempt was made to reduce the dimensionality of the pattern space while retaining salient features necessary for successful classification. The feature space dimensionality was denoted by N, implying N was smaller than that of the pattern space R. However, there is no conceptual reason that classification cannot be carried out in the pattern space and in fact is often so done. For purposes of continuity, then, we shall assume that the dimensionality of data into the classifier is given by N where, in fact, N may be equal to R for the case in which no feature selection has occurred.

3.1 Discriminant Functions

Consider the K pattern classes: $S_1, S_2, \ldots, S_k, \ldots, S_K$ with defining prototypes $\mathbf{y}_m^{(k)}$ where $m = 1, \ldots, M_K$ counts the number of prototypes within a given class. Ideally, one would like a function which measures each point in the pattern or feature space and assigns to that point a value as to its degree of membership to a given class. Such functions have been called characteristic functions in the context of fuzzy set theory [1], discriminant function in the context of pattern recognition, and probability density functions in statistical decision theory. Discriminant functions have the property that they partition the pattern or feature space into mutually exclusive regions, each region contributing to the domain of a class. Note that the regions corresponding to a given class need not be contiguous. The discriminant function will be defined such that for all points $\mathbf{x}$ within the region describing S_k, there exists a function $g_k(\mathbf{x})$ such that $g_k(\mathbf{x}) > g_j(\mathbf{x})$ for all $k \neq j$. Mathematically,

$$g_k(\mathbf{x}) > g_j(\mathbf{x}) \, \forall \, \mathbf{x} \in S_k \quad \text{and} \quad \forall k \neq j \tag{3.1}$$

Thus within region S_k, the kth discriminant function will have the largest value. The surface separating region S_k and S_j is given by $g_k(\mathbf{x}) - g_j(\mathbf{x}) = 0$ which is equivalent to those points in the space which have equal discriminant functions for both class S_k and S_j. There are $K(K - 1)/2$ such separating surfaces in a K class problem. Often, though, not all surfaces will be significant and redundant hyperplanes will develop. Figure 3.1 presents an example of such a situation [2]. Note that the number of separating surfaces is equal to the number of entries above the diagonal in an upper triangular matrix. Figure 3.2 indicates the discriminant function classifier and a possible separating surface in two-dimensional space. Parenthetically it should be pointed out that adding a constant to all discriminant functions leaves the decision surfaces unchanged as does any monotonic nondecreasing operation (i.e., logarithm, square, etc.). In addition, for a two-class problem ($K = 2$) a single discriminant function and threshold element suffices for classification

$$g(\mathbf{x}) = g_1(\mathbf{x}) - g_2(\mathbf{x}) \tag{3.2}$$

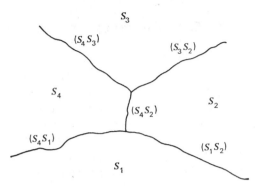

FIGURE 3.1.   Example of redundant decision surfaces (S_1, S_3).

When $g(\mathbf{x})$ is positive, class S_1 is determined and when $g(\mathbf{x})$ is negative, S_2 is determined. Actually one needs only $K - 1$ discriminant functions to separate K classes [3]. The construction and adjusting of discriminant functions is referred to as "training" or "learning." If the training is based upon statistics, parametric and certain nonparametric techniques are used. If the training is based on an assumed functional form for the discriminant function (i.e., linear, quadratic, etc.), distribution free techniques are employed.

Possibly the simplest assumed functional form for the discriminant function is that known as a linear discriminant function. Such a function can be represented in scalar and vector forms as

$$g_k(\mathbf{x}) = w_1^{(k)} x_1 + w_2^{(k)} x_2 + \cdots + w_N^{(k)} x_N + w_{N+1}^{(k)} \qquad (3.3)$$

or

$$g_k(\mathbf{x}) = \mathbf{w}_k^t \mathbf{x} \qquad (3.4)$$

Note that a scalar term $w_{N+1}^{(k)}$ has been added to the discriminant function for coordinate translation purposes. To make equation (3.4) a valid vector multiplication, the input vector $\mathbf{x}$ has been augmented to become $N + 1$ dimensional by $x_{N+1} = 1$. This will allow a translation of all linear discriminant functions to pass through the origin of the augmented space when desired. In other words the surface separating class S_j and S_k is also linear and defined as $g_k(\mathbf{x}) - g_j(\mathbf{x}) = 0$ or $(\mathbf{w}_k^t - \mathbf{w}_j^t)\mathbf{x} = 0$. One solution to this equation is given by $\mathbf{x} = \mathbf{0}$ thus indicating that the separating linear hyperplane indeed passes through the origin in augmented feature space. Figure 3.3 is such an example.

One of the simplest classification algorithms which utilizes a linear discriminant function is known as a minimum distance classifier. As a simple example of such a classifier let the average point of the prototypes defining a given class S_k be given by

$$\langle \mathbf{y}_k \rangle = \frac{1}{M_k} \sum_{m=1}^{M_k} \mathbf{y}_m^{(k)} \tag{3.5}$$

Then there exist K such points in N space. Let the Euclidean metric be assumed in the space and let the classifier assign an unknown

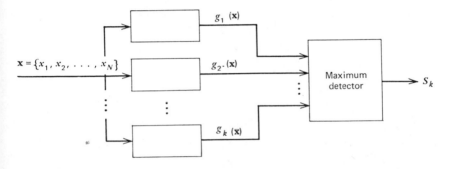

(a) A typical classifier

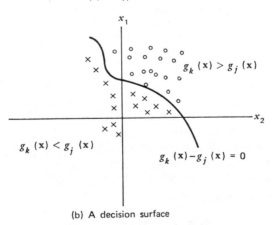

(b) A decision surface

FIGURE 3.2. Calculation and example of discriminant functions.

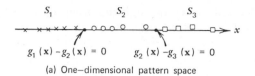

$$g_1(\mathbf{x}) - g_2(\mathbf{x}) = 0 \qquad g_2(\mathbf{x}) - g_3(\mathbf{x}) = 0$$

(a) One–dimensional pattern space

$$g_1(\mathbf{x}) - g_2(\mathbf{x}) = 0 \qquad g_2(\mathbf{x}) - g_3(\mathbf{x}) = 0$$

(b) Two–dimensional augmented pattern space

FIGURE 3.3.　Linear hyperplanes in augmented space.

point $\mathbf{x}$ to that class which has its average value $\langle \mathbf{y}_k \rangle$ closest to $\mathbf{x}$. Thus the decision rule becomes

$$\mathbf{x} \in S_j \quad \text{if} \quad d(\mathbf{x}, \langle \mathbf{y}_j \rangle) = \min_k d(\mathbf{x}, \langle \mathbf{y}_k \rangle) \tag{3.6}$$

But

$$d^2(\mathbf{x}, \langle \mathbf{y}_k \rangle) = (\mathbf{x} - \langle \mathbf{y}_k \rangle)^t (\mathbf{x} - \langle \mathbf{y}_k \rangle) \tag{3.7a}$$

$$= \mathbf{x}^t \mathbf{x} - 2\mathbf{x}^t \langle \mathbf{y}_k \rangle + \langle \mathbf{y}_k \rangle^t \langle \mathbf{y}_k \rangle \tag{3.7b}$$

According to the properties of a discriminant function we can subtract the constant $\mathbf{x}^t\mathbf{x}$ from the metric without changing the decision surfaces. However the algorithm calls for the minimum distance. By multiplying by $-\frac{1}{2}$ the modified distance squared function becomes a valid discriminant:

$$g_k(\mathbf{x}) = \mathbf{x}^t \langle \mathbf{y}_k \rangle - \tfrac{1}{2} \langle \mathbf{y}_k \rangle^t \langle \mathbf{y}_k \rangle \tag{3.8}$$

In the context of linear discriminants the elements of $\langle \mathbf{y}_k \rangle$ become the linear weights and $-\frac{1}{2}\langle\mathbf{y}_k\rangle^t\langle\mathbf{y}_k\rangle$ becomes the augmenting quantity. The decision surface becomes the perpendicular bisector separating points $\langle\mathbf{y}_j\rangle$ and $\langle\mathbf{y}_k\rangle$ for the surface between classes S_j and S_k. Figure 3.4 presents some examples for a 4-class and 7-class problem. Note in Figure 3.4a the redundant (unused) bisector or separating surface determined by classes S_4 and S_2. Also in Figure 3.4b there are 6 separating surfaces on the cube and there will be an additional surface at 45° to each of the 12 edges of the cube resulting in 18 separating surfaces. However, there are computationally $K(K-1)/2$ or 21 surfaces. The three redundant surfaces are the three bisectors in three-dimensional space separating geometrically opposing pairs of points.

One final comment is in order concerning linear discriminant functions. Remember that we have a known set of prototypes $\mathbf{y}_m^{(k)}$ assigned to each class S_k. If there exists linear discriminant functions $g_1, \ldots, g_k, \ldots, g_K$ such that $g_k(\mathbf{y}_m^{(k)}) > g_j(\mathbf{y}_m^{(k)})$ for all $m = 1, \ldots, M_k$ and for all $k \neq j$, then the classes are said to be *linearly separable*. It can be shown that such separating surfaces define convex regions.

Possibly the next step in sophistication in defining discriminant functions is given by the piecewise linear functions. The separating surfaces of piecewise linear machines no longer define convex regions in the pattern or feature spaces and consequently such machines do not possess some of the more elegant properties that linear machines have. The classic example for the piecewise linear machine is the minimum distance classifier with respect to prototypes. Thus if we wish to define the distance of an unknown $\mathbf{x}$ from a class S_k, one possibility becomes

$$d(\mathbf{x}, S_k) = \min_{m=1,\ldots,M_k} \{d(\mathbf{x}, \mathbf{y}_m^{(k)})\} \tag{3.9}$$

Thus the distance becomes the smallest distance between all of the prototypes of S_k and the unknown $\mathbf{x}$. The decision rule then becomes

$$\mathbf{x} \in S_j \quad \text{if} \quad d(\mathbf{x}, S_j) = \min_k d(\mathbf{x}, S_k) \tag{3.10}$$

The discriminant function corresponding to such an algorithm then becomes

$$g_k(\mathbf{x}) = \max_{m=1,\ldots,M_k} \{\mathbf{x}^t\mathbf{y}_m^{(k)} - \tfrac{1}{2}\mathbf{y}_m^{(k)t}\mathbf{y}_m^{(k)}\} \tag{3.11}$$

An example of such a surface is presented in Figure 3.5a.

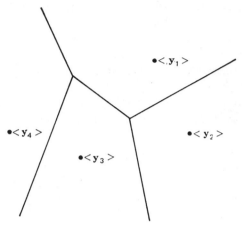

(a) Four classes ($K = 4$, $N = 2$)

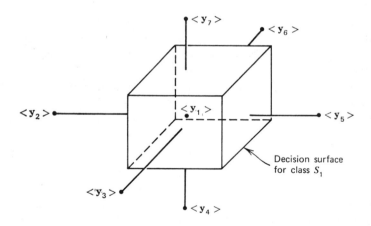

(b) Three classes ($K = 7$, $N = 3$)

FIGURE 3.4. Minimum distance classifiers.

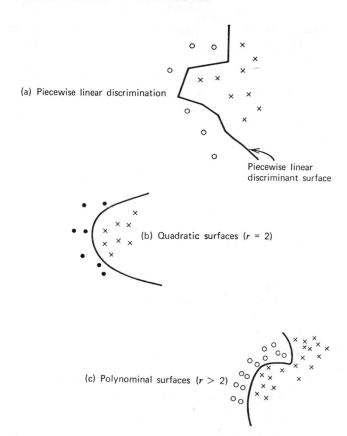

(a) Piecewise linear discrimination

Piecewise linear
discriminant surface

(b) Quadratic surfaces ($r = 2$)

(c) Polynominal surfaces ($r > 2$)

FIGURE 3.5. Nonlinear separating surfaces.

A quadratic discriminant function includes all coefficients of terms up to and including second orders. Thus there will be N linear terms, N square terms, $N(N-1)/2$ cross product terms, and one constant term. The discriminant function becomes

$$g_k(\mathbf{x}) = \sum_{n=1}^{N} w_{nn}^{(k)} x_n^2 + w_n^{(k)} x_n + \sum_{n=1}^{N-1} \sum_{j=n+1}^{N} w_{nj}^{(k)} x_n x_j + w_{N+1}^{(k)} \quad (3.12a)$$

or in vector form

$$g_k(\mathbf{x}) = \mathbf{x}^t [A_k] \mathbf{x} + \mathbf{x}^t [B_k] + w_{N+1}^{(k)} \quad (3.12b)$$

Such functions define class separating surfaces in terms of second order variables and are referred to as hyperhyperboloid surfaces. The discriminant function can be implemented as a linear function with respect to $(N + 1)(N + 2)/2$ variables using a preprocessor which computes the necessary quadratic terms. Thus

$$g_k(\mathbf{x}) = w_1^{(k)} f_1 + w_2^{(k)} f_2 + \cdots + w_T^{(k)} f_T + w_{T+1}^{(k)} \qquad (3.13)$$

where

$$\{f_1, \ldots, f_N\} = \{x_1^2, \ldots, x_N^2\}$$

$$\{f_{N+1}, \ldots, f_{2N}\} = \{x_1, \ldots, x_N\}$$

and

$$\{f_{2N+1}, \ldots, f_{N(N+3)/2}\} = \{x_1 x_2, x_1 x_3, \ldots, x_{N-1} x_N\}$$

The equation (3.13) representation for a quadratic discriminant function is then consistent with the ϕ function interpretation of Nilsson [4]. For higher order polynomial discriminant functions the above analogy can be pursued. In general for an rth order discriminant function there will exist $\binom{N+r}{r}$ coefficients and the size of f in equation (3.13) will be one less than that number in unaugmented space. By using such an interpretation it will be possible to describe rth order polynomial machines in terms of a preprocessor which computes $\mathbf{f}$ followed by a linear machine of dimensionality $\binom{N+r}{r}$. Note that such a formulation is still not applicable for piecewise linear machines because of the nonlinearity in their coefficients. Figure 3.5 includes some polynomial separating surfaces.

3.2 Linear Training Algorithms

Under the assumption that a set of prototype data is linearly separable, it is possible to develop algorithms to find the linear hyperplanes which properly separate the data. These algorithms are often referred to as "error-correction" training procedures and have the property of converging to the solution which linearly separates the prototypes into their correct classifications if indeed the data is so separable. Because the separating surfaces are linear it is possible to determine which side of the hyperplane $\mathbf{w}^t \mathbf{x} = 0$ the prototypes fall. For a two-class problem we have

$$\mathbf{w}^t\mathbf{x} > 0 \Rightarrow \mathbf{x} \in S_1 \qquad (3.14a)$$

$$\mathbf{w}^t\mathbf{x} < 0 \Rightarrow \mathbf{x} \in S_2 \qquad (3.14b)$$

If we can find a $\mathbf{w}$ such that

$$\mathbf{w}^t\mathbf{y}_m^{(1)} > 0 \qquad \text{for all} \qquad \mathbf{y}_m^{(1)} \in S_1 \qquad (3.15a)$$

and

$$\mathbf{w}^t\mathbf{y}_m^{(2)} < 0 \qquad \text{for all} \qquad \mathbf{y}_m^{(2)} \in S_2 \qquad (3.15b)$$

then the prototypes are linearly separable by the weight vector $\mathbf{w}$. It is possible to investigate the behavior of the training algorithms in "weight" space (a term introduced by Widrow [5]) as well as in pattern or feature space. To each weight vector in pattern space there exists a hyperplane passing through the origin such that $\mathbf{w}^t\mathbf{x} = 0$. To each prototype in weight space there exists a hyperplane passing through the origin such that $\mathbf{w}^t\mathbf{y}_m^{(k)} = 0$. In weight space each hyperplane dichotomizes the space such that the points on one side of the hyperplane are positive and those on the other are negative. Figure 3.6 is an example of such a weight space. By labeling each prototype in the weight space with an arrow pointing into the positive semispace and by searching for the intersection of the positive regions due to prototypes of class S_1 and negative

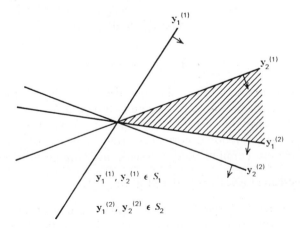

FIGURE 3.6. Two-dimensional weight space.

regions due to prototypes of class S_2 a solution region can be found such that any weight vector from that region satisfies the linearly separable solution. In Figure 3.6 the shaded region is the solution region. Obviously for nonlinearly separable data no region will exist. It should parenthetically be mentioned that a general or buffer zone can be defined to insure weight vector solutions which do not lie close to any prototype points in the pattern space. Thus

$$\mathbf{w}^t\mathbf{x} > d \tag{3.16a}$$

$$\mathbf{w}^t\mathbf{x} < -d \tag{3.16b}$$

would provide such a zone.

In order to train the weight vector we will use the following algorithm. If there exists a prototype from class S_1 such that $\mathbf{w}^t\mathbf{y}_m^{(1)} < 0$, we want to increase the value of the weight vector. If there exists a prototype from class S_2 such that $\mathbf{w}^t\mathbf{y}_m^{(2)} > 0$, we will decrease the weight vector. Therefore at the ith iteration if

$$\mathbf{w}(i)^t\mathbf{y}_m^{(1)} < 0 \tag{3.17a}$$

then

$$\mathbf{w}(i + 1) = \mathbf{w}(i) + \alpha\mathbf{y}_m^{(1)} \tag{3.18a}$$

if

$$\mathbf{w}(i)^t\mathbf{y}_m^{(2)} > 0 \tag{3.17b}$$

then

$$\mathbf{w}(i + 1) = \mathbf{w}(i) - \alpha\mathbf{y}_m^{(2)} \tag{3.18b}$$

Training occurs by cycling through the $M_1 + M_2$ prototypes, in any order, such that each prototype is tested at least once. Such a cycle is an iteration. The initial condition on $\mathbf{w}$, $\mathbf{w}(1)$ is arbitrary except for the fractional correction rule in which case $\mathbf{w}(1) \neq 0$. The three most common rules for selecting α are given below.

Fixed increment rule: $\alpha > 0$ and fixed $\tag{3.19a}$

Absolute correction rule: α is the smallest integer greater than $|\mathbf{w}(i)^t\mathbf{x}|/\mathbf{x}^t\mathbf{x}$ such that the new $\mathbf{w}(i + 1)$ will be on the proper side of the prototype hyperplane currently being tested. $\tag{3.19b}$

Fractional correction rule: α is chosen such that we move a fraction λ, normal to the hyperplane such that

$$|\mathbf{w}(i)^t\mathbf{x} - \mathbf{w}(i+1)^t\mathbf{x}| = \lambda|\mathbf{w}^t\mathbf{x}| \qquad (3.19c)$$

or

$$\alpha = \lambda \frac{|\mathbf{w}(i)^t\mathbf{x}|}{\mathbf{x}^t\mathbf{x}} \qquad (3.19d)$$

Note that the fixed increment rule with $\alpha = 1$ when iterated many times for the same prototype will result in the absolute correction rule. Note also that for the fractional correction rule for $0 < \lambda < 1$ we move toward the correct region in weight space but will never make it. For $\lambda = 2$ we reflect about the hyperplane an equivalent distance. The first two rules are guaranteed to converge to a linearly separable solution [7]. Figure 3.7 indicates the moves for the three different training procedures.

For greater than two-class problems $(K > 2)$ the weight space analogy can be pursued but visualization is difficult. However, the

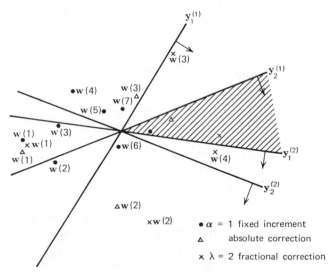

FIGURE 3.7. Three training procedures. Fixed increment terminates in seven steps. Absolute correction terminates in three steps. Fractional correction terminates in four steps.

updating algorithm becomes modified such that the solution results in a set of discriminant functions $g_k(\mathbf{x})$ such that

$$g_k(\mathbf{x}) > g_j(\mathbf{x}) \; \forall \; \mathbf{x} \in S_k \; \forall \; j \neq k \tag{3.20}$$

The separating surfaces between classes remains linear and $\mathbf{w}_k$ is the weight vector for class S_k. When the machine misclassifies $\mathbf{x}$ into S_j when it should be in S_k we want to modify $\mathbf{w}_k$ by an increase and modify $\mathbf{w}_j$ by a decrease. Thus

$$\mathbf{w}_k(i+1) = \mathbf{w}_k(i) + \alpha \mathbf{y}_{(m)}^{(k)} \tag{3.21a}$$

$$\mathbf{w}_j(i+1) = \mathbf{w}_j(i) - \alpha \mathbf{y}_m^{(k)} \tag{3.21b}$$

Again this generalized error correction procedure is guaranteed to find a set of solution weight vectors after a finite number of iterations if the prototypes are linearly separable. A point in passing should be made about the nonequivalence of this technique to the approach of finding a hyperplane separating class S_1 and not class S_1, class S_2 and not class S_2, etc., and combining to solve for the general K class problem. The difficulty of this approach is that the data may be linearly separable into K classes but there may not exist linear hyperplanes which separate out each class individually from the rest of the classes. Figure 3.8 presents such an example.

It was mentioned above that for the multiclass problem $(K > 2)$ two solution techniques exist. The first is to simultaneously solve for all discriminant functions as in equations (3.20) and (3.21). However, if we wish to linearly train a set of K polynomial discriminant functions of order r because of the nonlinear separability of the data, then a simultaneous training algorithm will force all surfaces to be as high an order polynomial as is necessary to separate the most complicated surface. This may introduce an unnecessary complication to the problem. Therefore, the second technique of separating multiclass data may be utilized. In this approach all separating surfaces are calculated, $(S_i S_j)$ many of which may be redundant. However, for a polynomial separating surface possibly only a few surfaces will require a large order of r while the others may separate linearly. Consequently, we trade off a forced rth order polynomial solution for separating all classes simultaneously, with a sequential pairwise solution where each surface will require the

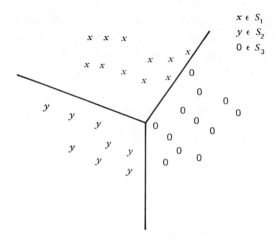

FIGURE 3.8.   Counterexample to the one class at a time procedure for the many class problem. There exist no linear hyperplanes such that the x's can be separated from the union of the y's and 0's.

minimum r for polynomial separation but redundant surfaces are calculated. Problem 7 illustrates this phenomenon in greater detail.

It is instructive to investigate one of the proofs that the fixed increment rule converges in a finite number of steps to a solution if the data is linearly separable. For simplicity of notation let $\alpha = 1$ (the increment) and let the initial weight vector guess be zero ($\mathbf{w}(0) = \mathbf{0}$). We will use a training sequence of prototypes for a two-class problem such that

$$\mathbf{y}'_m = \mathbf{y}_m \qquad \text{if} \quad \mathbf{y}_m \in S_1 \tag{3.22a}$$

$$\mathbf{y}'_m = -\mathbf{y}_m \qquad \text{if} \quad \mathbf{y}_m \in S_2 \tag{3.22b}$$

$$m = 1, \ldots, M_1 + M_2 \tag{3.22c}$$

and we will focus our attention only on those prototypes for which $\mathbf{w}(k + 1) \neq \mathbf{w}(k)$. In other words, our training sequence of prototypes will contain vectors for which new weights must be calculated at each stage. Let such a sequence be indexed by k and be denoted by P. The following theorem will then result [24].

THEOREM.   *Let S_1 and S_2 be classes of linearly separable proto-*
types. Let P be the training sequence. For the fixed increment ($\alpha = 1$)
error correction procedure and $\mathbf{w}(0) = \mathbf{0}$, the kth weight vector will
separate the data for a finite k.

The proof of the theorem is as follows. Because for every $\mathbf{y}_k'$ in P
we have $\mathbf{w}^t(k)\mathbf{y}_k' \leq 0$, the $(k + 1)$st weight vector will be

$$\mathbf{w}(k + 1) = \mathbf{w}(0) + \mathbf{y}_1' + \mathbf{y}_2' + \cdots + \mathbf{y}_k' \qquad (3.23a)$$

or

$$\mathbf{w}(k + 1) = \sum_{i=1}^{k} \mathbf{y}_i' \qquad (3.23b)$$

Let $\mathbf{w}_s$ be a solution weight vector. Let

$$a \triangleq \min_{y_i' \in P} \{\mathbf{w}_s^t \mathbf{y}_i'\} > 0 \qquad (3.24)$$

Taking the inner product of both sides of equation (3.23b) with $\mathbf{w}_s$
results in

$$\mathbf{w}_s^t \mathbf{w}(k + 1) = \sum_{i=1}^{k} \mathbf{w}_s^t \mathbf{y}_i' \qquad (3.25)$$

and

$$\mathbf{w}_s^t \mathbf{w}(k + 1) \geq ka \qquad (3.26)$$

From the Schwarz inequality we have

$$\|\mathbf{w}(k + 1)\|^2 \geq \frac{k^2 a^2}{\|\mathbf{w}_s\|^2} \qquad (3.27)$$

However we can compute $\|\mathbf{w}(k + 1)\|^2$ using a different method.
Note that

$$\mathbf{w}(i + 1) = \mathbf{w}(i) + \mathbf{y}_i' \qquad (3.28)$$

Therefore

$$\|\mathbf{w}(i + 1)\|^2 = \|\mathbf{w}(i)\|^2 + 2\mathbf{w}(i)^t \mathbf{y}_i' + \|\mathbf{y}_i'\|^2 \qquad (3.29)$$

But by definition $\mathbf{w}(i)^t \mathbf{y}_i' \leq 0$. Consequently

$$\|\mathbf{w}(i + 1)\|^2 - \|\mathbf{w}(i)\|^2 \leq \|\mathbf{y}_i'\|^2 \qquad (3.30)$$

Summing over all i results in

$$\|\mathbf{w}(k + 1)\|^2 \leq \sum_{i=1}^{k} \|\mathbf{y}_i'\|^2 \qquad (3.31)$$

or

$$\|\mathbf{w}(k+1)\|^2 \leq kE \tag{3.32}$$

where E equals the maximum energy in any of the prototypes in the training sequence P. Thus

$$E = \max_{y_i' \in P} \{\|\mathbf{y}_i'\|^2\} \tag{3.33}$$

We see from the results of equation (3.27) that each successive weight vector must increase in magnitude by the square of the iteration number k. But from the results of equation (3.32) we see that each successive weight vector must *not* increase in magnitude greater than the value of the iteration number. To avoid a contradiction from these two results we can solve for the terminal iteration k_t

$$k_t = \frac{E \|\mathbf{w}_s\|^2}{a^2} \tag{3.34}$$

which gives the terminal value of the iteration before a contradiction in the proof results. Consequently the theorem is proved. But more significantly it is interesting to investigate this bound on k. Unfortunately k is a function of a point in the solution space, $\mathbf{w}_s$, and consequently nothing can be said about the speed of convergence to a solution or about the number of trials necessary before it can be determined if indeed a set of data is linearly separable. Thus although we have found algorithms which are guaranteed to converge to a solution (if one exists) in a finite number of steps, "finite" can be a very large number. It therefore becomes useful to reformulate the question of linear separability in the context of a gradient approach utilizing a matrix algebra notation. In such a context let the matrix $[Y]$ be formed from the set of augmented prototypes $\mathbf{y}_m'$ as defined in equation (3.22) such that the rows of $[Y]$ are the prototypes. Consequently

$$[Y]^t = [\mathbf{y}_1^{(1)} \mathbf{y}_2^{(1)} \cdots \mathbf{y}_{M_1}^{(1)} - \mathbf{y}_1^{(2)} - \mathbf{y}_2^{(2)} \cdots -\mathbf{y}_{M_2}^{(2)}] \tag{3.35}$$

We are interested in obtaining a weight vector $\mathbf{w}$ such that

$$[Y]\mathbf{w} > 0 \tag{3.36a}$$

or equivalently

$$[Y]\mathbf{w} > \mathbf{z} > 0 \tag{3.36b}$$

The method of solution of equation (3.36) with which we will be interested is due to Ho and Kashyap [8, 9]. There are other methods for solving the inequality given in equation (3.36a) due to linear programming [10, 11] which lend themselves to digital computation and provide fast efficient means of separating known patterns. The technique with which we will be concerned utilizes a gradient method that adjusts $\mathbf{w}(k)$ and $\mathbf{z}(k)$ toward the direction of negative gradient such that

$$J(\mathbf{w}, \mathbf{z}) = \| [Y]\mathbf{w} - \mathbf{z} \|^2 \qquad \mathbf{z} > 0 \qquad (3.37)$$

is minimized. Taking partial derivatives results in

$$\frac{\partial J}{\partial \mathbf{w}} = [Y]^t([Y]\mathbf{w} - \mathbf{z}) \qquad (3.38a)$$

$$\frac{\partial J}{\partial \mathbf{z}} = (\mathbf{z} - [Y]\mathbf{w}) \qquad (3.38b)$$

Because $\mathbf{w}$ is unconstrained, a solution exists when

$$\mathbf{w} = ([Y]^t[Y])^{-1}[Y]^t\mathbf{z} \qquad (3.39)$$

An algorithm which approaches this gradient solution is

$$\mathbf{w}(k + 1) = \mathbf{w}(k) + \alpha[S][Y]^t \,|\mathbf{e}(k)| \qquad (3.40a)$$

$$\mathbf{z}(k + 1) = \mathbf{z}(k) + |\mathbf{e}(k)| + \mathbf{e}(k) \qquad (3.40b)$$

$$\mathbf{e}(k) = [Y]\mathbf{w}(k) - \mathbf{z}(k) \qquad (3.40c)$$

where $|\mathbf{e}(k)|$ implies componentwise magnitude and where $\mathbf{w}(0)$ is arbitrary, $\mathbf{z}(0) > 0$, and $\alpha > 0$ as in earlier algorithms. This algorithm is shown to converge in a finite number of steps bounded by a function of the matrix $[S]$ above [9]. For

$$[S] = ([Y]^t[Y])^{-1}, \qquad 0 < \alpha < 2 \qquad (3.41a)$$

the algorithm converges the fastest and when

$$\mathbf{w}(0) = ([Y]^t[Y])^{-1}[Y]^t\mathbf{z}(0) \quad \text{and} \quad \mathbf{z}(0) = (\mathbf{1}),$$

then the solution $\mathbf{w}(k)$ represents the best linear least square fit for a given $\mathbf{z}(k)$.

The algorithm given by equations (3.40) is best described by noting that a parallel set of gradient solutions are implemented simultaneously. First, for a fixed $\mathbf{z}$, equation (3.40a) is seen to be nothing more than the old weight vector updated by its gradient as determined by equation (3.38a) for $[S]$ as defined in equation (3.41a). This iteratively forces the weight vector towards the optimum global solution of equation (3.39). Now for a fixed $\mathbf{w}$, equation (3.40c) computes the error function which will have certain components negative and others positive. Those negative components correspond to the prototypes which are not on the correct side of the hyperplane. Consequently, for those negative components of $\mathbf{e}(k)$, no change in $\mathbf{z}(k)$ is allowed, see equation (3.40b). However, for those positive components of $\mathbf{e}(k)$, which correspond to correctly classified prototypes, it is now desirable to minimize $J(\mathbf{w}, \mathbf{z})$. However, in order to do this it is obvious that the corresponding components of $\mathbf{z}(k)$ must be increased toward the $[Y]\mathbf{w}(k)$ value. Thus, $\mathbf{z}(k)$ moves in the direction of steepest descent subject to the constraint $\mathbf{z} > 0$. Therefore, the algorithm of equations (3.40) can be interpreted as a simultaneous solution of two gradient techniques, one searching for a global optimum $(\mathbf{w})$ and the other searching for a constrained optimum $(\mathbf{z})$ in order that $J(\mathbf{w}, \mathbf{z})$ be minimized. The speed of convergence can be effected by

$$[S] = [I], \quad 0 < \alpha < \|[Y]^t[Y]\|^{-1} \tag{3.41b}$$

and the norm of a matrix can be defined as any of the following

$$\|[A]\| = \sum_{ij}^{N} |a_{ij}|$$

$$\|[A]\| = \max_{i} \sum_{j=i}^{N} |a_{ij}|$$

$$\|[A]\| = \left(\sum_{ij} |a_{ij}|^2\right)^{1/2} = \mathrm{tr}([A][A]^*)^{1/2}.$$

Here the algorithm is the simplest to implement but converges slower. Note that the constraint of equation (3.41a) requires the inversion of a matrix which may not exist. In such a case the generalized inverse must be used. Secondly, even if the inverse does exist it may be considerably difficult to compute if the pattern recognition problem is of large dimensions. The asymptotic property of the algorithm of equation (3.40) is shown to converge exponentially and [9]

$$k_t = (\log \|e(0)\|^2)/C \qquad (3.42)$$

where C is proportional only to a priori knowledge given by the prototypes. Thus it is possible from equation (3.42) to bound k_t firmly as opposed to the results of equation (3.34) where k_t was a function of the solution vector. Note also that the algorithm updates the $\mathbf{w}(k)$ vector componentwise such that only those prototypes which are still misclassified cause adjustment of the solution weight vector. This is accomplished by the factor $|e(k)| + e(k)$ which has components zero for correctly classified prototypes and thus there is no change for those components in the next weight vector.

It is instructive to compare the algorithms discussed so far for comparison purposes. The fixed increment rule of equation (3.19a) was presented in a one-at-a-time context in which each prototype was investigated singly. Such an algorithm has often been referred to as the "perceptron" algorithm and when implemented in a many-at-a-time environment becomes

$$\mathbf{w}(k + 1) = \mathbf{w}(k) + \alpha[Y]^t[\text{sgn} |e(k)| - \text{sgn } e(k)] \qquad (3.43)$$

The "relaxation" algorithm becomes

$$\mathbf{w}(k + 1) = \mathbf{w}(k) + \alpha[Y]^t[|e(k)| - e(k)] \qquad (3.44)$$

where in both cases

$$e(k) = [Y]\mathbf{w}(k) - \mathbf{1} \qquad (3.45)$$

where it may be desirable to normalize the error vector to remain within reasonable bounds for computation. Thus the "relaxation" algorithm, like the "perceptron" algorithm, is a many-at-a-time technique. The distance moved is proportional to the magnitude of misclassification as opposed to being simply proportional to the sign of classification and can be likened to the fractional correction rule investigated earlier. Note that of the three types of algorithms presented thus far, perceptron, relaxation, and gradient, only the latter lends itself to interpretation (best linear least squares fit) to nonlinearly separable data.

Before continuing to the subject of piecewise linear decision

surfaces, it is instructive to review just what is significant about the
training procedures described above. It could be argued that considerable effort has been spent on linearly separable data when, in
fact, a set of prototypes may be far from linearly separable. However,
it is important to point out that the training techniques so presented
are equally valid for training any set of linear coefficients. Therefore data may be quadratically separable, and discriminant functions
may have their quadratic and linear coefficients (see equation (3.13))
linearly trained. In fact any order polynomial discriminant function
can have its coefficients trained in a linear fashion, thus simulating
the ϕ machine of Nilsson, and we will see that by Taylor series
approximating the decision surfaces resulting from certain potential
function method techniques, it will be possible to linearly train
coefficients such that the resulting surfaces properly separate the
prototypes no matter how complex they are. Of course, the usefulness of such a procedure may be in question both from a computational complexity consideration as well as separability potential on
unknown patterns. For the interested reader further discussion of
this and other related topics can be found in Nilsson [5] and Cover
[23] in which the degrees of freedom of polynomial separating
surfaces might be a useful indicator of separability.

3.3 Piecewise Linear Machines

While it is possible to train coefficients of any order polynomial
linearly, piecewise linear machines do not lend themselves to the
same analysis. Nilsson [12] and Henrichon and Fu [13] both talk
about layered machines which can be described in terms of a piecewise linear decision surface. Possibly the easiest machine to describe
is a two-layer machine known as a "committee" machine such that
the second layer is a single linear surface whose weight vector is the
unity vector (1). The first layer consists of an odd number of linear
surfaces or threshold logic units (TLU's) whose outputs have been
clipped to describe which semispace the particular input falls (see
Figure 3.9). The machine is a committee machine because it takes a
fair vote for each linear discriminant function output to determine
the classification of an input. An example of nonlinearly separable

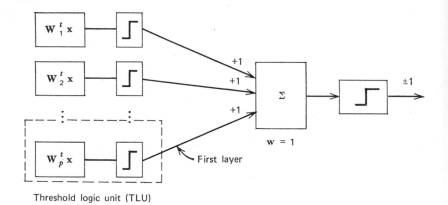

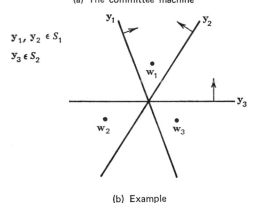

(a) The committee machine

$$\mathbf{y}_1, \mathbf{y}_2 \in S_1$$
$$\mathbf{y}_3 \in S_2$$

(b) Example

FIGURE 3.9. Committee machine.

$\mathbf{w}_1^t\mathbf{y}_1 > 0$	$\mathbf{w}_1^t\mathbf{y}_2 > 0$	$\mathbf{w}_1^t\mathbf{y}_3 > 0$
$\mathbf{w}_2^t\mathbf{y}_1 < 0$	$\mathbf{w}_2^t\mathbf{y}_2 > 0$	$\mathbf{w}_2^t\mathbf{y}_3 < 0$
$\mathbf{w}_3^t\mathbf{y}_1 > 0$	$\mathbf{w}_3^t\mathbf{y}_2 < 0$	$\mathbf{w}_3^t\mathbf{y}_3 < 0$
$\mathbf{y}_1 \in S_1$	$\mathbf{y}_2 \in S_1$	$\mathbf{y}_3 \in S_2$

data which is committee machine separable is also given in Figure 3.9 in the weight space. Nilsson [12] describes a training procedure for such a machine which has intuitive appeal. In addition he shows that it is always possible to properly dichotomize a set of data with two layers, thus indicating that additional layers would serve only to simplify the first layer. It should be parenthetically added that the results of the layered machine in reference [13] are piecewise linear surfaces parallel to the dimensions of the vector space. The properties of layered machines can be analyzed with switching function theory owing to the Boolean nature of the output at each layer. Thus the prototypes from pattern space are mapped by the first layer onto the vertices of a p-dimensional hypercube with coordinates ± 1. The hypercubes can then be investigated as to their separability condition in this layer. Finally it should be mentioned that a system of prototypes may not be committee machine separable but may still be successfully separated by a two-layered machine similar to that of Figure 3.9 but with the weight vector in the second layer augmented and properly adjusted. (see problems 2, 3, 4).

A second type of piecewise linear machine was mentioned earlier and is the minimum distance classifier with respect to prototypes. Such a machine can be likened to a nearest neighbor rule (NN) of which there has been considerable material published in the literature [14–17]. The simplest NN rule classifies an unknown in the category of its nearest neighbor. Variations on this theme include the k-nearest neighbor rule [18, 19] in which an unknown is classified according to the plurality (majority for 2 classes) of the k nearest neighbors. It has been shown [17] that the probability of error of such a rule is greater than the Bayes probability of error (see the following chapter) and less than twice that Bayes error. One of the major disadvantages of such a rule is that it requires a tremendous amount of storage as well as computation for a decision to be reached. As a suggestion to alleviate the storage and computational problems, the condensed nearest neighbor rule (CNN) has been proposed [20]. Such a rule makes use of a "consistent subset" of a set of data such that when the consistent subset is used as a reference set for the NN rule the remaining points in the simple set are correctly classified. While the theory is still lacking for such an approach, large storage requirement reductions have been reported using such an algorithm [20].

3.4 Potential Function Method

The potential function method for discriminant function definition is unlike that described in the previous discussion in that a polynomial surface is not assumed beforehand. Instead the method of superposition is utilized such that a function is defined for each prototype over the entire pattern space with variable $\mathbf{x}$. Such a function, known as a kernel in probability density function estimators, will be denoted $\psi(\mathbf{x}, \mathbf{y}_m^{(k)})$ where, again, $\mathbf{y}_m^{(k)}$ is the mth prototype defining class S_k. The sum of these individual kernel "potential" functions will then become our discriminant function:

$$g_k(\mathbf{x}) = \frac{\left(\sum_{m=1}^{M_k} \psi(\mathbf{x}, \mathbf{y}_m^{(k)}) \right)}{M_k} \tag{3.46}$$

Note that because the summation is only over a given class, S_k, the same method can be used to describe probability density functions in probability space or characteristic functions in fuzzy set space. Such a statement cannot be made for the discriminant functions described earlier by the various iterative training algorithms. The $\psi(\cdot)$ function may be different between classes or even between prototypes within a class and should reflect a decreasing influence of a sample point $\mathbf{y}_m^{(k)}$ upon points in the pattern space $\mathbf{x}$ as the distance $d(\mathbf{x}, \mathbf{y}_m^{(k)})$ between the two points increases. The average of these $\psi(\cdot)$ kernels or "potentials" of prototypes from a given class indicates a degree of membership of the point $\mathbf{x}$ in the class. An example might be

$$\psi(\mathbf{x}, \mathbf{y}_m^{(k)}) = \frac{1}{1 + ad^2(\mathbf{x}, \mathbf{y}_m^{(k)})} \tag{3.47}$$

Desirable characteristics of potential functions might be enumerated as follows.

(1) $\psi(\mathbf{x}, \mathbf{y})$ should be maximized for $\mathbf{x} = \mathbf{y}$.
(2) $\psi(\mathbf{x}, \mathbf{y})$ should be approximately zero for $\mathbf{x}$ distant from $\mathbf{y}$ in the region of interest.
(3) $\psi(\mathbf{x}, \mathbf{y})$ should be smooth (continuous) and decrease approximately monotonically with distance $d(\mathbf{x}, \mathbf{y})$.
(4) If $\psi(\mathbf{x}_1, \mathbf{y}) = \psi(\mathbf{x}_2, \mathbf{y})$ where $\mathbf{y}$ is a prototype, then patterns represented by $\mathbf{x}_1$ and $\mathbf{x}_2$ should have approximately the same "degree of similarity" to $\mathbf{y}$.

If a set of potential functions are determined such that a satisfactory discriminant function is obtained, then certain modifications to that function are possible. Thus if

$$g_k(\mathbf{x}) > g_j(\mathbf{x}) \tag{3.48a}$$

then

$$f(\mathbf{x}) + g_k(\mathbf{x}) > g_j(\mathbf{x}) + f(\mathbf{x}) \qquad \forall f(\mathbf{x}) \tag{3.48b}$$

and

$$f(\mathbf{x})g_k(\mathbf{x}) > g_j(\mathbf{x})f(\mathbf{x}) \qquad \forall f(\mathbf{x}) > 0 \tag{3.48c}$$

Therefore certain modifications for convenience are possible to the potential function. One example follows. Let

$$\begin{aligned}
\psi_1(\mathbf{x}, \mathbf{y}) &= \exp\{-(\mathbf{x} - \mathbf{y})^t(\mathbf{x} - \mathbf{y})\} \\
&= \exp\{-\|\mathbf{x} - \mathbf{y}\|^2\} \\
&= \exp\{-\|\mathbf{x}\|^2 - \|\mathbf{y}\|^2 + 2\mathbf{x}^t\mathbf{y}\} \tag{3.49}
\end{aligned}$$

Then a new, equally valid, potential function may be

$$\psi_2(\mathbf{x}, \mathbf{y}) = \exp\{\|\mathbf{x}\|^2\}\psi_1(\mathbf{x}, \mathbf{y}) \tag{3.50a}$$

$$\psi_2(\mathbf{x}, \mathbf{y}) = \exp\{2\mathbf{x}^t\mathbf{y} - \|\mathbf{y}\|^2\} \tag{3.50b}$$

which may be easier to compute because of being of a lower order in $\mathbf{x}$. This same technique was utilized in making the minimum distance classifier linear.

In order to be guaranteed of the generality and power of the potential function method, the following theorem and proof (due to Meisel [21]) is of interest.

THEOREM. *Let* $S_1 = \{\mathbf{y}_1^{(1)}, \mathbf{y}_2^{(1)}, \ldots, \mathbf{y}_{M_1}^{(1)}\}$ *be one class and* $S_2 = \{\mathbf{y}_1^{(2)}, \mathbf{y}_2^{(2)}, \ldots, \mathbf{y}_{M_2}^{(2)}\}$ *be another. There exists a potential function* $\psi(\mathbf{x}, \mathbf{y})$ *such that* $g_k(\mathbf{x})$ *classifies all points of* S_1 *and* S_2 *correctly.*

PROOF. Let D be the closest distance of all points in one class to points in the other. Then

$$D^2 = \operatorname*{Min}_{1 \leq i \leq M_1}\left\{\operatorname*{Min}_{1 \leq j \leq M_2}\{\|\mathbf{y}_i^{(1)} - \mathbf{y}_j^{(2)}\|^2\}\right\}$$

Let

$$\psi(\mathbf{x}, \mathbf{y}) = \exp\left\{-\frac{1}{\alpha}\|\mathbf{x} - \mathbf{y}\|^2\right\}$$

and let

$$\frac{1}{\alpha} > [\ln(\text{Max}\{M_1, M_2\})]/D^2$$

Then

$$g_2(\mathbf{y}_m^{(1)}) = \frac{1}{M_2} \sum_{i=1}^{M_2} \exp\left\{-\frac{1}{\alpha} \|\mathbf{y}_m^{(1)} - \mathbf{y}_i^{(2)}\|^2\right\}$$

which is the sum of the elements in class S_2 evaluated at the $\mathbf{y}_m^{(1)}$ point in class S_1. But

$$g_2(\mathbf{y}_m^{(1)}) \leq \underset{1 \leq i \leq M_2}{\text{Max}} \left\{\exp\left\{-\frac{1}{\alpha} \|\mathbf{y}_m^{(1)} - \mathbf{y}_i^{(2)}\|^2\right\}\right\}$$

and

$$g_2(\mathbf{y}_m^{(1)}) \leq \exp\left\{-\frac{1}{\alpha}\left(\underset{1 \leq i \leq M_2}{\text{Min}} \{\|\mathbf{y}_m^{(1)} - \mathbf{y}_i^{(2)}\|^2\}\right)\right\}$$

$$g_2(\mathbf{y}_m^{(1)}) \leq \exp\{-D^2/\alpha\}$$

$$g_2(\mathbf{y}_m^{(1)}) < \exp\{-\ln(\text{Max}\{M_1, M_2\})\}$$

by replacing $1/\alpha$ by its constraint defined earlier. But because $\text{Max}(M_1, M_2) \geqq M_1$ we have

$$g_2(\mathbf{y}_m^{(1)}) < \exp\{-\ln M_1\} = \frac{1}{M_1}$$

and by replacing the value unity with its exponential form

$$g_2(\mathbf{y}_m^{(1)}) < \frac{1}{M_1} \exp\left\{-\frac{1}{\alpha} \|\mathbf{y}_m^{(1)} - \mathbf{y}_m^{(1)}\|^2\right\}$$

$$< \frac{1}{M_1} \sum_{i=1}^{M_1} \exp\left\{-\frac{1}{\alpha} \|\mathbf{y}_m^{(1)} - \mathbf{y}_i^{(1)}\|^2\right\}$$

$$< g_1(\mathbf{y}_m^{(1)})$$

Therefore $g_1(\mathbf{y}_m^{(1)}) > g_2(\mathbf{y}_m^{(1)})$ for all m and consequently all points in class S_1 are correctly classified. Similarly by reversing the notation and subscripts, all the points in class S_2 will be correctly classified. Note that the potential functions and therefore discriminant functions are continuously differentiable.

The results of the proof indicate that any set of data can be properly separated. However, as before when using piecewise linear and higher order polynomial discriminant functions, the resulting surface may not separate unknowns successfully owing to the complicated nature of that surface. Thus the power of the potential function method will also be limited by the degree of clustering of the points in the original patterns. The discriminant function will be quite complex and will behave poorly for unknown points if the original training set was not well separated in the feature selection process. We will see application of the above technique in estimating density functions in the next chapter. Note also that the incremented correction rules presented earlier can be interpreted as subsets of the potential function method [22].

3.5 Problems

1. Given the following two-class set of prototypes

$$S_1 = \{(2, 2), (3, 1), (3, 3), (-1, -3), (4, 2), (-2, -2)\}$$
$$S_2 = \{(7, 1), (-2, 2), (7, 3), (-4, 2), (-4, 3), (8, 3)\}$$

(a) Determine if the two classes are linearly separable.

(b) If they are linearly separable, use a fixed increment, $\alpha = 1$, one-at-a-time algorithm with $\mathbf{w}(1) = \mathbf{0}$ to determine the separating boundaries.

(c) Classify the following points

$$Y_1 = (-1, -1)$$
$$Y_2 = (2, 0)$$
$$Y_3 = (5, 0)$$
$$Y_4 = (0, 3)$$

using a minimum distance classifier with respect to class means. Draw the decision surfaces in two-space.

(d) Is the classifier used in (c) linear?

(e) In two-space draw the decision surfaces for a minimum distance classifier with respect to prototypes.

(f) Classify the points of (c) using the surfaces of (e).

(g) Is the classifier of (e) linear?

2. A weight space is plotted with 4 prototype pattern hyperplanes
    below. The arrows point to the positive side of the hyper-
    planes.

    (a) P_1 and P_2 are members of Class 1.
        P_3 and P_4 are members of Class 2.
        Are the prototypes linearly separable?
    (b) P_1 and P_2 are members of Class 1.
        $-P_3$ and $-P_4$ are members of Class 2.
        Are the prototypes linearly separable?
    (c) For the case in which they are not linearly separable, will
        a committee machine provide a solution? If so, what size
        machine is necessary (lower bound)?
    (d) If a committee machine solution exists, indicate the weights
        on the weight space diagram.

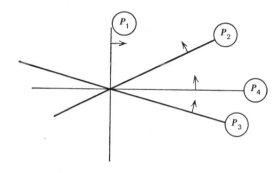

3. You are presented with the following prototypes in augmented
    form:

$$P_1 = (3, 1, 1)$$
$$P_2 = (4, 0, 1)$$
$$P_3 = (4, -\tfrac{1}{2}, 1)$$
$$P_4 = (5, 2, 1)$$
$$P_5 = (5, 3, 1)$$
$$P_6 = (1, 2, 1)$$
$$P_7 = (0, -4, 1)$$

and are informed that P_1, P_2, and P_3 are members of class S_1
and P_4, P_5, P_6, and P_7 are members of class S_2. You also

have learned that a layered machine might be a useful tool in dichotomizing the prototypes properly. You begin with the simplest such machine, 3 TLU's in the 1st layer and 1 TLU in the 2nd layer.

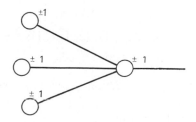

You have selected the TLU weight vectors to be

$$W_1 = -1, 1, 5$$
$$W_2 = 1, 1, -1$$
$$W_3 = -\tfrac{1}{2}, 1, 0$$

(a) Compute and plot the prototypes in the first layer space, i.e., each prototype will be characterized by a 3-sample code word of elements ±1.

(b) Will a committee machine separate these prototypes with the TLU's as shown?

(c) Will any layered machine separate these prototypes with the TLU's as shown?

(d) What single prototype must be removed for the first layer space to be linearly separable?

(e) Will a committee machine work now?

(f) What weight vector on TLU-4 (2nd layer), consisting only of elements ±1, will dichotomize the space properly (ignoring the removed prototype).

4. Using the same data and problem set up as in problem 3 show that by changing the sign of one of the dimensions in all the weight vectors, the first layer space is linearly separable.

(a) What are the new weight vectors?

(b) Compute and plot the prototypes in the first layer space.

(c) Find a weight vector for TLU-4 (2nd layer) which solves the problem for all seven prototypes.

(d) Will a committee machine suffice with the three TLU weight vectors in part (4a)?

5. Given three pattern classes, S_1, S_2, and S_3. Find linear discriminant functions for the sample points

$$\{(0, 1, -1, 2)\} \in S_1$$
$$\{(1, 1, 1, 1), (2, 1, 1, 1)\} \in S_2$$
$$\{(-1, 1, 0, 1)\} \in S_3$$

using the absolute correction algorithm one at a time, and $\mathbf{w}^{(k)}(0) = \mathbf{0}$ for all k.

6. Given the sample vectors

$$\mathbf{y}_1 = (1, 1, -1, 0, 2)$$
$$\mathbf{y}_2 = (0, 0, 1, 2, 0)$$
$$\mathbf{y}_3 = (-1, -1, 1, 1, 0)$$
$$\mathbf{y}_4 = (4, 0, 1, 2, 1)$$
$$\mathbf{y}_5 = (-1, 1, 1, 1, 0)$$
$$\mathbf{y}_6 = (-1, -1, -1, 1, 0)$$
$$\mathbf{y}_7 = (-1, 1, 1, 2, 1)$$

where

$$\{\mathbf{y}_2, \mathbf{y}_4, \mathbf{y}_5, \mathbf{y}_6\} \in S_1$$

and

$$\{\mathbf{y}_1, \mathbf{y}_3, \mathbf{y}_7\} \in S_2$$

If they are presented in numerical order repeatedly, give the sequence of weight vectors and the solution generated using $\mathbf{w}(0) = (1, 1, 1, -1, -1, 1)$ and

(a) Fixed increment $\alpha = 1$ one-at-a-time
(b) "Perception" $\alpha = 1$ many-at-a-time
(c) "Gradient" $\alpha = .02$, $[S] = [I]$ many-at-a-time
(d) "Relaxation" $\alpha = .025$ many-at-a-time
(e) "Gradient" $\alpha = 1.[S] = ([Y]^t[Y])^{-1}$ many-at-a-time
Note: It may be desirable to normalize by the norm of $\mathbf{e}(k)$ to speed convergence.

7. You are intrigued with the Φ machine approach and decide to linearly train the coefficients of an rth order polynomial using

the fixed increment one-at-a-time algorithm with $\alpha = 1$. The data given you is the following:

$$\{(1, 1), (0, -1), (4, 5)\} \in S_1$$
$$\{(2, 2), (0, 2), (2, 3)\} \in S_2$$
$$\{(-1, -1), (-2, 0)\} \in S_3$$

(a) Find the minimum r necessary for simultaneous separation of the data.

(b) Start with $\mathbf{w}_1(0) = \mathbf{w}_2(0) = \mathbf{w}_3(0) = \mathbf{0}$ and remembering that the dimension is a function of r and the pattern space $N = 2$, solve for the $\mathbf{w}_1$, $\mathbf{w}_2$, and $\mathbf{w}_3$ weight vectors. (Good luck!)

(c) Repeat 7a finding the minimum r_1, r_2, r_3 for individually separating surface $(S_1 S_2)$, $(S_2 S_3)$, $(S_3 S_1)$ respectively.

8. You are given the following two-class set of prototypes in augmented space:

$$\{(5, 5, 1), (5, 7, 1), (4, 9, 1), (6, 9, 1)\} \in S_1$$
$$\{(5, 2, 1), (2, 3, 1), (8, 3, 1), (9, 6, 1), (1, 6, 1)\} \in S_2$$

and having a sneaking suspicion that the data is separable.

(a) It is linearly separable?

(b) Is it quadratically separable?

(c) Go to a high enough polynomial and separate it. Let $\mathbf{w}(0) = \mathbf{0}$ and use any iterative algorithm you like.

9. Using the data of problem 8, classify the following points:

$$\mathbf{x}_1 = (0, 0, 1)$$
$$\mathbf{x}_2 = (0, 1, 1)$$
$$\mathbf{x}_3 = (5, 9, 1)$$
$$\mathbf{x}_4 = (2, -1, 1)$$
$$\mathbf{x}_5 = (3, 3, 1)$$
$$\mathbf{x}_6 = (0, 5, 1)$$

(a) Using the NN rule with respect to prototypes and a Euclidean distance.

(b) Using the $k - NN$ rule with respect to prototypes and a Euclidean distance with $k = 3$.

    (c) Repeat (a) using the city block distance (absolute value).

    (d) Repeat part (b) using the absolute value distance.

10. (a) Using the data of problem 6 find the discriminant functions for both classes using the potential function method. Follow the proof in the notes closely for this problem (i.e., properly determine $1/\alpha$ and select a similar kernel).

    (b) Prove that your discriminant functions are valid by evaluating them for each prototype.

11. How many separating surfaces in a K class problem?

12. What two words are descriptive of the minimum distance classifier with respect to prototypes?

13. Given the following means in two-space draw the decision surfaces for a minimum classifier.

$$\mathbf{m}_1 = (0, 0)$$
$$\mathbf{m}_2 = (1, 1)$$
$$\mathbf{m}_3 = (1, 2)$$
$$\mathbf{m}_4 = (2, 1)$$

14. Justify the use of augmented pattern space.

15. If a set of data is separable will the fixed increment rule always separate it?

16. Given a set of prototype data, is it always possible to properly separate it into the correct classes by decision surfaces?

17. Given a K class problem which is linearly separable, is it possible to separate the classes by two-class techniques concentrating on class S_k and class not S_k?

18. Repeat problem 17 where the two-class techniques concentrate on classes S_k and S_j.

19. What is a ϕ machine and what is its usefulness in linear training techniques?

20. Does there exist a potential function which will always separate data properly from two classes?

21. Given the following set of data

$(.5, 1.5, 0)$	$(.5, .5, -1.0)$
$(.5, 2.5, 0)$	$(1.5, .5, -.5)$
$(.5, 3.5, .5)$	$(1.5, 1.5, 0)$
$(1.5, 3.5, 1.0)$	$(1.5, 2.5, 0)$

Find a weight which will linearly separate the two classes using any training method. However, you must indicate the method used as well as the correct solution.

22. Determine the values of matrix $[A_k]$ and $[B_k]$ in equation (3.12b) in terms of the w's of equation (3.12a).

3.6 References

1. Zadeh, L. A., "Communication Fuzzy Algorithms," *Information and Control*, Vol. 12, p. 94–102 (1968).

2. Nilsson, N. J., *Learning Machines*, McGraw-Hill, New York, 1965, p. 19.

3. Nilsson, N. J., *ibid.*, p. 7.

4. Nilsson, N. J., *ibid.*, p. 30.

5. Nilsson, N. J., *ibid.*, Chapter 4.

6. Fu, K. S., *Sequential Methods in Pattern Recognition and Machine Learning*, Academic Press, New York, 1968, Chapter 1.

7. Nilsson, N. J., *op.cit.*, Chapter 5.

8. Ho, Y. C. and R. L. Kashyap, "An Algorithm for Linear Inequalities and its Applications," *IEEE Transactions Electronic Computers*, Vol. EC-14, pp. 683–688 (1965).

9. Mendel, J. M. and K. S. Fu, *Adaptive, Learning and Pattern Recognition Systems*, Academic Press, New York, 1970, Chapter 3.

10. Dantzig, G., *Linear Programming and Extensions*, Princeton University Press, Princeton, N.J., 1963.

11. Smith, F., "Pattern Classifier Design by Linear Programming," *IEEE Transactions on Computers*, Vol. C-17, No. 4 (April, 1968) pp. 367–372.

12. Nilsson, N. J., *op.cit.*, Chapter 6.

13. Henrichon, E. B., Jr. and K. S. Fu, "A Nonparametric Partitioning Procedure for Pattern Classification," *IEEE Transactions on Computers*, Vol. C-18, No. 7, pp. 614–623 (July 1969).

14. Duda, R. O. and H. Fossum, "Pattern Classification by Iteratively Determined Linear and Piecewise Linear Discriminant Functions," *IEEE Transactions on Electronic Computers*, Vol. EC-15, No. 2 (April 1966) pp. 220–232.

15. Peterson, D. W., "Some Convergence Properties of a Nearest Neighbor Rule," *IEEE Transactions on Information Theory*, Vol. IT-16, No. 1, pp. 26–31 (January 1970).

16. Chow, C. K., "A Recognition Method Using Neighbor Dependence," *IRE Trans. on Electronic Computers*, Vol. 11, pp. 683–690 (October 1962).

17. Cover, T. M. and P. E. Hart, "Nearest Neighbor Pattern Classification," *IEEE Trans. on Information Theory*, Vol. IT-13, No. 1, pp. 21–26 (January 1967).

18. Fix, E. and J. L. Hodges, Jr., "Discriminatory Analysis, Non-parametric Discrimination," USAF School of Aviation Medicine, Randolph Field, Texas, Project 21-49-004, Report 4, Contract AF41(128)-31 (February 1951).

19. Fix, E. and J. L. Hodges, Jr., "Discriminatory Analysis: Small Sample Performance," USAF School of Aviation Medicine, Randolph Field, Texas, Project 21-49-004, Report 11 (August 1952).

20. Hart, P. E., "The Condensed Nearest Neighbor Rule," *IEEE Transactions on Information Theory*, Vol. IT-14, No. 3, pp. 515–516 (May 1968).

21. Meisel, W. S., "Potential Functions in Mathematical Pattern Recognition," *IEEE Trans. on Computers*, Vol. C-18, No. 10, pp. 911–918 (October 1969).

22. Babu, C. C. and W. Chan, "On the Potential Function Method and the Increment Error Correction Rule in Pattern Classification," *IEEE Proceedings*, Vol. 57, No. 11 (Letters) pp. 2086–2088 (November 1969).

23. Cover, T. M., "Geometrical and Statistical Properties of Systems of Linear Inequalities with Applications in Pattern Recognition," *IEEE Trans. on Electronic Computers*, Vol. EC-14, No. 3, pp. 326–334 (1965).

24. Block, H. D., "The Perception: A Model for Brain Functioning I," *Reviews of Modern Physics*, Vol. 34, No. 1, pp. 123–135 (Jan. 1962).

3.7 Related Bibliography

Aizerman, M. A., E. M. Braverman and L. I. Rozonoer, "Theoretical Foundations of the Potential Function Method in Pattern Recognition Learning," *Automation and Remote Control*, vol. 25, no. 6, pp. 917–936 (June 1964).

Aizerman, M. A., E. M. Braverman and L. I. Rozonoer, "The Probability Problem of Pattern Recognition Learning and the Method of Potential Functions," *Automation and Remote Control*, vol. 25, no. 9, pp. 1175–1190 (1964).

Babu, C. C. and W. C. Chan, "An Algorithm for Pattern Classification Using Eigenvectors," IEEE Trans. Computers, vol. C-20, no. 5, pp. 575–578 (May 1971).

Bashkerov, O. A., E. M. Braverman and I. B. Muchnick, "Potential Function Algorithms for Pattern Recognition Learning Machines," *Avtomatika i Telemekhanika*, vol. 25, no. 5, pp. 692–695 (May 1964).

Braverman, E. M., "On the Method of Potential Functions," *Avtomatika i Telemekhanika*, vol. 26, no. 12, pp. 2130–2139 (December 1965).

Cadzow, J. A., "Synthesis of Nonlinear Decision Boundaries by Cascaded Threshold Gates," *IEEE Trans. on Computers*, vol. C-17, no. 12, pp. 1165–1172 (December 1968).

Chaplin, W. G. and V. S. Levadi, "A Generalization of the Linear Threshold Decision Algorithm to Multiple Classes," *Computer and Information Sciences II*, ed. Tou, Academic Press, New York, 1967, pp. 337–355.

Cover, T. M., "Estimation by the Nearest-Neighbor Rule," *IEEE Trans. Info. Theory*, vol. IT-14, no. 1, pp. 50–55 (January 1968).

Das, S. K., "A Method of Decision Making in Pattern Recognition," *IEEE Trans. on Computers*, vol. C-18, no. 4, pp. 329–333 (April 1969).

Drucker, H., "Computer Optimization of Recognition Networks," *IEEE Transactions on Computers*, vol. C-18, no. 10, pp. 918–923 (October 1969).

Fukunaga, K. and D. R. Olsen, "Piecewise Linear Discriminant Functions and Classification Errors for Multiclass Problems," *IEEE Trans. Information Theory*, vol. IT-16, no. 1, pp. 99–100 (January 1970).

Hellman, M. E., "The Nearest-Neighbor Classification Rule with a Reject Option," *IEEE Trans. SSC*, vol. SSC-6, no. 3, pp. 179–185, (July 1970).

Highleyman, W. H., "Linear Decision Functions, with Applications to Pattern Recognition," Ph.D. dissertation, Electrical Engineering Department, Polytechnic Institute of Brooklyn, New York, June 1961.

Highleyman, W. H., "Linear Decision Functions with Application to Pattern Recognition," *Proc. IRE*, vol. 50, no. 6, pp. 1501–1514, (June, 1962).

Hiva, H. R. and C. L. Sheng, "An Approach for the Decomposition of Higher Degree Φ-Functions by Using Imperfect Φ-Functions," *Proc. Syst. for Seventies*, Pittsburgh, October 14–17, 1970.

Hudson, J. F. P., *Piecewise Linear Topology*, Benjamin, New York, 1969.

Ibaraki, T. and S. Muroga, "Adaptive Linear Classifier by Linear Programming," *IEEE Trans. System Science and Cybernetics*, vol. SSC-6, no. 1, pp. 53–63 (January 1970).

Kaminuma, T. and S. Watanabe, "On the Development of a Well-Balanced Adaptive Linear Decision Function," *Proc. 3rd Hawaii Conf. Sys. Science*, pp. 111–114 (January 1970).

Kashyap, R. L., "Algorithms for Pattern Classification," Chapter 3 of *Adaptive, Learning and Pattern Recognition Systems*, ed. Mendel and Fu, pp. 81–113, Academic Press, New York, 1970.

Lambert, P. F., "Designing Pattern Categorizers with Extremal Paradigm Information," *Methodologies in Pattern Recognition*, ed. Watanabe, pp. 359–391, Academic Press, New York, 1969.

Meisel, W. S., "Potential Functions in Pattern Classification Algorithms," *Proc. IEEE Symp. on Adaptive Processes 1969*, pp. 3-d-1 to 3-d-6.

Mengert, P. H., "Solution of Linear Inequalities," *IEEE Transactions on Computers*, vol. C-19, no. 2, pp. 124–131 (February 1970).

Mucciardi, A. N. and E. E. Gose, "Evolutionary Pattern Recognition in Incomplete Nonlinear Multithreshold Networks," *IEEE Trans. on Elect. Computers*, vol. EC-15, no. 2, pp. 257–261 (April 1966).

Patrick, E. A. and F. P. Fischer, III, "A Generalized K-Nearest Neighbor Rule," *Info. and Control*, vol. 16, pp. 128–152 (April 1970).

Peterson, D. W. and R. L. Mattson, "A Method of Finding Linear Discriminant Functions for a Class of Performance Criteria," *IEEE Trans. Information Theory*, vol. IT-12, no. 3, pp. 380–387 (July 1966).

Sammon, J. W., Jr., "An Optimal Discriminant Plane," *IEEE Trans. on Computers*, vol. C-19, no. 9, pp. 826–829 (September 1970).

Smith, F. W., "Design of Multicategory Pattern Classifiers with Two-Category Design Procedures," *IEEE Trans. Computers* (short notes) vol. C-18, pp. 548–551 (June 1969).

Smith, F. W., "Optimality of Adaptive Algorithms for Pattern Classifier Design," *IEEE Symp. Adaptive Processes*, pp. 3-b-1 to 3-b-3 (1969).

Steinbuch, K. and U. A. W. Piske, "Learning Matrices and Their Applications," *IEEE Trans. on Electronic Computers*, pp. 846–862 (December 1963).

Wilson, D. L., "Nearest Neighbor Rules in Pattern Recognition," *Proc. of the 3rd Hawaii International Conf. on Syst. Sci.*, 1970 pp. 131–137.

Yau, S. S. and P. C. Chuang, "Feasibility of Using Linear Pattern Classifiers for Probabilistic Pattern Classes," *Proc. IEEE* (corres.), vol. 54, no. 12, pp. 1957–1959 (December 1966).

STATISTICAL
CLASSIFICATION

4.0   Introduction

The previous chapter was devoted to those algorithms and
classification procedures which were implementable
without reference to statistical assumptions. They were
referred to as "distribution free" techniques but it
should be emphasized that they often will have a statistical
interpretation. In fact some people prefer to interpret the
techniques developed in the context of distribution free
assumptions simply as nonparametric procedures in
statistical analyses with all statistics uniformly distributed.
In any event the material to be developed in this chapter
relates to the use of all statistical knowledge possible in
the solution of the pattern recognition classification

problem. In the context of the phases of mathematical pattern recognition the subject of statistical classification is probably the most advanced. There exists a considerable wealth of knowledge in the subjects of statistical communication, detection, and decision theory which can be applied to the pattern recognition problem. While it is not the intention to completely review these subjects, abstraction of many of their results will prove pertinent to the pattern classification problem.

The main objective in developing a statistical approach to certain pattern recognition problems is that it is often possible to accurately model certain processes in nature using statistical parameters of those processes. In addition it is obvious upon statement, but often ignored in practice, that a pattern recognizer wants to take all a priori knowledge of his problem into account in the solution of that problem. Often that knowledge is accurately couched in statistical terms. Finally, it is often desirable to evaluate existing systems in terms of their statistical performance. Thus percent correct classification or error rate will assume some underlying statistical basis if such a measure is going to be a meaningful evaluation parameter. Thus when it is desired to evaluate a distribution free, many-at-a-time error correction algorithm resulting in linear discriminant functions for nonlinearly separable data, statistical interpretations will provide such a measure.

Consequently the introduction of cost or loss functions as well as likelihood ratios and probability density functions becomes necessary. Bayes machines will be discussed followed by a section on parametric classification. Parametric classification assumes an underlying density, and simple estimates of a few parameters will define the densities and corresponding discriminant functions. Nonparametric classification will then be treated in which underlying densities are unknown but desired for discriminant function definition. Thus probability density and mode estimation become important and often stochastic approximation techniques become useful. Finally it should be pointed out that regardless of the name (distribution free, parametric, or nonparametric), the resulting discriminant function is defined by a set of parameters which must be determined from existing prototype and a priori information. Consequently all techniques are somewhat "parametric" in nature.

4.1 Classical Techniques

The underlying assumption in statistical pattern recognition problems is that there exists some multivariate probability density function whose parameters of definition may be unknown to us. It will then be our task to learn these parameters based upon the known prototypes. The multivariate probability density functions, $p(\mathbf{x})$, are defined over the N dimensional feature or pattern space (if no feature selection has been developed) and it will be assumed that the prototypes $\mathbf{y}_m^{(k)}$ of class S_k are selected from a multivariate distribution conditioned upon that class, $p(\mathbf{x}/S_k)$. In addition another statistic of interest will be the a priori probability of class S_k occurring, $P(S_k)$. This becomes particularly significant where, for instance, the probability of an "E" occurring is considerably larger than that for a "Z" ($P(\text{E}) \gg P(\text{Z})$) in a character recognition experiment. A crude estimate of $P(S_k)$, when the ease of prototype acquisition is proportional to the a priori class occurrence, might be

$$P(S_k) \approx M_k \bigg/ \sum_{k=1}^{K} M_k \qquad (4.1)$$

Again it is emphasized that this estimate is valid only if the number of prototypes per class is an indication of the importance of that class. Often the a priori probabilities are purposely set equal in order that the pattern recognition machine treat each class with the same a priori weight. This guarantees no initial bias which is often a good assumption for problems in which initial knowledge is limited.

In the use of decision theory a loss function will become quite relevant. Thus $C(S_i/S_k)$ will become the loss incurred when a pattern actually belonging to S_k is placed in class S_i. The loss function (also known as a cost function) has the advantage of providing a means of weighting specific recognition errors more heavily than others. Consequently the cost of a false alarm in a radar system would be considerably cheaper than the cost of a missed detection. In order to make use of the loss function, it will be useful to imbed it into a conditional average loss, $L(\mathbf{x}, S_k)$.

$$L(\mathbf{x}, S_k) = \sum_{i=1}^{K} C(S_k/S_i) p(S_i/\mathbf{x}) \qquad (4.2)$$

Thus this function is conditioned upon the observation $\mathbf{x}$ and can be interpreted as the loss associated with making observation $\mathbf{x}$ and assigning it to various classes S_k each weighed by the loss incurred by that particular classification. Also $L(\mathbf{x}, S_k)$ can be considered as an average of $C(S_k/S_i)$, the individual losses, each loss being weighted by the probability of the S_i class occurring having observed the point $\mathbf{x}$. If $L(\mathbf{x}, S_k)$ is minimized, then the machine becomes statistically optimum in a Bayes sense and is therefore often referred to as a Bayes machine. To minimize the conditional average loss the machine must assign $\mathbf{x}$ to the category S_k where $L(\mathbf{x}, S_k) \leq L(\mathbf{x}, S_i)$ for all $i = 1, \ldots, K$. Thus $L(\mathbf{x}, S_i)$ must be calculated for all classes and we will therefore end up with K conditional average losses. An obvious set of discriminant functions then becomes

$$g_k(\mathbf{x}) = -L(\mathbf{x}, S_k) \tag{4.3}$$

However a more convenient expression is obtained by using Bayes rule:

$$p(S_i/\mathbf{x}) = \frac{p(\mathbf{x}/S_i)P(S_i)}{p(\mathbf{x})} \tag{4.4}$$

Therefore

$$L(\mathbf{x}, S_k) = \sum_{i=1}^{K} C(S_k/S_i) \frac{p(\mathbf{x}/S_i)P(S_i)}{p(\mathbf{x})} \tag{4.5a}$$

and

$$L(\mathbf{x}, S_k) = (p(\mathbf{x}))^{-1} \sum_{i=1}^{K} C(S_k/S_i)p(\mathbf{x}/S_i)P(S_i) \tag{4.5b}$$

But $(p(\mathbf{x}))^{-1}$ is common to all conditional average losses (for each class) and consequently plays no role in the discriminant function. Therefore let

$$l(\mathbf{x}, S_k) = \sum_{i=1}^{K} C(S_k/S_i)p(\mathbf{x}/S_i)P(S_i) \tag{4.6a}$$

or

$$l(\mathbf{x}, S_k) = \sum_{i=1}^{K} C(S_k/S_i)p(\mathbf{x}, S_i) \tag{4.6b}$$

using Bayes rule in the form

$$p(\mathbf{x}/S_i)P(S_i) = p(\mathbf{x}, S_i) \tag{4.7}$$

We will simply refer to $l(\mathbf{x}, S_k)$ as a form of conditional average loss noting that the $p(\mathbf{x})$ statistic is missing. In terms of discriminant functions

$$g_k(\mathbf{x}) = -l(\mathbf{x}, S_k) \tag{4.8}$$

and the decision rule states that we place $\mathbf{x}$ in class S_k such that $g_k(\mathbf{x}) \geq g_i(\mathbf{x})$, $(l(\mathbf{x}, S_k) \leq l(\mathbf{x}, S_i))$, for all $i = 1, \ldots, K$. This decision rule has become known as the Bayes rule and the machine which implements such a decision surface is known as a Bayes machine.

This same decision rule can be used to minimize the overall risk for each class for the entire multivariate space. Up until now, the conditional average loss has simply been a value assigned to each class S_k at a given point $\mathbf{x}$ in the pattern space. Integrating over the entire decision space results in a risk

$$R(S_k) = \int L(\mathbf{x}, S_k)p(\mathbf{x}) \, d\mathbf{x} \tag{4.9}$$

where multidimensional integration is understood in the vector notation. The Bayes rule then minimizes the average loss or risk for each class. If the a priori statistics, $P(S_k)$, are unknown, then the optimum decision rule could not be implemented. Therefore to minimize the risk one chooses to minimize the maximum worst assumption possible on the distribution of $P(S_k)$ which is a uniform one $P(S_k) = K^{-1}$ for all $k = 1, \ldots, K$. This is known as the mini-max criterion on a priori statistics and the discriminant function of equation (4.8) is further simplified by ignoring all $P(S_k)$.

A specific loss function which has received considerable interest is the symmetric loss function

$$C(S_k/S_i) = 1 - \delta(i - k) \tag{4.10a}$$

where $\delta(i - k)$ is the Kronecker delta function. Thus

$$C(S_k/S_i) = \begin{cases} 0 & i = k \\ 1 & i \neq k \end{cases} \tag{4.10b}$$

This loss function states that we lose one unit for only misrecognition and nothing is lost for correct classification. Such a loss function reflects a certain amount of ambivalence on the part of the machine designer as to his interest in specific misclassifications. Consequently all misclassifications are equally as bad. The Bayes decision rule for the symmetric loss function becomes

$$l(\mathbf{x}, S_k) = \sum_{i=1}^{K} (1 - \delta(i - k))p(\mathbf{x}/S_i)P(S_i) \qquad (4.11a)$$

or

$$l(\mathbf{x}, S_k) = \sum_{i=1}^{K} p(\mathbf{x}/S_i)P(S_i) - \sum_{i=1}^{K} \delta(i - k)p(\mathbf{x}/S_i)P(S_i) \quad (4.11b)$$

and finally

$$l(\mathbf{x}, S_k) = p(\mathbf{x}) - p(\mathbf{x}/S_k)P(S_k) \qquad (4.11c)$$

$l(\mathbf{x}, S_k)$ is now minimized with respect to k by maximizing $p(\mathbf{x}/S_k)P(S_k)$. Therefore the Bayes decision rule becomes: choose S_k such that

$$p(\mathbf{x}/S_k)P(S_k) \geq p(\mathbf{x}/S_i)P(S_i) \qquad \forall i = 1, \ldots, K \qquad (4.12)$$

In the context of likelihood ratios we have

$$\lambda = \frac{p(\mathbf{x}/S_k)}{p(\mathbf{x}/S_i)} \qquad (4.13)$$

and the decision rule becomes: choose S_k such that

$$\lambda \geq \frac{P(S_i)}{P(S_k)} \qquad \forall i = 1, \ldots, K \qquad (4.14)$$

which is also known as the unconditional maximum likelihood decision. The discriminant function becomes

$$g_k(\mathbf{x}) = P(S_k)p(\mathbf{x}/S_k) \qquad (4.15a)$$

or as will become useful later

$$g_k(\mathbf{x}) = \log \{P(S_k)p(\mathbf{x}/S_k)\} \qquad (4.15b)$$

The decision surface $(S_k S_i)$ between class S_k and class S_i can be expressed as

$$g_k(\mathbf{x}) - g_i(\mathbf{x}) = 0 \qquad (4.16a)$$

or

$$\log\left\{\frac{P(S_k)p(\mathbf{x}/S_k)}{P(S_i)p(\mathbf{x}/S_i)}\right\} = 0 \qquad (4.16b)$$

Figure 4.1a presents a block diagram of the probability computer or pattern recognition machine for the Bayes classifier and a symmetric loss function.

A second type of loss function which might be of interest could be described by

$$C(S_k/S_i) = \begin{cases} -h_i & i = k \\ 0 & i \neq k \end{cases} \tag{4.17}$$

where $h_i > 0$. Such a loss function is equivalent to a diagonal matrix and can be interpreted as assigning a negative loss (or positive gain) to a correct decision and no loss (gain) to an incorrect decision. Thus it is possible to weigh the importance of guessing one class correctly over another class by assigning different values to h_i. The modified conditional average loss then becomes

$$l(\mathbf{x}, S_k) = - \sum_{i=1}^{K} h_i \delta(i - k) p(\mathbf{x}/S_i) P(S_i) \tag{4.18a}$$

or

$$l(\mathbf{x}, S_k) = -h_k p(\mathbf{x}/S_k) P(S_k) \tag{4.18b}$$

This implies a decision rule such that $\mathbf{x}$ is placed in class S_k when

$$h_k p(\mathbf{x}/S_k) P(S_k) \geq h_i p(\mathbf{x}/S_i) P(S_i) \qquad \forall i = 1, \ldots, K \tag{4.19a}$$

Thus in terms of likelihood ratios the test becomes: choose S_k such that

$$\lambda \geq \frac{h_i P(S_i)}{h_k P(S_k)} \qquad \forall i \in K \tag{4.19b}$$

It is interesting to investigate the probability of error for a multiclass pattern recognition problem in terms of the known statistics of the problem. Assuming a symmetric loss function and a Bayes decision algorithm, equation (4.12), the total probability of error can be equated with

$$P_e = \sum_{k=1}^{K} P(S_k) \int_{\bar{S}_k} p(\mathbf{x}/S_k) \, d\mathbf{x} \tag{4.20}$$

Here $\bar{S}_k$ is the complement of the region $S_k = \{x : P(S_k) p(\mathbf{x}/S_k) \geq P(S_i) P(\mathbf{x}/S_i) \forall i\}$. It is possible to relate this probability of error to the pairwise errors obtained from investigating the problem two

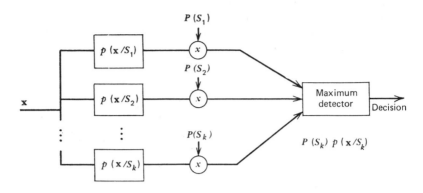

(a) Bayes classifier and a symmetric loss function

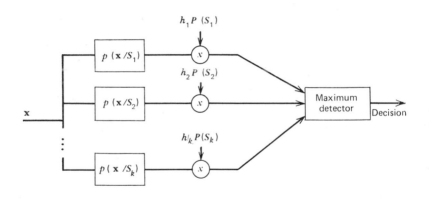

(b) Bayes classifier and a diagonal loss function

FIGURE 4.1.   Probability computers.

classes at a time. Let $Q_{ki} = \{x : P(S_k)p(\mathbf{x}/S_k) < P(S_i)p(\mathbf{x}/S_i)\}$. Then the pairwise error, $P_e(S_k, S_i)$ becomes

$$P_e(S_k, S_i) = P(S_k)\int_{Q_{ki}} p(\mathbf{x}/S_k)\, d\mathbf{x} + P(S_i)\int_{Q_{ik}} p(\mathbf{x}/S_i)\, d\mathbf{x} \quad (4.21)$$

Summing over all pertinent pairwise errors we have

$$\sum_{k>i} P_e(S_k, S_i) = \tfrac{1}{2}\sum_{k=1}^{K} P(S_k)\sum_{i=1}^{K}\int_{Q_{ki}} p(\mathbf{x}/S_k)\, d\mathbf{x} \quad (4.22a)$$

Where we have noted the symmetry of Q_{ki} and Q_{ik} and the emptiness of Q_{kk}. However because not all Q_{ki} are mutually exclusive and because the integrand is positive we have the inequality

$$2\sum_{k>i} P_e(S_k, S_i) \geq \sum_{k=1}^{K} P(S_k) \int_{\cup_i Q_{ki}} p(\mathbf{x}/S_k)\, d\mathbf{x} \qquad (4.22b)$$

But $(\cup_i Q_{ki}) = \bar{S}_k$, where $\cup_i$ is the union operator. Consequently

$$2\sum_{k>i} P_e(S_k, S_i) \geq \sum_{k=1}^{K} P(S_k) \int_{\bar{S}_k} p(\mathbf{x}/S_k)\, d\mathbf{x} \qquad (4.22c)$$

$$\geq P_e \qquad (4.22d)$$

Having found an upper bound for P_e, such a bound can be further simplified according to the following technique established earlier in the feature selection chapter. Specifically

$$P_e \leq 2\sum_{k>i} P_e(S_k, S_i) \qquad (4.23a)$$

$$\leq 2\sum_{k>i} P(S_k) \int_{Q_{ki}} p(\mathbf{x}/S_k)\, d\mathbf{x} + P(S_i) \int_{Q_{ki}} p(\mathbf{x}/S_i)\, d\mathbf{x} \qquad (4.23b)$$

$$\leq 2\sum_{k>i} \int_{-\infty}^{\infty} \min\{P(S_k)p(\mathbf{x}/S_k), P(S_i)p(\mathbf{x}/S_i)\}\, d\mathbf{x} \qquad (4.23c)$$

$$\leq 2\sum_{k>i} \int_{-\infty}^{\infty} \{P(S_k)P(S_i)p(\mathbf{x}/S_k)p(\mathbf{x}/S_i)\}^{\frac{1}{2}}\, d\mathbf{x} \qquad (4.24)$$

which follows from the fact that $\min(a, b) \leq (ab)^{\frac{1}{2}}$. Thus

$$P_e \leq 2\sum_{k>i} (P(S_k)P(S))^{\frac{1}{2}} \int_{-\infty}^{\infty} (p(\mathbf{x}/S_k)p(\mathbf{x}/S_i))^{\frac{1}{2}}\, d\mathbf{x} \qquad (4.25)$$

and in terms of the Bhattacharyya distance mentioned as a feature selection device

$$P_e \leq 2\sum_{k>i} (P(S_k)P(S_i))^{\frac{1}{2}} \exp\{-B(S_k, S_i)\} \qquad (4.26)$$

Figure 4.2 illustrates the proof for a three-class problem. Thus it is evident that maximizing $B(S_k, S_i)$ will minimize the upper bound on the multicategory probability of error and therefore would be a good criterion for feature selection.

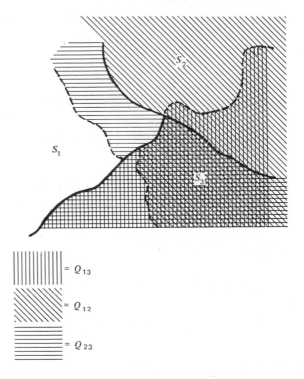

$$P_e = P(S_1)\int_{S_2 \cup S_3} p(\mathbf{x}/S_1)\, d\mathbf{x} + P(S_2)\int_{S_1 \cup S_3} p(\mathbf{x}/S_2)\, d\mathbf{x} + P(S_3)$$

$$\times \int_{S_1 \cup S_2} p(\mathbf{x}/S_3)\, d\mathbf{x}$$

$$\leq P_e(S_1, S_2) + P_e(S_1, S_3) + P_e(S_2, S_3)$$

$$= P(S_1)\int_{Q_{12}+Q_{13}} p(\mathbf{x}/S_1)\, d\mathbf{x} + P(S_2)\int_{Q_{21}+Q_{23}} p(\mathbf{x}/S_2)\, d\mathbf{x} + P(S_3)$$

$$\times \int_{Q_{31}+Q_{32}} p(\mathbf{x}/S_3)\, d\mathbf{x}$$

FIGURE 4.2.   Multiclass versus pairwise error probabilities ($N = 2$, $K = 3$).

4.2 Parametric Classification

Parametric classification refers to the development of statistically defined discriminant functions in which the underlying probability density functions are assumed known. It then remains to simply estimate a set of parameters which will then completely describe the densities as a function of the known prototypes. The most obvious such assumption is the density function given by the Gaussian or normal distribution. Intuitively it may be quite appealing to assume such a distribution because often nature provides us with samples which apparently follow such statistics. Probably a more honest statement of the reason for selecting normal statistics is the relative ease with which analyses can be handled under such assumptions. However, before proceeding a word of caution must be uttered. The parametric pattern recognition machine will only be as useful as the validity of the known (assumed) underlying densities. No matter how elegant the mathematics, if the prototypes and unknowns are not samples from the assumed statistics, the classification accuracy will suffer accordingly. Therefore, assuming we know for a fact that the underlying distribution is Gaussian, let us proceed.

In general we define a vector which is the mean of a set of points in N dimensional space to be

$$\mu = \mathscr{E}\{\mathbf{x}\} \tag{4.27}$$

where the $\mathscr{E}\{\cdot\}$ is the expectation operator. Similarly we can define a covariance matrix for a set of data points to be given by

$$[\Phi] = \mathscr{E}\{(\mathbf{x} - \mu)(\mathbf{x} - \mu)^t\} \tag{4.28}$$

which is often referred to as the expectation taken over the outer product of mean zero data $\mathbf{x} - \mu$. The covariance matrix is real, symmetric, and positive definite for real processes and if it has an inverse it will be given as $[\Phi]^{-1}$. The N variate normal distribution then becomes

$$p(\mathbf{x}) = \frac{1}{(2\pi)^{N/2} |\Phi|^{1/2}} \exp\{-\tfrac{1}{2}(\mathbf{x} - \mu)^t [\Phi]^{-1}(\mathbf{x} - \mu)\} \tag{4.29a}$$

where $|\Phi|$ is the determinant of $[\Phi]$ and the factor preceding the exponential is a normalization constant guaranteeing the unit integrability of $p(\mathbf{x})$. This distribution is often simplified notationally to the form

$$p(\mathbf{x}) = N(\boldsymbol{\mu}, [\Phi]) \qquad (4.29b)$$

and when the exponent is equal to a constant, the "lines" (contours) of equal probability become hyperellipsoids. Figure 4.3 displays some typical one- and two-dimensional normal distributions.

In the context of the pattern recognition environment, we are particularly interested in the conditional density $p(\mathbf{x}/S_k)$ due to our a priori knowledge of the correct classification of the known proto-types. In this case the conditional distributions become

$$p(\mathbf{x}/S_k) = \frac{1}{(2\pi)^{N/2} |\Phi_k|^{1/2}} \exp\{-\tfrac{1}{2}(\mathbf{x} - \boldsymbol{\mu}_k)^t [\Phi_k]^{-1}(\mathbf{x} - \boldsymbol{\mu}_k)\} \qquad (4.30)$$

where we have a mean and covariance matrix for each class of prototypes. It becomes evident that to completely specify the density

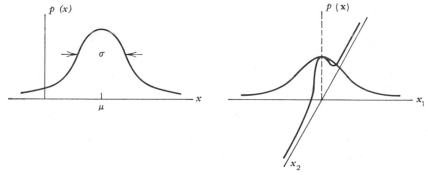

(a) One–and two–dimensional normal distribution

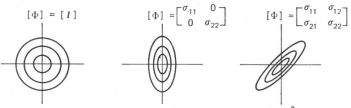

Note: σ_{nn} is a variance and therefore equivalent to σ_n^2

(b) Lines of equal probability ($N = 2$)

FIGURE 4.3. Normal distributions.

function all we need are the first (mean) and second (covariance) order statistics. The mean and covariance now take on values

$$\mu_k = \mathscr{E}\{y_m^{(k)}\} \tag{4.31a}$$

$$[\Phi_k] = \mathscr{E}\{(y_m^{(k)} - \mu_k)(y_m^{(k)} - \mu_k)^t\} \tag{4.31b}$$

Using the above notation we can now develop the discriminant functions given by the Bayes machine solution presented in the earlier section. Specifically for the symmetric loss function, $C(S_k/S_i) = 1 - \delta(i - k)$, we had discriminant functions given by

$$g_k(x) = P(S_k)p(x/S_k) \tag{4.32a}$$

or

$$g_k(x) = \log\{P(S_k)p(x/S_k)\} \tag{4.32b}$$

Choosing the latter for reasons of analytic simplicity, we obtain the Bayes machine solution for the symmetric loss function to be

$$g_k(x) = \log P(S_k) - \frac{N}{2} \log 2\pi - \tfrac{1}{2} \log |\Phi_k|$$

$$- \tfrac{1}{2}((x - \mu_k)^t[\Phi_k]^{-1}(x - \mu_k)) \tag{4.33a}$$

However the term $N/2 \log 2\pi$ is common to all such discriminant functions independent of k and consequently can be removed. Thus

$$g_k(x) = -\tfrac{1}{2}x^t[\Phi_k]^{-1}x + x^t[\Phi_k]^{-1}\mu_k - \tfrac{1}{2}\mu_k^t[\Phi_k]^{-1}\mu_k$$

$$+ \log P(S_k) - \tfrac{1}{2} \log |\Phi_k| \tag{4.33b}$$

where use has been made of the symmetry of $[\Phi_k]^{-1}$ due to the symmetry of $[\Phi_k]$. The quadratic discriminant function of equation (4.33) can often be simplified if additional assumptions about the statistics of the problem can be made. Specifically if the covariance functions of each class are the same, a condition which commonly occurs in communication systems where deterministic signals are perturbed by additive Gaussian noise, the discriminant functions become

$$g_k(x) = x^t[\Phi]^{-1}\mu_k - \tfrac{1}{2}\mu_k^t[\Phi]^{-1}\mu_k + \log P(S_k) \tag{4.34}$$

Here the common terms, $-\tfrac{1}{2}x^t[\Phi]^{-1}x$, and $-\tfrac{1}{2} \log |\Phi|$ have been eliminated and the discriminant function becomes linear. In terms of earlier notation the weight vector becomes

$$\mathbf{w} = [\Phi]^{-1}\boldsymbol{\mu}_k$$

$$w_{N+1} = -\tfrac{1}{2}\boldsymbol{\mu}_k[\Phi]^{-1}\boldsymbol{\mu}_k + \log P(S_k)$$

If we wanted to concentrate on a two-class problem the discriminant function separating the classes becomes

$$g(\mathbf{x}) = g_1(\mathbf{x}) - g_2(\mathbf{x}) \tag{4.35a}$$

or

$$g(\mathbf{x}) = \mathbf{x}^t[\Phi]^{-1}(\boldsymbol{\mu}_1 - \boldsymbol{\mu}_2) - \tfrac{1}{2}\boldsymbol{\mu}_1^t[\Phi]^{-1}\boldsymbol{\mu}_1 + \tfrac{1}{2}\boldsymbol{\mu}_2^t[\Phi]^{-1}\boldsymbol{\mu}_2 + \log\frac{P(S_1)}{P(S_2)}$$

$$\tag{4.35b}$$

Note that the last three terms are constant depending on prototypes defining $\boldsymbol{\mu}_1$ and $\boldsymbol{\mu}_2$ as well as a priori distributions. They can be calculated before presenting the machine with an unknown $\mathbf{x}$. Finally we can further simplify the multicategory discriminant function of equation (4.34) if in addition to the covariance matrices being equal over all classes, they are also equal to the identity matrix, $[\Phi] = [I]$. In such a situation we obtain (assuming equally likely a priori statistics, $P(S_k) = (1/K)\forall k$), the following

$$g_k(\mathbf{x}) = \mathbf{x}^t\boldsymbol{\mu}_k - \tfrac{1}{2}\boldsymbol{\mu}_k^t\boldsymbol{\mu}_k \tag{4.36}$$

This discriminant function is immediately recognized as the minimum distance classifier discussed in the previous chapter. This results in a correlation or matched filter decision algorithm.

Figure 4.4 presents some typical decision boundaries for various assumed means and covariance properties of the normal distribution. The separating surfaces have been drawn under the assumption of equal a priori statistics. A simple shift in the existing surfaces results if this assumption is false.

It should be mentioned at this point that the means and covariance which completely define the Gaussian distribution can be estimated from the sample prototypes. Thus if the expectation operator, $\mathscr{E}\{\cdot\}$, is taken as an average over prototypes, the estimates of the

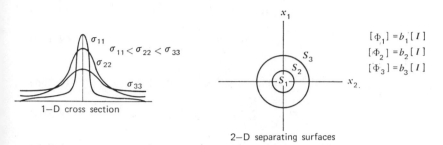

(a) Equal means, uncorrelated covariances

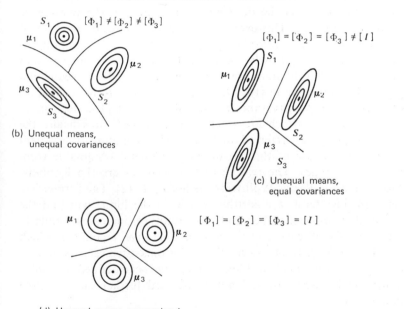

(b) Unequal means,
unequal covariances

(c) Unequal means,
equal covariances

(d) Unequal means, uncorrelated
and equal covariances

FIGURE 4.4. Some typical separating surfaces for $N(\mu_k, [\Phi_k])$, $(N = 2, k = 3)$.

means and covariance matrices become

$$\boldsymbol{\mu}_k = \langle \mathbf{y}_m^{(k)} \rangle \tag{4.37a}$$

$$= \frac{1}{M_k} \sum_{m=1}^{M_k} \mathbf{y}_m^{(k)} \tag{4.37b}$$

and

$$[\Phi_k] = \langle (\mathbf{y}_m^{(k)} - \boldsymbol{\mu}_k)(\mathbf{y}_m^{(k)} - \boldsymbol{\mu}_k)^t \rangle \tag{4.38a}$$

$$= \frac{1}{M_k} \sum_{m=1}^{M_k} (\mathbf{y}_m^{(k)} - \boldsymbol{\mu}_k)(\mathbf{y}_m^{(k)} - \boldsymbol{\mu}_k)^t \tag{4.38b}$$

Under the assumption that the prototypes indeed were obtained from normally distributed data, these estimates are then reasonable for use in specifying the discriminant functions in the parametric training procedure. However, if the data is nonstationary or if sequential learning is desirable it is possible to develop more refined estimates which, for slowly varying distributions tend to track that variation. Such techniques are particularly meaningful in sequential probability ratio testing [1, 2] (see Chapter 6). Often the techniques of stochastic approximation are utilized for parametric determination of variables which are stochastically defined. Specifically the methods have been referred to as noisy hill climbing or gradient techniques because of the use of noisy estimates obtainable from known prototypes. The two classical techniques are the Robbins-Monro and the Kiefer-Wolfowitz methods [11, 12]. The former is a zero crossing iterative algorithm which, in the limit, will find the parameter of interest as the number of prototypes increases. Similarly the Kiefer-Wolfowitz technique is an iterative technique which searches for the zero of a derivative and is thus often referred to as a noisy gradient method. Both techniques have been defined for multi-dimensional spaces but will not be pursued further due to space limitations.

4.3   Nonparametric Classification

Nonparametric techniques in statistical decision models are often resorted to when underlying probability densities are unknown. Thus if a priori knowledge of the problem does not lend itself to a safe density assumption, a variety of nonparametric procedures may be utilized to develop the discriminant functions necessary for classification. However if it is unknown as to what degree of polynomial the discriminant function should be to successfully separate the known prototypes and if we desire a statistical interpretation as to the validity of the resulting decision surfaces, we may resort to the use of the average risk (mentioned earlier) in defining our discriminants. Thus, the objective in this discussion is to minimize the risk by appropriate selection of separating hyperplanes. The results of these techniques should then be relatable to the earlier derived discriminant functions on a purely distribution free basis. Finally by selecting a particular order multidimensional polynomial as the separating boundary it will be possible to relate that surface, in a probability measure, to data which may be nonseparable with such discriminant functions. Thus we will be able to relate how good a particular linear decision surface is to nonlinearly separable data. The development will be formulated in a two-class ($k = 2$) environment and then generalized to the multicategory situation for linear discriminant functions. Amari [3] has discussed higher order functions and the reader is reminded of the generality of the linear techniques afforded by the use of the ϕ function preprocessor. Koford and Groner [4] have also investigated the linear optimal pattern classifier.

Recall that the risk for a two-class problem can be stated in terms of

$$R = P(S_1)\int_{S_2} p(\mathbf{x}/S_1)C(S_2/S_1)\,d\mathbf{x}$$

$$+ P(S_2)\int_{S_1} p(\mathbf{x}/S_2)C(S_1/S_2)\,d\mathbf{x} \tag{4.39a}$$

and the regions of integration are given, as earlier, to be $S_k = \{\mathbf{x}:P(S_k)p(\mathbf{x}/S_k) \geq P(S_i)p(\mathbf{x}/S_i)\forall i\}$. However, at this point it will be expedient to develop a loss function which is also a function of the discriminant weight vectors in augmented space $\mathbf{w}$. Thus

$$R(\mathbf{w}) = P(S_1)\int_{S_2} p(\mathbf{x}/S_1)C(\mathbf{x}, \mathbf{w}, S_2/S_1)\,d\mathbf{x}$$

$$+ P(S_2)\int_{S_1} p(\mathbf{x}/S_2)C(\mathbf{x}, \mathbf{w}, S_1/S_2)\,d\mathbf{x} \tag{4.39b}$$

This will allow us to minimize the risk by properly adjusting the individual weight vector components. Assuming $R(\mathbf{w})$ is differentiable with a global minimum with respect to $\mathbf{w}$, we therefore search for a solution

$$\nabla R(\mathbf{w}) = 0 \qquad (4.40)$$

where

$$\nabla = \left(\frac{\partial}{\partial w_1}, \ldots, \frac{\partial}{\partial w_{N+1}} \right) \qquad (4.41)$$

The risk will have a solution of the following form

$$\nabla R(\mathbf{w}) = P(S_1) \int_{S_2} p(\mathbf{x}/S_1) \nabla C(\mathbf{x}, \mathbf{w}, S_2/S_1) \, d\mathbf{x}$$

$$+ P(S_2) \int_{S_1} p(\mathbf{x}/S_2) \nabla C(\mathbf{x}, \mathbf{w}, S_1/S_2) \, d\mathbf{x} + f(S_1, S_2) \quad (4.42a)$$

where the first two terms of the gradient risk are due to the variation of the loss function over the properly defined regions with $\mathbf{w}$ and the third term is due to the functional dependence of the gradient on the boundaries of the sets $\{S_k\}$. However, this dependence can be eliminated by simply requiring that the loss on the boundaries be zero. Under that assumption

$$\nabla R(\mathbf{w}) = P(S_1) \int_{S_2} p(\mathbf{x}/S_1) \nabla C(\mathbf{x}, \mathbf{w}, S_2/S_1) \, d\mathbf{x}$$

$$+ P(S_2) \int_{S_1} p(\mathbf{x}/S_2) \nabla C(\mathbf{x}, \mathbf{w}, S_1/S_2) \, d\mathbf{x} \quad (4.42b)$$

Loss functions of particular interest usually are defined monotonically proportional to the distance that a point is misclassified. The distance from a particular hyperplane to the point $\mathbf{x}$ is given by

$$d = \|g(\mathbf{x})\| \Big/ \left(\sum_{n=1}^{N} w_n^2 \right)^{1/2} \qquad (4.43a)$$

$$= \|\mathbf{w}^t \mathbf{x}\| / \|\mathbf{w}'\| \qquad (4.43b)$$

where $g(\mathbf{x})$ is the linear discriminant function and $\mathbf{w}'$ is the augmented vector with $w_{N+1} = 0$. Thus if $C(\mathbf{x}, \mathbf{w}, S_k/S_i) = C(d, S_k/S_i)$, some monotonically increasing function of d, then we can further evaluate the gradient. For the linear loss function

$$C(d, S_1/S_2) = \begin{cases} \mathbf{w}^t\mathbf{x}/\|\mathbf{w}'\| & \mathbf{w}^t\mathbf{x} > 0 \\ 0 & \mathbf{w}^t\mathbf{x} \leq 0 \end{cases} \tag{4.44a}$$

$$C(d, S_2/S_1) = \begin{cases} 0 & \mathbf{w}^t\mathbf{x} \geq 0 \\ \mathbf{w}^t\mathbf{x}/''\|\mathbf{w}'\| & \mathbf{w}^t\mathbf{x} < 0 \end{cases} \tag{4.44b}$$

Thus

$$\nabla(\mathbf{w}^t\mathbf{x}/\|\mathbf{w}'\|) = \|\mathbf{w}'\|^{-3}(\|\mathbf{w}'\|^2\mathbf{x} - (\mathbf{w}^t\mathbf{x})\mathbf{w}') \triangleq q(\mathbf{w}, \mathbf{x}) \tag{4.45}$$

Consequently

$$\nabla R(\mathbf{w}) = P(S_2)\int_{S_1} p(\mathbf{x}/S_2)q(\mathbf{w}, \mathbf{x})\, dx$$

$$- P(S_1)\int_{S_2} p(\mathbf{x}/S_1)q(\mathbf{w}, \mathbf{x})\, dx \tag{4.46}$$

Amari [3] points out that considering the family of distance loss functions, $C(d) = d^r$, has the following interpretation. For $r = 2$ the loss criterion is to minimize the sum of the squared distances of misclassified points (i.e., a least squares criterion). As r increases, the criterion becomes one of minimizing the maximum of the distances of misclassified points or a minimax criterion. Finally as r decreases, the criterion becomes one of simply minimizing the number of misclassified patterns which implies a symmetric loss function. Meisel [5] has suggested the loss function

$$C(d) = \begin{cases} 0 & d \leq 0 \\ d^2 & 0 \leq d \leq a \\ 2ad - a^2 & d > a \end{cases} \tag{4.47}$$

which has the feature that distances misclassified far from the hyperplane don't dominate owing to their square terms.

To proceed further in evaluation of the gradient technique requires knowledge of the statistics, $P(S_k)$ and $p(\mathbf{x}/S_k)$. However under the nonparametric assumption, this knowledge is not available. If we assume that an iterative procedure is desirable we can specify a delta increment in weight vector such that

$$\mathbf{w}(i + 1) = \mathbf{w}(i) + \alpha\Delta\mathbf{w}(i) \tag{4.48}$$

Conceivably this $\Delta\mathbf{w}(i)$ should be proportional to the negative of $\nabla R(\mathbf{w})$ if we are to attain the minimum risk. However because $\nabla R(\mathbf{w})$ is a function of unknown statistics we will have to be content to settle for an average type of gradient which averages out the unknown distributions thereby resulting in a probabilistic-descent method as opposed to the deterministic steepest descent method conventionally used when the gradients are known. One technique for such a solution is obtained when $R(\mathbf{w})$ is approximated by a summation over prototypes rather than an integration over densities. Then

$$\tilde{R}(\mathbf{w}) = \sum_{k=1}^{2} \frac{1}{M_k} \sum_{m=1}^{M_k} C(\mathbf{w}, \mathbf{y}_m^{(k)}, S_k/S_i) \qquad (4.49)$$

and the gradient of this function becomes the value to which $\Delta\mathbf{w}(i)$ becomes proportional. Consequently

$$\mathbf{w}(i+1) = \mathbf{w}(i) - \alpha\nabla\tilde{R}(\mathbf{w}(i)) \qquad (4.50)$$

and for the linear loss functions developed earlier

$$\mathbf{w}(i+1) = \mathbf{w}(i) - \alpha\sum_{k=1}^{2} \frac{1}{M_k} \sum_{J(\mathbf{w}(i))} q(\mathbf{w}(i), \mathbf{y}_m^{(k)}) \qquad (4.51)$$

where $J(\mathbf{w}(i))$ is the set of integers for which misclassification occurs on the (i)th iteration. The algorithm defined by equation (4.51) can be interpreted as a many-at-a-time technique in that the change in weight vector at each stage of the iteration is proportional to an average of all the gradients of loss functions of misclassified points.

Of course any other previously described loss functions would have a corresponding many-at-a-time iterative algorithm. Figure 4.5 depicts some loss functions and associated pattern space. Generalization of the above procedure to multicategory problems is straightforward and follows the techniques developed in the previous chapter. Thus there will be K weight vectors or hyperplanes and each is adjusted according to whether a prototype belonging to that particular class is correctly classified or not. Consequently if a point, $\mathbf{y}_m^{(k)}$, is classified as a member of class S_j on the average, then the weight vector $\mathbf{w}_k$ is moved toward that point and $\mathbf{w}_j$ is moved away from that point proportional to their respective gradients.

While the probabilistic-descent method provides a technique for determining optimal decision surfaces in an average risk sense, often

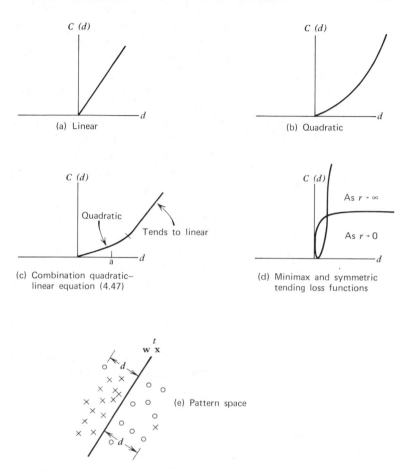

FIGURE 4.5.   Some loss functions for linear discriminant functions.

it is more desirable to develop estimates of the probability densities which are assumed unknown at the outset of the pattern recognition problem. By probability density estimation is meant the construction, in this case nonparametric, of a function in N dimensional space which is proportional to a density function (usually multimodal). Most often the data points or prototypes defining the pattern recognition problem are incorporated in the construction of such a function. If the point classes are known, then the constructed functions will be conditional densities and the problem will fall into the class of supervised pattern recognition techniques. If the data point classifications are unknown, then the density function estimated becomes an unconditional distribution and can be used to determine modes or characteristics of an unsupervised pattern recognition problem, a topic to be discussed in further detail in the following chapter. In any event the motivation toward developing probability density estimation techniques is the search for distributions which can be used in the statistically optimum classifier based on likelihood ratios.

The techniques to be discussed shortly can be couched in terms of the potential function methods discussed earlier in distribution free classification. In that context the discriminant function, and in this case the probability density function, being sought was equated with the superposition of a set of "potential" or kernel functions in N dimensional space centered upon known prototype locations. Thus

$$p_{M_k}(\mathbf{x}/S_k) = \frac{1}{M_k} \sum_{m=1}^{M_k} \psi(\mathbf{x}, \mathbf{y}_m^{(k)}) \qquad (4.52a)$$

The kernel $\psi(\cdot)$ has been investigated by Parzen [6] for one dimension as to certain conditions under which equation (4.52) indeed becomes a valid probability density.

Constraints on the kernel such that

(a) $\sup |\psi(x)| < \infty$

(b) $\int_{-\infty}^{\infty} |\psi(x)| \, dx < \infty$

(c) $\int_{-\infty}^{\infty} \psi(x) \, dx = 1$

(d) $\lim_{x \to \infty} x\psi(x) = 0$

along with the requirement that

(e) $\lim_{M_k \to \infty} h(M_k) = 0$

guarantee that

$$p(\mathbf{x} \mid S_k) = \lim_{M_k \to \infty} \left\{ \frac{1}{M_k h} \sum_{m=1}^{M_k} \psi\{(x - y_m^{(k)})/h\} \right\} \qquad (4.52b)$$

holds at points of continuity of $p(\cdot)$.

Any potential function satisfying the above constraints will provide a valid estimate to the density function in the limit as $M_k \to \infty$. Examples of some other functions which might be useful are given below in scalar notation. While Parzen's work was for one dimension, Murthy [7] has extended the work to N dimensions.

Potential–kernel functions

Case	$\psi(x)$	Description (centered at prototype)
1	$\psi(x) = \begin{cases} \frac{1}{2} & \|x\| \le 1 \\ 0 & \|x\| > 1 \end{cases}$	Rectangle
2	$\psi(x) = \begin{cases} 1 - \|x\| & \|x\| \le 1 \\ 0 & \|x\| > 1 \end{cases}$	Triangle
3	$\psi(x) = (2\pi)^{-\frac{1}{2}} \exp(-x^2/2)$	Gaussian function
4	$\psi(x) = \frac{1}{2} \exp(-\|x\|)$	Exponential decay
5	$\psi(x) = (\pi(1 + x^2))^{-1}$	Cauchy distribution
6	$\psi(x) = (2\pi)^{-1} \left(\dfrac{\sin x/2}{x/2} \right)^2$	Sinc function squared

Valid kernels in N dimensions could be the N product of the scalar kernels above. Of course the above list is not complete. However, it is interesting to note the presence of case 6 in which the potential function is not monotonic decreasing but in fact has a periodic structure. However its envelop is indeed similar in characteristic to the traditional concept of a potential function. Examples of the use of such kernels are presented in Figure 4.6.

While Parzen has laid much of the probability theoretic work necessary for valid application of the potential function method to density function estimation, Specht has developed a useful example

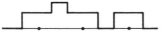

(a) Rectangle   (b) Triangle

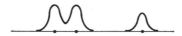

(c) Gaussian function   (d) Exponential decay

(e) Cauchy function   (f) Sinc function squared

FIGURE 4.6. Some one-dimensional potential functions.

of the technique in pattern recognition application through the specific use of the Gaussian kernel [8]. Thus

$$\psi(\mathbf{x}, \mathbf{y}_m^{(k)}) = (2\pi\sigma^2)^{-N/2} \exp\{-(\mathbf{x} - \mathbf{y}_m^{(k)})^t(\mathbf{x} - \mathbf{y}_m^{(k)})/2\sigma^2\} \quad (4.53)$$

which results in a conditional density estimate of

$$p(\mathbf{x}/S_k) = \frac{(2\pi\sigma^2)^{-N/2}}{M_k} \sum_{m=1}^{M_k} \exp\{-(\mathbf{x} - \mathbf{y}_m^{(k)})^t(\mathbf{x} - \mathbf{y}_m^{(k)})/2\sigma^2\} \quad (4.54)$$

σ will be referred to as a "smoothing parameter" because of the effect of a change in σ on the density function. Specht shows that as σ varies from 0 toward infinity the density goes from a set of delta functions, located one at each prototype, to a very smooth Gaussian shaped curve. However, the density function of equation (4.54) can be approximated by a polynomial to define a polynomial discriminant function which will then allow sequential (nonstored) use of known prototypes. For an rth order polynomial in N space we will need $\binom{N+r}{r}$ coefficients. If r is small and still a good approximation to the Gaussian kernel probability density function, then there will be an advantage in such a technique. However, the improper choice of r will result in a poor approximation to the kernel function because a polynomial can tend toward plus or minus infinity whereas the kernel function tends toward zero. Expanding the exponent of the terms in $p(\mathbf{x}/S_k)$ we obtain

$$p(\mathbf{x}/S_k) = \frac{(2\pi\sigma^2)^{-N/2}}{M_k} \sum_{m=1}^{M_k} \exp(-\mathbf{x}^t\mathbf{x} - \mathbf{y}_m^{(k)t}\mathbf{y}_m^{(k)} + 2\mathbf{x}^t\mathbf{y}_m^{(k)})/2\sigma^2 \quad (4.55a)$$

or

$$p(\mathbf{x}/S_k) = \frac{(2\pi\sigma^2)^{-N/2}}{M_k} \exp(-\mathbf{x}^t\mathbf{x}/2\sigma^2) \sum_{m=1}^{M_k} \exp(\mathbf{x}^t\mathbf{y}_m^{(k)}/\sigma^2) \exp(C_m^{(k)})$$

$$(4.55b)$$

where

$$C_m^{(k)} = -\|\mathbf{y}_m^{(k)}\|^2/2\sigma^2$$

By expanding the exponent in $\mathbf{x}$ in terms of an rth order polynomial we obtain

$$p(\mathbf{x}/S_k) \cong \frac{(2\pi\sigma^2)^{-N/2}}{M_k} \exp(-\mathbf{x}^t\mathbf{x}/2\sigma^2) \sum_{m=1}^{M_k} \exp(C_m^{(k)}) \sum_{h=0}^{r} (\mathbf{x}^t\mathbf{y}_m^{(k)})^h/\sigma^{2h}h!$$

$$(4.55c)$$

Because of the common terms preceding the summation, the discriminant function for a Bayes symmetric loss function machine becomes

$$g_k(\mathbf{x}) = \frac{P(S_k)}{M_k} \sum_{m=1}^{M_k} \exp(C_m^{(k)}) \sum_{h=0}^{r} (\mathbf{x}^t\mathbf{y}_m^{(k)})^h/\sigma^{2h}h! \quad (4.56)$$

By expanding the inner product $(\mathbf{x}^t\mathbf{y}_m^{(k)})^h$ we can determine the coefficients of an rth order polynomial described as

$$f_k(\mathbf{x}) = D_{0\cdots0}^{(k)} + D_{10\cdots0}^{(k)}x_1$$

$$+ D_{010\cdots0}^{(k)}x_2 + \cdots + D_{z_1z_2\cdots z_N}^{(k)}x_1^{z_1}x_2^{z_2}\cdots x_N^{z_N} \quad (4.57)$$

where the coefficients $D_{z_1 z_2 \ldots z_N}$ are subscripted by a lexicographic counting system where the set $\{z_i\}$ are integers referring to the power to which the respective dimension is raised. The discriminant function can now be related to the polynomial $f(\mathbf{x})$ by the following inner product expansion

$$g_k(\mathbf{x}) = \frac{P(S_k)}{M_k} \sum_{m=1}^{M_k} \exp(C_m^{(k)}) \sum_{h=0}^{r} \left[+ \cdots \frac{\sigma^{-2h}}{z_1! \, z_2! \cdots z_N!} \right.$$

$$\left. \times y_{1m}^{z_1} \cdots y_{Nm}^{z_N} x_1^{z_1} \cdots x_N^{z_N} + \cdots \right] \tag{4.58}$$

where

$$\sum_{n=1}^{N} z_n = h \tag{4.59}$$

and the summation within the brackets is meant to indicate the sum over all possible combinations of exponents such that the constraint $\sum_{n=1}^{N} z_n = h$ is maintained. By interchanging orders of summation on m and h the coefficients $\{D^{(k)}\}$ can be shown to be

$$D_{z_1 z_2 \ldots z_N}^{(k)} = \frac{\sigma^{-2h}}{z_1! \cdots z_N!} M_k^{-1} \sum_{m=1}^{M_k} y_{1m}^{z_1} \cdots y_{Nm}^{z_N} \exp(C_m^{(k)}) \tag{4.60}$$

and the superscript on the prototype for $\mathbf{y}_m^{(k)}$ has been suppressed for notational convenience. While the mathematical notation is quite cumbersome, keep in mind that the computer algorithm need only do bookkeeping for which the lexicographic notation is best suited. As an example, for a three-dimensional pattern space and second order polynomial, the coefficients $\{D_{000}, D_{100}, D_{010}, D_{001}, D_{200}, D_{020}, D_{002}, D_{110}, D_{011}, D_{101}\}$ need only be computed from the known prototypes, and because the coefficients $\{D^k\}$ are linear in prototypes (see equation (4.60)) storage requirements are eliminated.

The discriminant function thus defined has the advantage that it is an estimate of a smooth function which only grows linearly with new prototypes. In addition the coefficients of the polynomial are adjusted by adding the effects of each pattern one-at-a-time in a noniterative procedure (i.e., one pass is sufficient). Also by increasing the smoothing parameter, σ, the number and order of coefficients

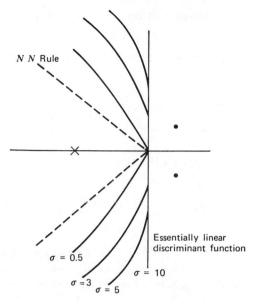

FIGURE 4.7. Polynomial discriminant function (after Specht [8]).

necessary for a given accuracy become drastically reduced. As σ becomes small the true delta function distribution will result in a point of probability at each prototype. This results in "nearest neighbor" classification. As σ becomes large the discriminant functions become strictly linear. Thus it is possible to go from the piecewise linear discriminant function (essentially an infinite order polynomial) to a linear discriminant function as a function of σ. Figure 4.7 demonstrates the phenomenon in two-space. It is also possible to continually update the discriminant function with new data in order to track nonstationary statistics which may be varying with time by applying a "time constant" $\exp(-a/m)$ as a weight on previous coefficients.

Finally it is of interest to investigate the effect upon the potential function by the polynomial approximation [9]

$$\psi(\mathbf{x}, \mathbf{y}) = \exp(-\|\mathbf{x}\|^2 - \|\mathbf{y}\|^2) \sum_{h=0}^{r} \frac{(2(\mathbf{x}^t\mathbf{y}))^h}{h!} \qquad (4.61)$$

Taking partial derivatives with respect to x_n yields

$$\frac{\partial \psi}{\partial x_n}(\mathbf{x}, \mathbf{y}) = -2x_n \exp(-\|\mathbf{x}\|^2 - \|\mathbf{y}\|^2) \sum_{h=0}^{r} \frac{(2(\mathbf{x}^t\mathbf{y}))^h}{h!}$$

$$+ \exp(-\|\mathbf{x}\|^2 - \|\mathbf{y}\|^2) \sum_{h=1}^{r} \frac{h(2(\mathbf{x}^t\mathbf{y}))^{h-1}}{h!} 2y_n \quad (4.62a)$$

or

$$\frac{\partial \psi}{\partial x_n}(\mathbf{x}, \mathbf{y}) = 2 \exp[-\|\mathbf{x}\|^2 - \|\mathbf{y}\|^2]$$

$$\times \left[(y_n - x_n) \sum_{h=0}^{r-1} \frac{(2(\mathbf{x}^t\mathbf{y}))^h}{h!} - x_n \frac{(2(\mathbf{x}^t\mathbf{y}))^r}{r!} \right] \quad (4.62b)$$

Thus it is evident that the partials do not go to zero at $\mathbf{x} = \mathbf{y}$. Thus the approximated potential functions do not have a maximum centered on the prototype. However as r increases, the

$$\lim_{r \to \infty} (2(\mathbf{x}^t\mathbf{y}))^r/r!$$

should approach zero, in which case taking more and more terms in the polynomial expansion causes the potential function to be - closer to a maximum at $\mathbf{x} = \mathbf{y}$.

Another nonparametric probability estimation technique which has been successfully applied to pattern recognition data is that given by Sebestyen and Edie [10]. While space limitations prohibit a complete exposition of their work a brief description will be presented in order to highlight certain important features. They describe an economical algorithm for estimating densities as adaptive generalized N dimensional histograms developed from sequentially introduced samples. One of the objectives is the minimization of the number of points necessary for storage of the histograms. The efficient storage of N dimensional functions can often be implemented by a variable sample and hold function such that only the center and width of the storage cell need be retained. This is similar to run length coding and requires an adaptive distance function which measures the neighborhood of large cells with a larger yardstick than those neighborhoods of smaller cells. Such a function is given by

$$d(\mathbf{x}, \mathbf{C}_m) = \sum_{n=1}^{N} \left(\frac{x_n - c_{mn}}{\sigma_{mn}} \right) \tag{4.63}$$

where $\mathbf{x}$ is an arbitrary point in N space, $\mathbf{C}_m$ is the center of the mth cell, and σ_{mn} is a scale factor depending on the cell identity, m, and the dimension n. Thus the distance to a cell center is quadratic in each dimension properly scaled for that dimension and cell. The intuitive justification for such a technique is that a measure of past experience can be built up and described by an adaptive N dimensional histogram. In those regions in which the data is concentrated the cells themselves will give a measure of the past. However for those points in N dimensional space far from clustering centers, a local density function must be assumed. In this case a Gaussian assumption is made for the tails of the cells away from concentrations of data. An algorithm is developed to adaptively define the number and cell size by a sequential method based upon the quadratic form mentioned above. The algorithm states that if the next data vector falls within the threshold of the mth cell, it is used to readjust the mean of that cell, $\mathbf{C}_m$. If it falls sufficiently outside the established cells it is used to form a new cell center. If it is not sufficiently far away it is tagged and saved for further "fine tuning" when greater global structure has been determined. Thus a type of "guard zone" effect will be developed. The samples which were temporarily stored in the guard zones are reprocessed after a certain number of cells have been established. An iterative procedure is again developed defining new guard zones and temporarily unassigned data sample points and the process is repeated. The algorithm tends to cause cell centers to migrate towards local modes in the probability densities thus acting as an effective clustering technique as well as density function approximates.

4.4 Problems

1. We are given a three-class problem and are told to use statistical theory to generate our discriminant functions. We decide to

design a Bayes machine and the nature of the pattern recognition problem suggests the following loss function matrix (assume equally likely a priori statistics):

$$C(S_i/S_k) = \begin{bmatrix} 0 & 1 & 3 \\ 1 & 0 & 2 \\ 3 & 2 & 0 \end{bmatrix}$$

We also discover that the conditional statistics, given the classes, are componentwise independent

$$p(\mathbf{x}/S_k) = \prod_{n=1}^{N} p(x_n/S_k)$$

Where N is the dimensionality of our feature or pattern space. The component conditional statistics are uniformly distributed as

$$p(x_n/S_k) = \begin{cases} \dfrac{1}{k} & 0 \leq x_n \leq k \\ 0 & \text{otherwise} \end{cases} \forall k$$

(a) Derive the three discriminant functions $g_i(x) = -l(\mathbf{x}, S_i)$ for all i.

(b) Assuming a one-dimensional pattern space, $N = 1$, draw the three decision functions (discriminant functions) for the real line. Partition the line accordingly.

(c) In two-dimensional pattern space what class does the unknown $\mathbf{x} = (1.5, 2.5)$ belong to?

(d) Repeat parts (a) and (b) for the symmetic loss function.

2. Let the loss function for two classes be

$$C(S_i/S_k) = \begin{cases} -K_1 & i = k \\ K_2 & i \neq k \end{cases}$$

where $K_1 > 0$, $K_2 > 0$.

Derive the decision function $l(\mathbf{x}, S_i)$ which minimizes the loss. Explain the effect of K_1 and K_2.

3. Given the symmetric loss function and the probability law for a one-dimensional pattern space for a 3-class problem

$$p(x, S_i) = \frac{1}{3\sqrt{2\Pi}} [e^{-x^2/2} \delta(i-1) + e^{-(x-2)^2/2} \delta(i-2)$$
$$+ e^{-(x+1)^2/2} \delta(i-3)]$$

find the optimum decision rule (regions).

4. Show that the decision function minimizing the loss function

$$C(S_i/S_k) = -h_i \delta(i-k)$$

with $h_i = 1$ is the same as for the symmetric loss function for any number of pattern classes.

5. Prove that the optimum separating surface (for the h_i loss function with $h_1 = h_2$ and equally likely probabilities of occurrence of classes $P(1) = P(2)$ is linear if the two classes arise from multivariate Gaussian distributions with *equal* covariance matrices.

6. In a two-class and two-dimensional problem let the set of prototypes for the classes be

$$S_1 = \{\mathbf{P}_1^1, \mathbf{P}_2^1, \mathbf{P}_3^1\}$$
$$S_2 = \{\mathbf{P}_1^2, \mathbf{P}_2^2, \mathbf{P}_3^2, \mathbf{P}_4^2\}$$

where

$$S_1 = \{(0, 0), (0, 1), (1, 1)\}$$
$$S_2 = \{(-1, 0), (-1, -1), (-\tfrac{1}{2}, -\tfrac{1}{2}), (0, -1)\}$$

assume $p(\mathbf{x}/S_1)$ and $p(\mathbf{x}/S_2)$ are bivariate Gaussian distributions and the number of prototypes in each class is indicative of the a priori probabilities, $p(S_1)$, $p(S_2)$.
   (a) Give expressions for $p(\mathbf{x}/S_1)$ and $p(\mathbf{x}/S_2)$ by estimating the necessary parameters from the sample prototypes.
   (b) Find the equation of the optimum separating surface for a symmetric loss function. Sketch it and the prototypes.

7. For the same problem as above, two more prototypes are presented.

$$(0, \tfrac{1}{2}) \in S_1$$
$$(-1, -\tfrac{1}{2}) \in S_2$$

(a) What is the new optimum separating surface?

(b) Sketch it and all the prototypes.

8. You have decided to use a parametric classification procedure because of a strong suspicion that your prototypes are behaving like shot noise. Therefore, you decide to use Poisson statistics. In addition, the features (dimensions) appear to be statistically independent. Thus:

$$p(x_n) = e^{-a_n} \frac{(a_n)^{x_n}}{x_n!} \qquad n = 1, \ldots, N$$

Where x_n takes on only integer values, and

$$p(\mathbf{x}) = \prod_{n=1}^{N} p(x_n)$$

(a) How many parameters must be estimated from the prototypes?

(b) What are the parameters which must be estimated?

(c) How high an order moment does one need to evaluate for this problem?

9. Find the function $q(\mathbf{w}(i), \mathbf{x})$ used for updating the weight vector in the probabilistic descent algorithm for optimizing the average risk for the following loss functions.

(a) $C(d) = \begin{cases} 0 & d \leq 0 \\ d^2 & d > 0 \end{cases}$

(b) $C(d) = \begin{cases} 0 & d \leq 0 \\ d^2 & 0 < d \leq a \\ 2ad - a^2 & d > a \end{cases}$

10. Given the following loss function:

$$C(S_k/S_i) = \begin{cases} 0 & k = i \\ 1 & k = 1, i = 2 \\ 2 & k = 2, i = 1 \end{cases}$$

Further given the a priori probabilities

$$p(S_1) = \tfrac{1}{4}$$
$$p(S_2) = \tfrac{3}{4}$$

and the conditional probabilities

$$p(x/S_1) = \begin{cases} \tfrac{1}{2} & \tfrac{1}{2} \leq x \leq \tfrac{5}{2} \\ 0 & \text{otherwise} \end{cases}$$

$$p(x/S_2) = \begin{cases} \dfrac{2}{\Pi}\sqrt{1 - x^2} & -1 \leq x \leq 1 \\ 0 & \text{otherwise} \end{cases}$$

Find the optimal decision function in the range $-1 \leq x \leq \tfrac{5}{2}$ such that the Bayes risk is minimized, i.e., specify the decision at each point x for the region $(-1, \tfrac{5}{2})$.

11. Write the N variate normal distribution expression for $p(x)$ not as $N(\mu, [\Phi])$.

12. Derive the Bayes machine solution for a symmetric loss function and Gaussian statistics (most general case for the kth discriminant function).

13. For a K class problem with normally distributed statistics of uncorrelated equal variance dimensions and equal a priori statistics, write the kth discriminant function.

14. Is the discriminant function of problem 13 quadratic?

15. Conceptually describe the probabilistic descent method of risk minimization due to Amari.

16. Describe the properties of the kernel of the Parzen estimator.

17. Is a $(\sin x/x)^2$ function a valid Parzen kernel?

18. What are the advantages of Specht's polynomial discriminant function method?

19. What are the disadvantages of Specht's polynomial discriminant function method?

20. What kernel is used in the method of problem 18?

21. What approximations are used in the method of problem 18?

22. Does the approximated kernel of problem 21 have a maximum at the respective prototype in N space?

4.5 References

1. Nilsson, N. J., *Learning Machines*, McGraw-Hill, New York, 1965, Chapter 3.

2. Mendel, J. M. and K. S. Fu, *Adaptive, Learning, and Pattern Recognition Systems, Theory and Application*, Academic Press, New York, 1970.

3. Amari, S., "A Theory of Adaptive Pattern Classifiers," *IEEE Trans. on Electronic Computers*, Vol. EC-16, No. 3, pp. 299–307 (June 1967).

4. Koford, J. S. and G. F. Groner, "The Use of an Adaptive Threshold Element to Design a Linear Optimal Pattern Classifier," *IEEE Trans. on Information Theory*, Vol. IT-12, No. 1, pp. 42–50 (January 1966).

5. Meisel, W. S., private communications.

6. Parzen, E., "On Estimation of a Probability Density Function and Mode," *Annals of Mathematical Statistics*, Vol. 33, pp. 1065–1076 (1962).

7. Murthy, V. K., "Nonparametric Estimation of Multivariate Densities with Applications," *An Introduction to Multivariate Statistical Analyses*, Wiley, New York, 1958.

8. Specht, D. F., "Generation of Polynomial Discriminant Functions for Pattern Recognition," *IEEE Trans. on Electronic Computers*, Vol. EC-16, No. 3, pp. 308–319 (June 1967).

9. Meisel, W. S., "Potential Functions in Mathematical Pattern Recognition," *IEEE Trans. on Computers*, Vol. C-18, No. 10, pp. 911–918 (October 1969).

10. Sebestyen, G. and J. Edie, "An Algorithm for Non-Parametric Pattern Recognition," *IEEE Trans. on Electronic Computers*, Vol. EC-15, No. 6, pp. 908–915 (December 1966).

11. Robbins, H. and S., Monro, "A Stochastic Approximation Method," *Ann. Math. Stat.*, Vol. 22, No. 1, pp. 400–407 (1951).

12. Keifer, J. and Wolfowitz, J., "Stochastic Estimation of the Maximum of a Regression Function," *Ann. Math. Stat.*, Vol. 23, No. 3 (1952).

4.6 Related Bibliography

Abend, K., "Compound Decision Procedures for Pattern Recognition," *Proc. NEC*, pp. 777–780 (1966).

Abramson, N. and D. Braverman, "Learning to Recognize Patterns in a Random Environment," *IRE Trans. on Information Theory*, vol. 8, pp. 58–63 (September 1962).

Abramson, N., D. Braverman, and G. Sebestyen, "Pattern Recognition and Machine Learning," *IEEE Trans. on Information Theory*, vol. IT-9, pp. 257–261 (October 1965).

Bledsoe, W. W., "Some Results on Multicategory Pattern Recognition," *JACM*, vol. 13, pp. 304–316 (April 1966).

Carlyle, J. W. and J. B. Thomas, "On Nonparametric Signal Detectors," *IEEE Trans. on Information Theory*, pp. 146–152 (April 1964).

Chow, C. K., "On Optimum Recognition Error and Reject Trade-off," *IEEE Trans. on Information Theory*, vol. IT-16, no. 1, pp. 41–46 (January 1970).

Cooper, P. W., "Hyperplanes, Hyperspheres, and Hyperquadratics as Decision Boundaries," Chapter 4, *Computer and Information Sciences*, Ed. Tou and Wilcox, Spartan and Cleaver-Hume, 1964.

Cooper, P. W., "The Hyperplane in Pattern Recognition," *Cybernetica* **5**, pp. 215–238 (1962) also *Info. and Control*, vol. 5, pp. 324–347 (1962).

Cover, T. M., "Geometrical and Statistical Properties of Systems of Linear Inequalities with Applications in Pattern Recognition," *IEEE Trans. on Electronic Computers*, vol. EC-14, no. 3, pp. 326–334 (1965).

Cover, T. M., "Learning in Pattern Recognition," *Methodologies in Pattern Recognition*, Ed. Watanabe, pp. 111–132, Academic Press, New York, 1969.

Dvoretzky, A., "On Stochastic Approximation," *Proc. 3rd Berkeley Symp. on Math. Stat. and Prob.*, J, Neyman, ed., University of California Press, Berkeley, Calif., 1956, pp. 95–104.

Fukunaga, K. and T. F. Krile, "Calculation of Bayes Recognition Error for Two Multivariate Gaussian Distributions," *IEEE Trans. on Computers*, vol. C-18, no. 3, pp. 220–229 (March 1969).

Glaser, E. M., "Signal Detection by Adaptive Filters," *IRE Trans. on Information Theory*, vol. IT-7, pp. 87–98 (April 1961).

Ho, Y. C. and A. K. Agrawala, "On Pattern Classification Algorithms Introduction and Survey," *Proc. IEEE*, vol. 56, no. 12, pp. 2101–2114 (December 1968).

Ito, T., "Note on a Class of Statistical Recognition Functions," *IEEE Trans. on Computers*, vol. C-18, no. 1, pp. 76–79 (January 1969).

Jarvis, R. A., "Adaptive Global Search in Time-Varying Environment; Pattern Recognition Supervision," *IEEE SSC*, vol. SSC-6, pp. 209–217 (July 1970).

Kanal, L. N. and N. C. Randall, "Recognition System Design by Statistical Analysis," *Proc. 19th National Meeting ACM*, August 1964.

Keehn, D. G., "A Note on Learning for Gaussian Properties," *IEEE Transactions*, vol. IT-11, no. 1, pp. 126–132 (January 1965).

Lainiotis, D. G., "A Class of Upper Bounds on Probability of Error for Multi-Hypotheses Pattern Recognition," *Proc. IEEE Symp. on Adaptive Processes 1969*, pp. 3-a-1 to 3-a-3.

Lainiotis, D. G., "On a General Relationship Between Estimation, Detection and the Bhattacharyya Coefficient," *IEEE Trans. Info. Theory*, vol. IT-15, no. 4, pp. 504–505 (July 1969).

Lakshmivarahan, S. and M. A. L. Thathachar, "Pattern Classification Using Stochastic Approximation Techniques," *IEEE Trans. on Computers*, vol. C-19, no. 7, pp. 649–651 (July 1970).

Loftsgaarden, D. O. and C. P. Quesenberry, "A Nonparametric Estimate of a Multivariate Density Function," *Ann. Math. Stat.* **36,** 1049–1051 (1965).

Murthy, V. K., "Estimation of Probability Density," *Ann. Math. Stat.*, **36**, 1027–1031 (1965).

Noguchi, S., N. Kazuyki, and J. Oizumi, "The Evaluation of the Statistical Classifier," *Methodologies in Pattern Recognition*, ed. Watanabe, Academic Press, New York, 1969, pp. 437–456.

Robbins, H., "The Empirical Bayes Approach to Statistical Decision Problems," *Ann. Math. Statistics*, **35**, 1–20 (1964).

Robbins, H. and S. Munro, "A Stochastic Approximation Method," *Ann. Math. Statistics*, **22**, 400–407 (1951).

Rosenblatt, M., "Remarks on Some Nonparametric Estimates of a Density Function," *Ann. Math. Stat.* **27**, 832–837 (1956).

Scudder, H. J., "Probability of Error of Some Adaptive Pattern Recognition Machines," *IEEE Trans. on Info. Theory*, vol. IT-11, pp. 363–371 (July 1965).

Sebestyen, G. S., "Pattern Recognition by an Adaptive Process of Sample Set Construction," *IRE Intern. Symp. Infor. Theory*, vol. IT-8, pp. 582–591 (September 1962).

Specht, D. F., "Vectorcardiographic Diagnosis Using the Polynomial Discriminant Method of Pattern Recognition," *IEEE Trans. on Biomedical Engineering*, vol. BME-14, pp. 90–95 (April 1967).

Spragins, J. D., Jr., "A Note on the Iterative Application of Bayes' Rule," *IEEE Trans. on Info. Theory*, vol. IT-11, pp. 544–549 (October 1965).

Talbert, L. R., "The Sum-Line Extrapolative Algorithm and Its Application to Statistical Classification Problems," *IEEE Trans. on SSC*, vol. SSC-6, no. 3, pp. 229–239 (July 1970).

Tsypkin, Y. Z., "Use of the Stochastic Approximation Method in Estimating Unknown Distribution Densities from Observations," *Automation and Remote Control*, vol. 27, no. 3, pp. 432–434 (March 1966).

Wainsky, M. N. and L. Kurz, "Nonparametric Detection Using Dependent Samples," *IEEE Trans. Information Theory*, vol. IT-16, no. 3, pp. 355–358 (May 1970).

Watson, G. S. and M. R. Leadbetter, "On the Estimation of a Probability Density, I," *Ann. Math. Stat.* **34**, 480–491 (1963).

Wee, W. G., "Generalized Inverse Approach to Adaptive Multi-class Pattern Classification," *IEEE Trans. Computers*, vol. C-17, no. 12, pp. 1157–1164 (December 1968).

Wee, W. G. and K. S. Fu, "An Adaptive Procedure for Multiclass Pattern Classification," *IEEE Trans. on Computers*, vol. C-17, no. 2, pp. 178–182 (February 1968).

Whittle, P., "On the Smoothing of Probability Density Functions," *J. Royal Stat. Soc.* (Ser. B) **20,** 334–343 (1958).

NONSUPERVISED LEARNING

5.0 Introduction

To this point we have discussed pattern recognition entirely within the context of supervised learning in the sense that prototypes were known as to their correct classification. However, in many data analysis applications such classification information is not available but it is still desirable to learn something of the nature of the process for which the data is descriptive. Thus the subject of nonsupervised learning encompasses an attempt to apply recognition techniques to unclassified data. Meaningful results from such an exercise might be descriptions of the number of classes or clusters the data naturally falls into, or the modes the data appears to describe. Once clusters are defined, the supervised learning techniques discussed up to this chapter become meaningful.

The topic of nonsupervised learning has a rich and varied history in both multidimensional data analysis and statistical decision theory. The techniques of nonsupervised learning are often referred to as mode seeking, unsupervised learning, subset generation, numerical taxonomy, learning without a teacher, or cluster analysis. We can roughly define clustering to be the nonsupervised classification of objects which amounts to the process of generating classes without any knowledge of prototype classification. The essential characteristic is the sorting of the data into subsets such that each subset contains data points that are as much alike as possible. In N dimensional space clusters can be likened to areas in which the density of samples is high compared to surrounding regions. Mode estimation becomes a useful tool in finding and describing cluster centers and more will be said about this subject shortly. For meaningful results some a priori assumptions or knowledge must be available. For instance the number or size of classes may be known or possibly the uniformity or degree of similarity versus dissimilarity within the classes might be available. Using statistical decision theory nonsupervised learning implies that given a sequence of samples known only to have been drawn from the aggregate of K classes, it is possible by examining only these samples to estimate the unknown statistics necessary to define the desired decision surfaces in N dimensional space. Of course, it is often not possible to learn anything in an unsupervised environment, but in many important instances of interest statistical decision techniques do provide useful results. In addition to the availability of statistical techniques, some distribution free procedures are also useful for cluster seeking applications [1].

5.1 Distribution Free Learning

One of the drawbacks of cluster analysis is the fact that there does not exist an objective quantitative performance criterion with which to evaluate the results of any unsupervised learning. In other words there is no error rate as in pattern recognition problems with known prototypes. Thus the fidelity of one technique over another for comparative purposes is ill defined. However, in order to do any clustering it is necessary to define a measure of similarity between two samples usually with the properties of a distance function. The simplest distance measure between two points, x_i and x_j, is probably the Euclidean or Cartesian distance

$$d^2(x_i, x_j) = (x_i - x_j)^t(x_i - x_j) \qquad (5.1)$$

When the relative size of dimensions has no corresponding significance, then it may be more useful to normalize dimensions (coordinate axes) before defining a similarity measure (see Chapter 1). The Euclidean distance measure is particularly susceptible to the problem of multiple dimensions of a variety of units (apples and oranges). Correlation techniques are particularly susceptible to pattern normalization. Certain other distance or similarity measures which might be considered are listed below:

Weighted Euclidean Distance:

$$d^2(x_i, x_j) = \sum_{n=1}^{N} \alpha_n(x_{ni} - x_{nj})^2 \qquad (5.2)$$

Correlation:

$$d(x_i, x_j) = x_i^t x_j \qquad (5.3)$$

Similarity Ratio:

$$d(x_i, x_j) = \frac{x_i^t x_j}{x_i^t x_i + x_j^t x_j - x_i^t x_j} \qquad (5.4)$$

Normalized Correlation:

$$d(x_i, x_j) = \frac{x_i^t x_j}{((x_i^t x_i)(x_j^t x_j))^{1/2}} \qquad (5.5)$$

This list is by no means exhaustive and the distance or similarity measure must be properly selected for a specific task.

Once an appropriate similarity measure has been selected it then becomes necessary to develop a criterion for cluster formation. Again because such a criterion will be highly data-dependent it becomes useful to apply iterative techniques rather than one-pass methods. Clustering can be based upon entropy considerations,

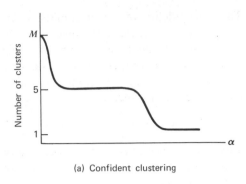

(a) Confident clustering

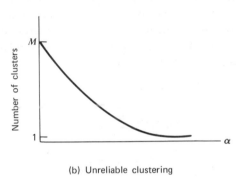

(b) Unreliable clustering

FIGURE 5.1. Clustering sensitivity.

average distances within and outside of clusters, and a host of other suitably adopted guidelines. It will become desirable to measure the sensitivity of a clustering algorithm to some parameter (α) such that a reasonable degree of confidence can be placed on the technique in question. Specifically it often occurs that α could describe some thresholding or radius effect in which it is possible to obtain as many clusters as data points, M, ($\alpha = 0$) or one cluster ($\alpha \rightarrow \infty$) monotonically in α. Figure 5.1 indicates the desirable and undesirable effects of the parametric sensitivity to α. Figure 5.1a might correspond to data of the form in Figure 5.2a while Figure 5.1b could correspond to that of Figure 5.2b. Unfortunately, no real analytic convergence properties exist for most of the cluster seeking techniques although plenty of experimental evidence is available for intuitive justification.

Scaling and linear transformations (rotations and translations) will have considerable effect on the resulting clusters. However, it is important to point out that clustering techniques will often afford greater insight into data structures than conventional methods such as factor or principal components analysis [1]. This is because of the lack of iterative adjustment associated with these latter approaches.

The chain method [2, 3] is a useful technique when the number of calculations must be minimized and it is a priori known that the clusters are tight and widely separated. In this method the first sample is taken as representative of the first cluster and the next sample distance is computed from the first cluster. If that distance is less than a threshold, say α, it is placed in the first class, otherwise a second cluster is formed. The method repeats with all samples

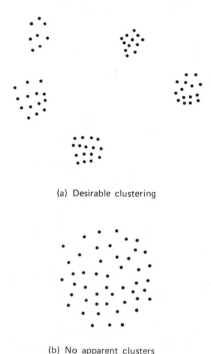

(a) Desirable clustering

(b) No apparent clusters

FIGURE 5.2. Two-space clustering.

by calculating the distance between each new sample and the representative of the clusters (i.e., the first sample found for each new cluster). If the distance is greater than the threshold for each old cluster, a new class is formed.

The method would be appropriate for the data of Figure 5.2a but obviously what is gained in simplicity of the method is lost in the requirement of stringent a priori assumptions.

If the number of clusters is known a priori, then there is one clustering technique which guarantees a type of convergence [2]. The data is partitioned such that the average spread of the clusters is minimized. Let $\mathscr{C}_j^k$ be the set of points comprising the kth cluster at the jth iteration where $\mathbf{C}_j^k$ is the cluster center. A two-step iteration is defined by the following procedure [4].

(a) Assign one of the M data points $\mathbf{x}_i$ to only one cluster according to its nearest center

$$\mathbf{x}_i \in \mathscr{C}_j^k \quad \text{iff} \quad d(\mathbf{x}_i,\ \mathbf{C}_j^k) = \min_l d(\mathbf{x}_i,\ \mathbf{C}_j^l) \qquad (5.6a)$$

Here l enumerates all clusters.

(b) Define the cluster centers such that

$$\mathbf{C}_{j+1}^k \Rightarrow \sum_{\mathbf{x}_i \,\in\, \mathscr{C}_j^k} d(\mathbf{x}_i, \mathbf{C}_{j+1}^k) = \min_{\mathbf{y}} \sum_{\mathbf{x}_i \,\in\, \mathscr{C}_j^k} d(\mathbf{x}_i, \mathbf{y}) \qquad (5.6b)$$

(c) repeat for each $\mathbf{x}_i$ one at a time until cluster and cluster centers become unchanged.

In other words the new cluster center is that point which minimizes the average similarity measure for elements within the cluster. When the similarity measure is taken to be the Euclidean distance function, $\mathbf{C}_j^k$ becomes the mean vector of the kth cluster at the jth iteration. The distance (similarity) from each pattern to each new cluster is computed and the iteration repeated by reassigning patterns when necessary. The convergence mentioned earlier implies that the mean distance between patterns and cluster centers is continually decreasing in the algorithm. Initial cluster centers may be defined with a priori knowledge, otherwise a good choice is the mean of all the data points. The converged cluster centers can then be used in defining a discriminant function for classification purposes of new data. The inherent drawback of the process is that if the total number of clusters, K, is off by a single number, the averaging process in the iteration can average two clusters on top of a third. See problem 2.

An alternative approach which could be classified as a potential function method is the vector field approach to cluster analysis [5]. Here a gravitational field analogy is developed and a single parameter (α) results which allows interpretation of local sensitivity (where each point is a cluster) to global sensitivity (where all points form one class). From physics it is known that the gravitational force between two objects is proportional to their masses and reciprocal distance of separation

$$F = m_1 m_2 d^{-2} \tag{5.7a}$$

where d is the distance between mass m_1 and m_2. For unit masses m_1, m_2, and a generalized force law

$$F = d^{\alpha} \tag{5.7b}$$

where $\alpha \leq 0$.

Assuming each sample in N dimensional space is a unit mass contributing a force at each point $\mathbf{y}$ in the space, that force can be represented with N components

$$f_n = \sum_{m=1}^{M} [d(\mathbf{x}_m, \mathbf{y})]^{\alpha} \left[\frac{x_{mn} - y_n}{d(\mathbf{x}_m, \mathbf{y})} \right] \tag{5.8}$$

where the first term is the magnitude of the force and the second term is the direction cosine. Note here the close analogy to potential functions. The force component f_n can be reduced to

$$f_n = \sum_{m=1}^{M} \left[\sum_{n=1}^{N} (x_{nm} - y_n)^2 \right]^{(\alpha-1)/2} (x_{nm} - y_n) \tag{5.9}$$

and reference [5] has algorithms to simplify the computational complexity of evaluating the force vector, $\mathbf{F}(\mathbf{y}) = f_1, \ldots, f_N$, at any point $\mathbf{y}$. The advantage of the technique is that for $\alpha = 0$, one cluster results and as α becomes more negative, the field becomes more sensitive to local samples. Eventually α will be so negative that each sample becomes a node and therefore a class or cluster by itself.

Cluster centers will tend to have zero fields only if the data tends to be tightly clustered. There will be other zero field points between clusters which will be gravitational balance points and which must not be interpreted as cluster centers. Field gradients can be useful for the purpose. A combination of the field technique and statistical approaches using Gaussian data has yielded useful cluster identification [6].

5.2   Mode Estimation

Often it is desirable, in unsupervised learning, to discover the modes of underlying distributions as an aid in cluster identification. The concept of a "mode" can be interpreted as the position of the center of a local maximum in a probability distribution. Modes define regions of high concentrations of patterns and can be used to describe classes when the above probability distribution is unconditional, (nonsupervised learning), or subclasses when the distribution is conditional, conditioned on known classifications, (supervised learning). Using the method of potential functions, Parzen [7] shows that a consistent estimate of the mode is

$$\tilde{M}_J = \arg(\max\{p_M(x)\}). \tag{5.10}$$

If the potential function kernel is

$$\psi(y) = \begin{cases} \frac{1}{2} & |y| \geq 1 \\ 0 & \text{otherwise} \end{cases}$$

then the estimated probability density function is made up of boxes or rectangles centered at the learning sample data points and the mode estimate becomes the center of that interval which contains the most observations. The estimate is based on M samples and converges in probability $(p_M(x) \to p(x))$ to the true value. This idea has been extended to multiple mode estimation in one dimension [8] where a histogram is developed such that different modes occupy disjoint regions. Also adaptive histogram techniques are useful for the mode definition [9].

The histogram techniques tend to be quite consumptive of computer time and storage, though and as a compromise an eigenvector projection method can often be useful [10]. An iterative procedure is suggested such that the sample covariance matrix is diagonalized to determine its eigenvectors. Then the unsupervised data is projected onto the eigenvectors (in order of decreasing eigenvalues) and one-dimensional mode estimation techniques are utilized. Discovered modes can then be removed and regions defined such that further

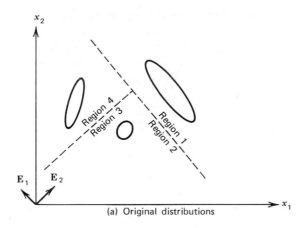

(a) Original distributions

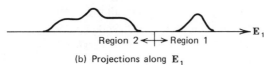

Region 2 ← | → Region 1

(b) Projections along E_1

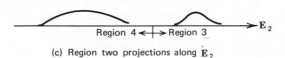

Region 4 ← | → Region 3

(c) Region two projections along E_2

FIGURE 5.3. A two-dimensional mode-seeking example (after Mendel and Fu [10]).

modes may be determined. New eigenvector projections can be
iterated through as old projections are exhausted as to their mode
revealing potential. Figure 5.3 indicates such a technique in two
dimensions.

5.3   Minimum Spanning Trees

The techniques discussed above have an inherent limitation in that
they are nonadaptive in terms of dimensions or coordinates. Thus,
certain clusters may, in fact, be strings or sheets of data wandering
through N dimensional space but their structure would remain
unknown if techniques were not developed to discover this intrinsic
dimensionality of the cluster. The technique of the minimum
spanning tree (MST) can often be utilized for investigating such
clusters, examples of which are illustrated in Figure 5.4. This
section is devoted to the MST approach while the following section
develops further intrinsic relationships amongst data.

The MST approach results from a graph theoretic analysis of
arbitrary point sets of data [11–13]. The MST is defined to be that
tree or connection of all points in the set to their closest neighbors
such that the entire tree is minimum. The resulting tree is unique
in the sense that the total length of the tree is minimum but equi-
distant points may be rearranged. Being a bit more precise, we can
define an *edge* to be a connection between two points. Then a *path*
becomes a sequence of edges joining two points (and may pass
through many other nodes). A *loop* is a closed path which allows a
series of edges to terminate on the same point. A *connected set* has
paths between any pair of points. A *spanning tree* is a connected
set with no loops which contains all points of the problem. Finally,
if we assign a weight to each edge which is the distance between the
points the edge connects, then the *minimal spanning tree* (MST) of a
set is that spanning tree with the sum of the weights of the edges of
the tree a minimum. Figures 5.5 and 5.6 present examples of two
such trees.

Because the minimum spanning tree is unique to a set of points in
terms of a minimum total weight, it is possible to use the tree as a
basis for certain cluster detection techniques combining both

distance properties and density properties described below. By removing the branch points from the minimum spanning tree one will obtain the *main diameter* which by definition will be the path of the MST with the largest number of points. Attached to the points of the main diameter might be the numeric maximum number of points branching from the node (see Figures 5.5 and 5.6). Now by using various combinations of neighborhood distances and density of points attached to various nodes, it may be possible to discover and separate clusters successfully. Thus, in the examples of Figures 5.5 and 5.6 a combination of local minimum on the main diameter histogram and inconsistent distance between points with the local

(a) Helix: intrinsically one-dimensional in three-space

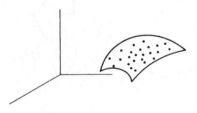

(b) Hemisphere: surface cluster in three-space intrinsically two-dimensional

(c) Spiral clusters: intrinsically one–dimensional in two–space

FIGURE 5.4. Nonlinearly clustering data.

minimum serves to successfully separate the data between points
A and *B*. Of course, in Figure 5.5 the inconsistent distance of edge
AB serves as a dominant clue as to the break between clusters,
whereas, in Figure 5.6 inconsistent distances are not as obvious as
the local minimum in the main diameter point density histogram.
Zahn [11] has shown many other uses of the MST of a point set
for cluster analysis with considerable success.

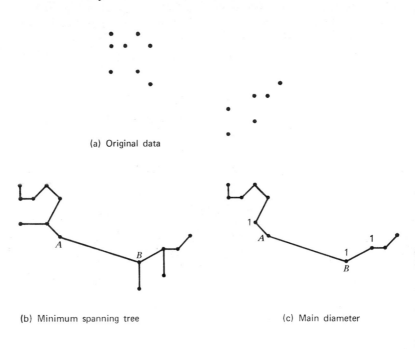

(a) Original data

(b) Minimum spanning tree   (c) Main diameter

(d) Main diameter histogram

FIGURE 5.5 Naturally separated clusters.

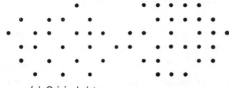

(a) Original data

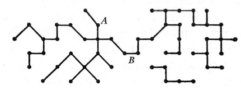

(b) Minimum spanning tree

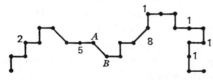

(c) Main diameter

(d) Main diameter histogram

FIGURE 5.6. Naturally touching clusters.

5.4 Intrinsic Dimensionality

The MST approach used above implicitly utilized local properties at the expense of global properties, (inconsistent distances and node densities). More explicitly, it may be desirable to destroy global relationships while maintaining local character in order that clustering and intrinsic dimensionality might be obtained. Thus, in order that one might discover the intrinsic dimensionality relationships indicated in the data of Figure 5.4 it becomes useful to study proximity analysis and rank preservation transformations. The underlying motivation for the study is the intuitive belief that the coordinates of the pattern space have little to do with the intrinsic structure describing prototype generation. It is desirable to obtain a clustering equal to the intrinsic dimensionality of the collection of signals comprising the prototypes independent of any given set of basis vectors. In other words we would like a measure which is only a property of the collection of prototypes and not a function of the particular coordinate system one chooses in order to expand or represent the prototypes. This problem has been attacked from two different disciplines, engineering [14] and psychology [12–21], with surprisingly similar results. The psychological development is historically older and will be described first.

The subject of proximity analysis is developed around the desire to form metric structures out of nonmetric data. Specifically the psychological concepts of similarity, nearness, degree of proximity, substitutability, association, and many others, all are subjective nonmetric notions but all have a commonality in that they are usually pair ranked by human subjects in psychological experiments. Thus, if there are M objects, a subject may be asked to describe similarity measures or other notions to the objects and such measures are usually a function of the objects taken two at a time. Thus, one obtains a total of $M(M-1)/2$ different measures assuming the psychological notions are symmetric (if A is similar to B then B is similar to A) and ignoring self-similarities. The $M(M-1)/2$ different values are not unlike the $M(M-1)/2$ different interpoint distances between a point set of M elements. The major difference between the distances and similarity measures is a metric versus nonmetric space upon which the two objects (prototypes) are described. In the psychological applications it becomes desirable to find a metric structure relating the nonmetric concepts and a technique for such a process becomes that of ranking. Thus, if the similarity between objects m and p is denoted $S(m, p)$ and if all such similarities are defined and ranked in monotonic fashion, then it would be desirable to maintain such a ranking in a reduced feature or clustering space. Because the number of different ranks or constraints increase as M^2 whereas the number of objects increase linearly with M, it is expected that a considerable dimensionality reduction could be obtained by simply keeping ranking order constant in a reduced space. Thus, in the psychological context of proximity analysis one is searching for: (a) an intrinsic dimensionality, (b) an orthogonal coordinate system upon which that dimensionality can be related, and (c) the shape of the monotonic function relating proximity measures to distance. The monotonicity constraint will imply that the rank of the $M(M - 1)/2$ proximities should be the inverse rank order of the $M(M - 1)/2$ distances of the M objects on the reduced space. Thus

$$S(i, m) > S(p, j) \Rightarrow d(i, m) < d(p, j) \qquad (5.11)$$

It is known that the upper bound on the number of dimensions necessary to describe $M(M - 1)/2$ different rankings is $M - 1$ [15]. In fact, for an iterative procedure it is possible to start with M points located at the vertices of the regular simplex in $(M - 1)$ space. In this case, all distances are equal; in two dimensions, the regular simplex is the equilateral triangle, in three dimensions, the data points describe the four vertices of a regular tetrahedron. Note, as Shepard has pointed out [16, 17], that a trivial solution to the ranking problem results in $M - 1$ space as the vertices of the triangle (in two-space) can be perturbed to obtain any of the three possible rankings desired. See Figure 5.7.

One method of reducing the dimensionality is by increasing the variance of the M points as they are perturbed and arranged in the proper rank order. Bennett [14] has noted that for points uniformly distributed in a sphere of radius a in N dimensions the normalized interpoint distance

$$d = \frac{|d(A, B)|}{a} \qquad (5.12)$$

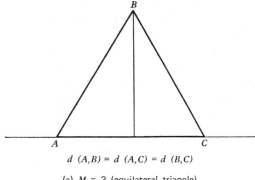

$$d\ (A,B) = d\ (A,C) = d\ (B,C)$$

(a) $M = 3$ (equilateral triangle)

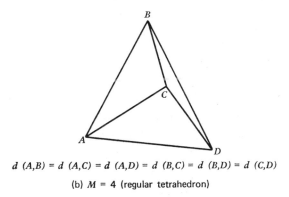

$$d\ (A,B) = d\ (A,C) = d\ (A,D) = d\ (B,C) = d\ (B,D) = d\ (C,D)$$

(b) $M = 4$ (regular tetrahedron)

FIGURE 5.7. Regular simplexes where all similarities (distances) are identical.

is distributed as

$$P_N(d) = {}_2N_{Nd}(N - 1)I_{1-d^2}(\tfrac{1}{2}N + \tfrac{1}{2}, \tfrac{1}{2})$$

where $I_x(p, q)$ is the incomplete beta function [22, 23]. The variance of this distribution (which is asymptotically normal for N) suggests that a displacement of points which increases the variance of the interpoint distances will tend to reduce the linear dimensionality of the displaced points. Shepard [20] points out the situation when the points are not uniformly distributed but are spherically normally distributed. The original iterative algorithm [16, 17] for the psychological ranking problem was to perturb the M points in order to maintain rank order and then to perturb the M points in order to increase their interpoint variance. Since increasing the interpoint variance is counter to maintaining rank monotonicity, when the two operations tend to balance, the solution is terminated. The terminating criterion was based upon a measure of how badly misranked the resulting proximities were. Because the process has been carried out in $(M - 1)$ space no dimensionality reduction has as yet been accomplished. After iterating the perturbations to maintain rankings and to increase variances, the final dimensionality is determined by the familiar eigenvector matrix diagonalization process. A flow chart of the technique follows. Shepard's experimental results [17] are quite encouraging and one particular aspect

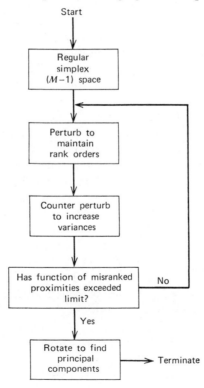

is worth discussing. Because the psychologist does not know the metric relationship, $d(i, m)$, with respect to the proximity measure, $S(i, m)$, other than through a ranking criterion, he is interested in recovering that information as well. Shepard has taken artificial proximity data and selected a variety of monotonic relationships and has successfully recovered the functional forms. Example of the relation between proximities and distances used were

$$S(i, m) = \exp\{-(1.4)d^2(i, m)\} \qquad (5.13a)$$

$$S(i, m) = \exp\{(-d(i, m)\} \qquad (5.13b)$$

$$S(i, m) = f\{d(i, m)\} \qquad (5.13c)$$

where $f\{\cdot\}$ is a monotonic piecewise linear function. The importance of this result is that any monotonic functional relationship seems to be a valid relation for the iterative procedure to be successful. In fact it will be suggested later that in the pattern recognition environment any monotonic function of Euclidean distance will be a valid distance function for nonlinear iterative techniques.

Kruskal [18, 19] has improved the work by Shepard in the technique for terminating the iteration. Shepard terminated based upon a measure of the number of misranked proximities but, because proximity space is not metric, such a criterion may be in doubt. Kruskal introduced the concept of a measure of stress upon which to evaluate the progress of the algorithm, and it is related to the earlier criterion used by Sammons (Chapter 2). Kruskal's motivation is that of maintaining monotonicity on the scatter diagram of dissimilarity versus distance. Whenever the variance-increasing perturbation violates the monotonicity criterion a new distance estimate, $\hat{d}$, is developed to redefine a monotone curve on the scatter diagram. For such monotone relations the stress, as given below, will be equal to zero. Thus, the difference between the original distances and the estimated distances to maintain monotonicity at each iteration becomes

$$E = \sum_{p=1}^{M} \sum_{m=1}^{M} (d(\mathbf{y}_p, \mathbf{y}_m) - \hat{d}(\mathbf{y}_p, \mathbf{y}_m))^2 \qquad (5.14)$$

While E as given by equation (5.14) is invariant under rigid motions (rotations, translations, and reflections), it is not invariant to uniform stretching. However, because rank orders are independent of such stretching, so should be the criterion for divergence from rank orders. Thus, the stress becomes

$$
E = \left\{ \frac{\sum_{p=1}^{M} \sum_{m=1}^{M} (d(\mathbf{y}_p, \mathbf{y}_m) - \hat{d}(\mathbf{y}_p, \mathbf{y}_m))^2}{\sum_{p=1}^{M} \sum_{m=1}^{M} d(\mathbf{y}_p, \mathbf{y}_m)^2} \right\}^{\frac{1}{2}}
\tag{5.15}
$$

By using the stress of equation (5.15) and minimizing with respect to the $\hat{d}(\mathbf{y}_p, \mathbf{y}_m)$ distance with a steepest descent technique a solution will be obtained. The distances $\hat{d}$ are a priori defined to be constrained to be monotonically ranked and related according to their psychological proximities and are varied within that constraint to minimize E. The minimum stress becomes

$$
E_{\min} = \min_{\substack{\text{all} \\ \hat{d} \text{ satisfy} \\ \text{monotonicity}}} \{E\}
\tag{5.16}
$$

However, the feature space dimensionality has not been determined until a rotation has been performed. Note that for $N > M - 1$, $E = 0$ because all possible rank orders are possible in such a space. As N decreases the minimum stress, $E_{\min}$, will increase and Kruskal has suggested that the elbow in the curve of N versus $E_{\min}$ will tell what dimension to use. Incidentally, because the stress of equation (5.15) is invariant to the above mentioned rigid body motions and uniform compression, it is possible to start the iterations by placing the center of gravity of the prototypes at the origin and stretching or shrinking the space so the root mean squared distance of points from the origin is equal to unity.

The above arguments have proven quite successful in certain psychological data and it is interesting to see a quite similar result that has been independently derived in the engineering literature by Bennett [14]. In the context of a pattern space which is a priori defined to be a metric space there is no need to relate subjective psychological evaluations (proximity analysis) to the set of proto-types defining a given class. Instead it is possible to start with the rank orders of the distances in the original pattern space defined by the M prototypes. The objective now is to reduce the dimensionality of the prototype space defined by the different $M(M - 1)/2$ ranks. Thus, the original basis vectors which define the pattern space (and which are usually defined by a transducer system) are only used to define the ranked distances. It becomes possible to use the pattern space as a starting space for the iteration technique for maintaining distance rank orders and increasing variances simultaneously. The locus of points resulting from the iterative transformation will then define the intrinsic dimensionality. Assuming a Euclidean metric, the example in Figure 5.8a in two-space could be the initial conditions

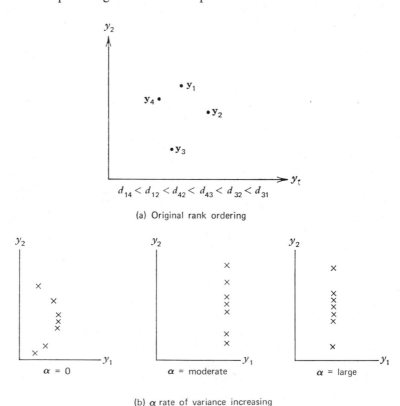

$$d_{14} < d_{12} < d_{42} < d_{43} < d_{32} < d_{31}$$

(a) Original rank ordering

$\alpha = 0$

$\alpha = $ moderate

$\alpha = $ large

(b) α rate of variance increasing

FIGURE 5.8. Pattern space rank orderings.

for the algorithm. Let

$$d(p, m) = f\left\{\left(\sum_{n=1}^{N}(y_{np} - y_{nm})^2\right)^{\frac{1}{2}}\right\} \qquad (5.17)$$

where $f\{\cdot\}$ is any monotonic nondecreasing function. Let

$$\bar{d} = \frac{1}{M(M-1)}\sum_{p=1}^{M}\sum_{m=1}^{M}d(p, m) \qquad (5.18)$$

such that $\bar{d}$ is the mean of the intrapoint distances. In order to increase the variance in the distances, those $d(p, m)$ less than $\bar{d}$ should be reduced while those $d(p, m)$ greater than $\bar{d}$ should be increased. A differential element is calculated at each iteration such that

$$\Delta_v(p, m) = \alpha(d(p, m) - \bar{d})/\bar{d} \qquad (5.19)$$

where α is a parameter governing the rate of increase of the variance of the new points. The normalized variance for the points is given by

$$\sigma^2 = \frac{2}{M(M-1)}\sum_{p=1}^{M}\sum_{m=1}^{M}(d(p, m) - \bar{d})^2/\bar{d}^2 \qquad (5.20)$$

and the factor α determines how this variance $\sigma^2(i)$ increases as a function of the ith iteration. Figure 5.8b indicates the effect of the value of α upon the dimensionality reduction. It is evident that if α is too large, then the dimensionality will be over-reduced at the expense of maintaining rank orders. In fact, in the limit the increasing variance criterion will result in a one-dimensional space in which two or at most three separate clusters result, each moving further away from the other and each becoming more and more tightly packed. The appropriate choice of α, then, must be made to define the correction factor, $\Delta_v(p, m)$ in determining the new prototype positions. Thus, the position on the mth point after the ith variance iteration becomes

$$y_{nm}(i + 1) = y_{nm}(i) + \frac{1}{2}\sum_{p=1}^{M} - (y_{np}(i) - y_{nm}(i))\Delta_v(p, m) \quad (5.21)$$

Because increasing variances may distort the ranked distances and because global structure is to be sacrificed for local structure, only those points within some sphere of radius β, centered at each prototype point $\mathbf{y}_m$ in the original pattern space will have their ranked distances maintained. Thus at each iteration a second differential element will be calculated which is a function of the number of misranked points within the original β radius after the variance-increasing algorithm. The appropriate prototype points are then moved to lessen the number of misranked prototypes. For local structure maintenance the sphere of radius β is placed on each prototype and assume that there are N_m other prototypes within the sphere centered at $\mathbf{y}_m$ and let the set of these prototypes be described by $\eta_m = \{\mathbf{y}_p : d(p, m) < \beta\}$. Then there are $N_m(N_m - 1)/2$ rank distances associated with these prototypes. Let R_{mpq} be the rank of the distance $d(p, q)$ where the p, q indices range over the points in η_m including of course $\mathbf{y}_m$. The range of the ranks, R_{mpq}, will be from 1 to $N_m(N_m - 1)/2$. Let R'_{mpq} be the new rankings of the points in η_m after the variance-increasing iteration. Then a measure of the degree of misranking becomes

$$\Delta_R(m, p, q) = (R_{mpq} - R'_{mpq})\gamma \qquad (5.22)$$

and γ is a parameter governing the rate of maintenance of the original ranking. Thus the position of the mth point after the ith ranking iteration becomes

$$y_{nm}(i + 1) = y_{nm}(i) - \frac{1}{2}\sum_{p=1}^{N_m}\sum_{q=1}^{N_m}(y_{np}(i) - y_{nm}(i))\Delta_R(m, p, q) \qquad (5.23)$$

where the double summation is used to "integrate" out the ranks of all the points within the set of η. A possible flow chart for the computation is seen on facing page, where ε is used as a termination parameter.

The transformation that results from such an algorithm will be nonlinear in nature but can be expressed as approximating that of a similarity transformation. Because the rank order of distances is invariant under rigid body motion and uniform expansions, if all rank orders were maintained, then a similarity transform would result. However, only rank orders within a radius β are attempted to be maintained and, consequently, as β increases the transformation becomes more and more that of similarity transform but with corresponding lower variances and higher dimensionality feature spaces.

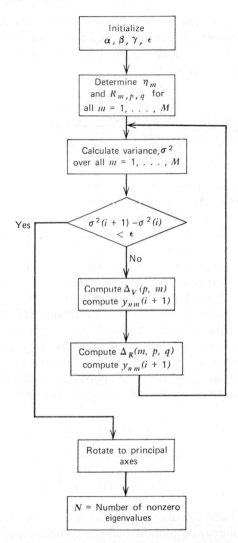

Certain experimental difficulties result from the selection of the radius β above as well as the rate of variance increase α which have led to another approach to the definition of the iterative nonlinear transformation. Again the objective is to maintain local structure at the expense of global framework and an index of continuity C has been introduced by Carroll [21] for this purpose. The motivation

for such a measure lies in the intuitive concept that as the prototypes become more and more alike their differences become smaller
and smaller. This is similar to the definition of continuity. The
index of continuity becomes

$$
C = \frac{\displaystyle\sum_{m=1}^{M} \sum_{p=1}^{M} \frac{d^2(\mathbf{y}_m, \mathbf{y}_p)}{d^2(\mathbf{v}_m, \mathbf{v}_p)} \, \mathbf{w}_{m,p}}{\displaystyle\sum_{m=1}^{M} \sum_{p=1}^{M} \left(\frac{1}{d^2(\mathbf{v}_m, \mathbf{v}_p)}\right)^2}
\tag{5.24a}
$$

where v_m is the new point obtained from y_m and w_{mp} is a weighting
function and the denominator is chosen so that C is independent
of the scale of the new feature space. It has been shown [24] that C
is minimum when $d(\mathbf{y}_m, \mathbf{y}_p)/d(\mathbf{v}_m, \mathbf{v}_p)$ is constant for all m, p.
However, this is nothing more than the linear transformation
involving only translations, rotations, and scale changes. For
nonlinear transformations C will be an inverse measure of the
continuity (or smoothness) of the transformation. When the new
space is constrained to be of lower dimensionality than the old,
then in general the absolute minimum will not be attainable [25].
The weighting factor, $w_{m,p}$, is most often taken as $\{d(\mathbf{v}_m, \mathbf{v}_p)\}^{-2}$ in
order that local structure be maintained. Thus points far apart in
the new space have less effect, proportional to the reciprocal of
their separation, than points closer together. The index of continuity
then becomes

$$
C = \frac{\displaystyle\sum_{m=1}^{M} \sum_{p=1}^{M} \frac{d^2(\mathbf{y}_m, \mathbf{y}_p)}{d^4(\mathbf{v}_m, \mathbf{v}_p)}}{\left(\displaystyle\sum_{m=1}^{M} \sum_{p=1}^{M} \frac{1}{d^2(\mathbf{v}_m, \mathbf{v}_p)}\right)^2}
\tag{5.24b}
$$

A variety of individuals [21, 24–26] have used this index as a
criterion for minimization in the iterative context mentioned earlier.
Both steepest descent and Monte Carlo techniques as well as a
"direct search" method have been used to minimize the constraint
C. Carroll [21] has pointed out how the method can be used to
puncture higher dimensional symmetric objects, spheres and toroids,
to reduce the dimensionality of such surfaces.

The nonlinear transformations described in this section have been mainly concerned with preserving local information at the expense of global structure. Thus, the transformations should be approximately conformal. In addition, the clusters or prototypes of the data should unfold to an essentially simple form, hyperellipsoidal rather than curvilinear; and the transformation should result in linear separation.

Thus far we are restricted to nonsupervisory learning problems utilizing these techniques. Of course, the intrinsic dimensionality clustering algorithms could be used on each set of known prototypes in a supervised environment, resulting in K different intrinsic dimensions and iteratively defined transformations, one for each class S_k. However, these nonlinear clustering results have not been advanced to the point where interclass structure is also included in the definition of the transformation.

5.5 Statistical Nonsupervised Learning

It is often possible to view the nonsupervised learning problem in the context of statistical decision theory. Because a priori knowledge is not available as to prototype classification, distributions are unconditional in nature and are often referred to as mixture statistics. A mixture statistic then is an overall density descriptive of the unsupervised learning task. Initially, it might seem futile to attempt to learn or adapt from such unconstrained statistics. However, work has been done in this area in recent years and it has been shown possible (under certain general conditions) to achieve adaptation without supervision. Cooper and Cooper [27] have presented early work along these lines with considerable success. In one application they concentrate on a two-class problem in which the mixture distribution of independent samples of both classes is examined. A criterion of minimum total probability of misclassification is used and solutions to a variety of assumed distributions and classifications are developed.

First, consider the case of the bimodal one-dimensional Gaussian mixture distribution in which it is assumed that the variance of each class is the same and a priori statistics are equal. Then the mixture density becomes

$$p(x) = \tfrac{1}{2}[N(\mu_1, \sigma^2) + N(\mu_2, \sigma^2)] \qquad (5.25a)$$

$$= \frac{1}{\sqrt{2\pi\sigma^2}} e^{-(a^2/2\sigma^2)} e^{-(1/2\sigma^2)(x-\mu)^2} \cosh[(a/\sigma^2)(x - \mu)] \quad (5.25b)$$

where $2a = \mu_2 - \mu_1$, $\mu = \tfrac{1}{2}(\mu_1 + \mu_2)$, and the proper decision boundary is the value μ. The simplest estimate of μ is the sample mean

$$\hat{\mu} = \frac{1}{M} \sum_{m=1}^{M} x_m \qquad (5.26)$$

For unknown a, σ, and m, the simultaneous solution of three equations, each which has variables within and outside of hyperbolic functions, is necessary for a maximum likelihood estimator.

For the case of two N dimensional spherically symmetric multivariate Gaussian distributions which differ only in the mean vector location, the optimum decision boundary separating the classes is the $N - 1$ dimensional plane (hyperplane) which perpendicularly bisects the vector connecting the two means. The bimodal distribution becomes

$$p(\mathbf{x}) = \frac{1}{(2\pi)^{N/2}\sigma^N} \exp - (1/2\sigma^2)$$
$$\times \exp\{-(1/2\sigma^2)(\mathbf{x} - \boldsymbol{\mu})^t (\mathbf{x} - \boldsymbol{\mu})\}$$
$$\times \cosh[(1/\sigma^2)\mathbf{a}^t(\mathbf{x} - \boldsymbol{\mu})] \qquad (5.27)$$

where again $\boldsymbol{\mu} = \tfrac{1}{2}(\boldsymbol{\mu}_1 + \boldsymbol{\mu}_2)$ and $2\mathbf{a} = \boldsymbol{\mu}_2 - \boldsymbol{\mu}_1$. The solution is obtained by estimating $\boldsymbol{\mu}$ and determining the principal axis of the bimodal distribution which is equivalent to calculating the eigenvector corresponding to the largest eigenvalue in the overall covariance matrix.

Again $\hat{\boldsymbol{\mu}}$ can be simply estimated as

$$\hat{\boldsymbol{\mu}} = \frac{1}{M} \sum_{m=1}^{M} \mathbf{x}_m \qquad (5.28)$$

and the values of a_i are shown to be

$$a_i^2 = \phi_{ii} - \sigma^2 \qquad (5.29)$$

when ϕ_{ii} are the diagonal estimates of the correlation matrix

$$[\hat{\phi}] = \frac{1}{M-1} \sum_{m=1}^{M} (\mathbf{x}_m - \hat{\mu})(\mathbf{x}_m - \hat{\mu})^t \tag{5.30}$$

Additional results are obtained for nonsymmetric (ellipsoidal) component covariance matrices for the N dimensional Gaussian assumption. In fact for ellipsoidally symmetric and monotone component distributions (of which the multivariate Gaussian is an example) the hyperplane which passes through the mean, μ, of the mixtures provides the optimum decision boundary, and thus unsupervised learning can be extended to these cases [27].

Even more general results can be obtained for the unsupervised learning of discriminant functions under the assumption of unknown common component densities $p(x)$ separated by an unknown distance, $2a$. In the one-dimensional case the sequence of random variables $\{x_m\}$ define the density, $g(x)$, in the limit as more and more samples are taken. In fact the mixture density $g(x) = \frac{1}{2}[p(x-a) + p(x+a)]$ can be related to the component density through the use of characteristic functions (the Fourier transform of a density function). Thus $\hat{g}_M(s) = \cos(as)\hat{p}(s)$ where $\hat{g}_M(s)$ is the Fourier transform of $g_M(x)$, the empirical distribution function of the statistically independent samples, x_m.

$$g_M(x) = \frac{1}{M} \sum_{m=1}^{M} D(x - x_m) \tag{5.31}$$

where $D(x - x_m)$ = rectangle Parzen estimator. Thus the zeros of $\hat{g}_M(s)$ will be those of $\cos(as)$ and if $\hat{p}(s)$ does not have periodic zeros, a valid estimate of a can be obtained from the periodicity of $\cos(as)$.

5.6 Conclusions

The techniques presented thus far in this chapter are meant only to provide the reader with some of the more common approaches to the complex problems of nonsupervised learning. There exist many other approaches which are beyond the scope in space and concept of an introductory pattern recognition text. Such areas as unsupervised stochastic approximation are left as topics of independent study for the interested reader. However, the subject of nonsupervised learning will be considered again in the following chapter in the context of sequential processes after some introductory material on sequential supervised learning.

5.7 Problems

1. You are interested in investigating the potential of the chain method of clustering. The data is presented to you in the following sequence.

$$x_1 = (1, 0)$$
$$x_2 = (1, 1)$$
$$x_3 = (0, 1)$$
$$x_4 = (0, 0)$$
$$x_5 = (3, 1)$$
$$x_6 = (4, 1)$$
$$x_7 = (4, 0)$$
$$x_8 = (3, 0)$$

(a) What data points belong to what clusters for a threshold of 3?

(b) Repeat part (a) for a threshold of 1.5

(c) Repeat part (a) for a threshold of .5

(d) If a ninth point, $x_9 = (2, 1/2)$, is added, in what cluster does it fall when starting the algorithm with x_1 and threshold 1.5?

(e) Repeat part (d) for the data in the reversed order. This is an example which is referred to as a bridge.

2. Utilize the convergence clustering algorithm which minimizes average cluster spread on the following 3-cluster data.

$x_1 = (6, 0)$	$x_9 = (-7, 6)$	$x_{17} = (9, 0)$
$x_2 = (-4, -5)$	$x_{10} = (7, 0)$	$x_{18} = (-7, -5)$
$x_3 = (-5, 5)$	$x_{11} = (-5, 8)$	$x_{19} = (-7, 7)$
$x_4 = (-6, 6)$	$x_{12} = (-5, -6)$	$x_{20} = (7, -1)$
$x_5 = (-6, -3)$	$x_{13} = (-6, 8)$	$x_{21} = (-6, -6)$
$x_6 = (7, 1)$	$x_{14} = (-6, -7)$	$x_{22} = (-7, 4)$
$x_7 = (-5, -4)$	$x_{15} = (8, -1)$	$x_{23} = (-5, 7)$
$x_8 = (8, 0)$	$x_{16} = (-7, -8)$	$x_{24} = (8, 1)$

(a) Using the points in the order presented determine the three cluster centers $\mathbf{C}^1$, $\mathbf{C}^2$, $\mathbf{C}^3$ with the following initial conditions

$$\mathbf{C}^1(0) = (8, 8)$$
$$\mathbf{C}^2(0) = (-8, -8)$$
$$\mathbf{C}^3(0) = (-8, 8)$$

and $d^2(x_i, x_j) = (x_i - x_j)^t(x_i - x_j)$

(b) Repeat the algorithm with the data conditions of part (a) but with the incorrect assumption of a 2-cluster problem.

3. The never ending quest of the student suggests that your instructor once again has deceived you. He told you that for a one-dimensional bimodal mixture distribution comprised of univariate common variance Gaussian component distributions, the simplest estimator for a decision boundary in unsupervised learning is to determine the mean, $\hat{\mu} = \dfrac{1}{M} \sum_{m=1}^{M} x_m$. However the maximum likelihood estimator is another function

$$\hat{\mu} = \frac{1}{M} \sum_{m=1}^{M} x_m - \frac{a}{M} \sum_{m=1}^{M} \tanh[(a/\sigma^2)(x_m - \hat{\mu})]$$

Prove this fact by differentiating the function

$$L = \sum_{m=1}^{M} \log p(x_m)$$

with respect to μ and setting the partial derivative equal to zero. Here $p(x)$ is the mixture distribution.

4. Assume a two-class nonsupervised learning task is to be performed on unknown common component density $p(x)$ shifted by an unknown amount $2a$. Assume that the a priori distribution of class S_1 is $P(S_1) = q$. Solve for the characteristic function of the mixture distribution.

5. For the same assumptions as in problem 4 but with $P(S_1) = \frac{1}{2}$, how would you estimate the shift, a, when you know:

(a) $p(x)$ is uniformly distributed.

(b) $p(x)$ is triangularly distributed.

(c) $p(x)$ is Gaussianly distributed.

(d) $p(x)$ is exponentially decaying distributed.

(e) Solve for (a), (b), (c), and (d) where possible.

6. Using the minimum spanning tree, its main diameter histogram, and the use of inconsistent distances, cluster the following data.

$x_1 = (-5, 10)$	$x_2 = (-1, 5)$	$x_3 = (2, 3)$
$x_4 = (2.5, 9.2)$	$x_5 = (-1, 9)$	$x_6 = (4, 3)$
$x_7 = (-2.5, 11)$	$x_8 = (.5, 7)$	$x_9 = (5, 4)$
$x_{10} = (0, -2)$	$x_{11} = (-2, -4)$	$x_{12} = (1, 4)$
$x_{13} = (0, -4)$	$x_{14} = (-3, -4.5)$	$x_{15} = (2, 4)$
$x_{16} = (-3, -3)$	$x_{17} = (-4, -6)$	$x_{18} = (3, 5)$
$x_{19} = (0, 11)$	$x_{20} = (-5, -5)$	$x_{21} = (2, 6)$
$x_{22} = (0, 10)$	$x_{23} = (-6, -7)$	$x_{24} = (2, 7)$
$x_{25} = (0, -5)$	$x_{26} = (-5, -8)$	$x_{27} = (1, 8)$
$x_{28} = (-1.5, -5)$	$x_{29} = (3.5, -9)$	$x_{30} = (1.5, 10)$
$x_{31} = (6.5, 6)$	$x_{32} = (-2, -7)$	$x_{33} = (3, 11)$
$x_{34} = (4.5, 6)$	$x_{35} = (-1, -8)$	$x_{36} = (3, 10)$
$x_{37} = (7, -5)$	$x_{38} = (-1, -9)$	$x_{39} = (4, 8)$
$x_{40} = (7.1, -5)$	$x_{41} = (0, 1)$	$x_{42} = (3, 7)$
$x_{43} = (7, -3)$	$x_{44} = (0, 3)$	$x_{45} = (6, 8)$
$x_{46} = (5, -3)$	$x_{47} = (0, 5)$	$x_{48} = (6, 10)$
$x_{49} = (4, -2)$	$x_{50} = (1, -4)$	$x_{51} = (3.1, 11)$
$x_{52} = (-4, 5)$	$x_{53} = (3, -3)$	$x_{54} = (0, 1.1)$
$x_{55} = (-4, 7)$	$x_{56} = (2, -6)$	$x_{57} = (4.3, 8)$
$x_{58} = (-3, 6)$	$x_{59} = (3, -5)$	$x_{60} = (1, 8.2)$
$x_{61} = (-2.5, 7.5)$	$x_{62} = (4, -6)$	
$x_{63} = (-2, 4)$	$x_{64} = (6, -6)$	
$x_{65} = (1, -8)$	$x_{66} = (5, -8)$	
$x_{67} = (1, -10)$	$x_{68} = (2.5, -8.5)$	
$x_{69} = (5, -10)$	$x_{70} = (3, -10)$	
$x_{71} = (7, -8)$	$x_{72} = (7, -6)$	

(a) How many clusters result?

(b) List the connections which define the main diameter.

(c) Draw the main diameter histogram.

(d) Between what points do you separate clusters?

5.8 References

1. Ball, G. H., "Data Analysis in the Social Sciences: What About the Details?," *Proc. FJCC*, pp. 533–599, December 1965.

2. Nagy, G., "State of the Art in Pattern Recognition," *Proc. IEEE*, Vol. 56, No. 5, pp. 836–861, May 1968.

3. Casey, R. G. and G. Nagy, "Advances in Pattern Recognition," *Scientific American*, Vol. 224, No. 4, pp. 56–72, April 1971.

4. Ball, G. H. and D. J. Hall, "ISODATA, A Novel Method of Data Analysis and Pattern Classification," *International Communication Conference*, Philadelphia, Pennsylvania, June 1966.

5. Butler, G. A., "A Vector Field Approach to Cluster Analysis," *Pattern Recognition*, Vol. 1, No. 4, pp. 291–300, July 1969.

6. Roese, J. A., "Application of Adaptive Clustering Techniques to Multivariate Normal Data," MS thesis, University of California, San Diego, Department of Information Science, 1969.

7. Parzen, E., "On Estimation of a Probability Density Function and Mode," *Annals of Mathematical Statistics*, Vol. 33, pp. 1065–1076, 1962.

8. Henrichon, E. G. and K. S. Fu, "On Mode Estimation in Pattern Recognition," *Proc. 7th Symposium Adaptive Processes*, Los Angeles, California, 1968.

9. Sebestyen, G. and J., Edie, "An Algorithm for Non-Parametric Pattern Recognition," *IEEE Transactions on Electronic Computers*, Vol. EC-15, No. 6, pp. 903–915, December 1966.

10. Mendel, J. M. and K. S. Fu, *Adaptive, Learning, and Pattern Recognition Systems—Theory and Application*, Chapter 3, p. 73, Academic Press, New York, 1970.

11. Zahn, C. T., "Graph-Theoretical Methods for Detecting and Describing Gestalt Clusters," *IEEE Trans. on Computers*, Vol. C-20, No. 1, pp. 68–86, January 1971.

12. Kruskal, J. B., Jr., "On the Shortest Spanning Subtree of a Graph and the Traveling Salesman Problem," *Proc. Amer. Math. Soc.*, No. 7, pp. 48–58, 1956.

13. Gower, J. C. and G. J. S. Ross, "Minimum Spanning Trees and Single Linkage Cluster Analysis," *Appl. Statistics*, Vol. 18, No. 1, pp. 54–64, 1969.

14. Bennett, R. S., "The Intrinsic Dimensionality of Single Collections," *IEEE Trans. PGIT*, Vol. IT-15, No. 5, pp. 517–525, September 1969.

15. Bennett, J. F. and W. L. Hays, "Multidimensional Unfolding: Determining the Dimensionality of Ranked Preference Data," *Psychometrika*, Vol. 25, No. 1, pp. 27–43, March 1960.

16. Shepard, R. N., "The Analysis of Proximities: Multidimensional Scaling with an Unknown Distance Function—I," *Psychometrika*, Vol. 27, No. 2, pp. 125–140, June 1962.

17. Shepard, R. N., "The Analysis of Proximities: Multidimensional Scaling with an Unknown Distance Function—II," *Psychometrika*, Vol. 27, No. 3, pp. 219–246, September 1962.

18. Kruskal, J. B., "Multidimensional Scaling by Optimizing Goodness of Fit to a Non-Metric Hypothesis," *Psychometrika*, Vol. 29, No. 1, pp. 1–27, March 1964.

19. Kruskal, J. B., "Nonmetric Multidimensional Scaling: A Numerical Method," *Psychometrika*, Vol. 29, No. 2, pp. 115–129, June 1964.

20. Shepard, R. N., "Metric Structures in Ordinal Data," Journal of Mathematical Psychology, Vol. 3, pp. 287–315, 1966.

21. Shepard, R. N. and J. D. Carroll, "Parametric Representation of Nonlinear Data Structures," *Proceedings of the International Symposium on Multivariate Analysis*, ed. P. R. Krishnaiah, Academic Press, New York, 1966.

22. Hammersley, J. M., "The Distribution of Distance in a Hypersphere," *Annals Mathematical Statistics*, Vol. 21, pp. 447–452, 1950.

23. Lord, R. D., "The Distribution of Distance in a Hypersphere," *Ann. Math. Stat.*, Vol. 25, pp. 794–798, 1954.

24. Calvert, T. W. and T. Y. Young, "Randomly Generated Nonlinear Transformations for Pattern Recognition," *IEEE Trans. SSC*, Vol. SSC-5, No. 4, pp. 266–273, October 1969.

25. Calvert, T. W., "Nonorthogonal Projections for Feature Extraction in Pattern Recognition," *Proc. IEEE Symposium on Adaptive Processes*, pp. 3-g-1 to 3-g-5, 1969.

26. Bennett, R. S., "Nonlinear Representations for Parametrically Similar Signals," Symposium on Information Processing, Purdue University, Vol. II, pp. 410–422, April 28–30, 1969.

27. Cooper, D. B. and P. W. Cooper, "Nonsupervised Adaptive Signal Detection and Pattern Recognition," *Information and Control*, Vol. 7, pp. 416–444, 1964.

5.9   Related Bibliography

Augustson, J. G. and J. Minker, "An Analysis of Some Graph Theoretical Cluster Techniques," *JACM*, vol. 17, pp. 571–588, (October 1970).

Ball, G. H., "A Comparison of Some Cluster-Seeking Techniques," Tech. Report No. RADC-TR-66-514, Stanford Research Institute, Menlo Park, California (November 1966).

Bonner, R. E., "On Some Clustering Techniques," *IBM J. Res. and Dev.*, vol. 8, pp. 22–32 (January 1964).

Braverman, E. M., "The Method of Potential Functions in the Problem of Training Machines to Recognize Patterns Without a Trainer," *Automation and Remote Control*, vol. 27, pp. 1748–1771 (October 1966).

Chernoff, H., "Estimation of the Mode," *Ann. Inst. Stat. Math. Tokyo* 16, pp. 31–41 (1964).

Cole, A. J. and D. Wishart, "An Improved Algorithm for the Jardine-Sibson Method of Generating Overlapping Clusters," *Computer Journal*, vol. 13, pp. 156–163 (May 1970).

Cooper, P. W., "Nonsupervised Learning in Statistical Pattern Recognition," *Methodologies of Pattern Recognition*, pp. 97–109, ed. Watanabe, Academic Press, New York, 1969.

Dorofeyuk, A. A., "Teaching Algorithms for a Pattern Recognition Machine Without a Teacher based on the Method of Potential Functions," *Automation and Remote Control*, vol. 27, pp. 1728–1737 (October 1966).

Fortier, J. J. and H. Solomon, "Clustering Procedures," prepared under Contract 2-10-165 with the U.S. Office of Education, pp. 493–506.

Fralick, S. C., "The Synthesis of Machines which Learn Without a Teacher," Stanford Tech. Report 61303-8 (April 1964).

Fu, K. S., "Mode Estimation in Pattern Recognition," Chapter 2, pp. 68–75 in *Adaptive, Learning and Pattern Recognition Systems*, ed. Mendel and Fu, Academic Press, New York, 1970.

Fukunaga, K. and W. L. G. Koontz, "A Criterion and an Algorithm for Grouping Data," *IEEE Trans. on Comp.*, vol. C-19, no. 10, pp. 917–923 (October 1970).

Gitman, I. and M. D. Levine," An Algorithm for Detecting Uni-model Fuzzy Sets and Its Application as a Clustering Technique," *IEEE Trans. on Computers*, vol. C-19, no. 7, pp. 583–593 (July 1970).

Grenander, V., "Some Direct Estimates of the Mode," *Ann. Math. Stat.* 36, pp. 131–138 (1965).

Hall, D. J., G. F. Ball and D. E. Wolf, "PROMENADE—An Interactive Graphic Computer System for Sorting Multivariate Data into Groups," *Symp. on Information Processing*, Purdue, p. 423 (April 28–30, 1969).

Hancock, J. C. and E. A. Patrick, "Iterative Computation of A Postori Probability for M-ary Nonsupervised Adaptation," *IEEE PGIT* (corresp.), vol. IT-2, pp. 483–484 (October 1966).

Hara, K., "An Unsupervised Algorithm for Adaptive Pattern Classification," *Proceed. 3rd Hawaii International Conference on System Sciences*, p. 119 (January 1970).

Hilborn, C. G. and D. G. Lainiotis, "Unsupervised Learning, Min. Risk Pattern Classification for Dependent Hypothesis and Dependent Measurements," *IEEE Trans SSC*, vol. SSC-5, pp. 109–115 (April 1969).

Mucciardi, A. N. and E. L. Gose, "An Algorithm for Automatic

Clustering in N Dimensional Spaces Using Hyperellipsoidal Cells," *Proc. Syst. for Seventies*, Pittsburgh, (October 4–16, 1970).

Patrick, E. A., "On a Class of Unsupervised Estimation Problems," *IEEE PGIT*, vol. IT-14, no. 3, pp. 407–415 (May 1968).

Patrick, E. A., and G. Carayannopoulos, "Codes for Unsupervised Learning of Source and Binary Channel Probabilities," *Information and Control*, vol. 14, pp. 358–376 (1969).

Patrick, E. A. and J. P. Costello, "On Unsupervised Estimation Algorithms," *Proc. 1969 IEEE International Symp. on Info. Theory* (January 1969).

Patrick, E. A. and F. P. Fischer II, "Cluster Mapping with Experimental Computer Graphics," *IEEE Trans. on Computers*, vol. C-18, no. 11, pp. 987–991 (November 1969).

Patrick, E. A. and J. C. Hancock, "Nonsupervised Sequential Classification and Recognition of Patterns," *IEEE PGIT*, vol. IT-12, pp. 362–372 (July 1966).

Patrick, E. A. and J. C. Hancock, "The Nonsupervised Learning of Probability Spaces and Recognition of Patterns," *IEEE Intern. Con.*, New York, (March 1965).

Patrick, E. A. and L. Y. L. Shen, "Iterative Use of Problem Knowledge for Clustering and Decision Making," *IEEE Transactions on Computers*, vol. C-20, no. 2, pp. 216–222.

Rosenfeld, A., et al., "An Application of Cluster Detection to Text and Picture Processing," *IEEE Trans. on Information Theory*, vol. IT-15, no. 6, pp. 672–681 (November 1969).

Ruspini, E. H., "A New Approach to Clustering," *Information and Control*, vol. 15, pp. 22–32 (July 1969).

Sammon, J. W., Jr., "Iterative Pattern Analysis and Classification," *CSI Report No. 69–28*, also *IEEE Trans. on Computers*, vol. C-19, no. 7, pp. 594–616 (July 1970).

Sokol, R. R. and P. H. A. Sneath, *Principles of Numerical Taxonomy*, W. H. Freeman and Co., San Francisco, California, 1963.

Spooner, R. L. and D. Joarsma, "An Unsupervised Learning Problem Using Limited Storage Capacity," *IEEE Trans. on SSC*, vol. SSC-6, no. 2, pp. 151–152 (April 1970).

Spragins, J., "Learning Without a Teacher," *IEEE PGIT*, vol. IT-12, pp. 223–229 (April 1966).

Torgerson, W. S., *Theory and Methods of Scaling*, Wiley, New York, 1958.

Venter, J. H., "On Estimation of the Mode," *Ann. Math. Stat.* 38, pp. 1446–1455 (1967).

Yakowitz, S. J., "Unsupervised Learning and the Identification of Finite Mixtures," *IEEE Trans. on Information Theory*, vol. IT-16, no. 3, pp. 330–338 (May 1970).

Young, T. Y. and G. Coraluppi, "On Estimation of a Mixture of Normal Density Functions," *IEEE Symposium on Adaptive Processes*, pp. 6-c-1 to 6-c-3 (1969).

Young, T. Y. and G. Coraluppi, "Stochastic Estimation of a mixture of Normal Density Functions Using an Information Criterion," *IEEE Trans. Information Theory*, Vol. IT-16, No. 3, pp. 258–263 (May 1970).

SEQUENTIAL
LEARNING

6.0 Introduction

The material in previous chapters has been implicitly
nonsequential in nature both in the data gathering and
recognition phases. Specifically a fixed size pattern space
(R) is assumed and in both the distribution free and
statistical classification chapters a fixed number of
prototypes are assumed available. Thus no sequential
learning, in the sense of decision making based on a
varying number of features, is undertaken. Consequently,
Bayes machines result and fixed feature space dimensions
are assumed as inputs to the pattern classifier. This chapter is devoted to attempting to apply learning techniques
in a sequential manner such that decisions can be made on

fewer features at a correspondingly earlier phase of the pattern recognition process. Thus it will become desirable to select pertinent features for classification as early as possible, eliminating the use of redundant information. Conceptually it would be desirable to use a sequential learning technique to define an optimal ordering of available features for classification purposes. Towards this end it is instructive to study the Wald sequential probability ratio test (SPRT) as a background for the pattern recognition application [1]. However, a modification to this test will become useful to the pattern recognition problem where a limited number of features are available or where the expense in time or cost of taking additional features is prohibitive.

6.1 Sequential Probability Ratio Test

The sequential probability ratio test (SPRT) of Wald is inherently a two-class ($K = 2$) technique which may be generalized either by solving a many-class problem two at a time or by resorting to multihypothesis ratio testing. However for our purposes investigation of the two-class technique will suffice. The two-class problem to be solved is simply, does the pattern $\mathbf{x}$ (assumed to be a random variable) belong to class S_1 or S_2? The test is to be made sequentially in the sense that $\mathbf{x}$ is a vector and sequential observation of its components x_n will be utilized. It will be desirable to obtain some degree of confidence in the test and consequently error rates e_{ij} will be defined. Here e_{ij} is the probability of error associated with assigning the vector to class S_i when in fact it was a member of class S_j for all $i \neq j$ ($i, j = 1, 2$). For a fixed sample size (dimensionality $= N$) nonsequential method the Neyman-Pearson result to this problem [2] utilizes the likelihood ratio

$$\lambda_N = \frac{p(\mathbf{x} \mid S_1)}{p(\mathbf{x} \mid S_2)} \tag{6.1}$$

The Wald solution to the sequential version of this problem makes use of the sequential likelihood ratio λ_n such that

$$\lambda_n = \frac{p(x_1, x_2, \ldots, x_n \mid S_1)}{p(x_1, x_2, \ldots, x_n \mid S_2)} \tag{6.2a}$$

or

$$\lambda_n = \frac{p_n(\mathbf{x} \mid S_1)}{p_n(\mathbf{x} \mid S_2)} \tag{6.2b}$$

where $p_n(\mathbf{x} \mid S_i)$ is multivariate n-dimensional. The decision for this solution is

$$\lambda_n \geq A \qquad \text{choose } S_1$$
$$B < \lambda_n < A \qquad \text{select another sample (feature)}$$
$$\lambda \leq B \qquad \text{choose } S_2$$

where A, B are constant stopping boundaries depending on the desired errors e_{ij}. In order to see this, consider the upper stopping boundary A. Ignoring the overshoot of λ_n we can assume

$$\lambda_n = A \tag{6.3}$$

upon stopping. Thus

$$p_n(\mathbf{x} \mid S_1) = A p_n(\mathbf{x} \mid S_2) \tag{6.4}$$

and

$$\int_{X_1} p_n(\mathbf{x} \mid S_1)\, d\mathbf{x} = A \int_{X_1} p_n(\mathbf{x} \mid S_2)\, d\mathbf{x} \tag{6.5}$$

where X_1 is the region of integration contributing to the decision S_1. Note that the n dimensional space is partitioned into 3 mutually exclusive regions X_1, X_2, and C where the region C is the decision region to continue taking more samples. This partitioning should be contrasted to the two-region partition (S_1, S_2) or fixed sample (nonsequential) techniques such as the fixed sample Bayes or Neyman-Pearson tests (see Chapter 4). Figure 6.1 indicates a possible interpretation of this partitioning. Continuing with our investigation of the boundary A, we have

$$\int_{X_1} p_n(\mathbf{x} \mid S_1)\, d\mathbf{x} = 1 - e_{21} \tag{6.6a}$$

and

$$\int_{X_1} p_n(\mathbf{x} \mid S_2)\, d\mathbf{x} = e_{12} \tag{6.6b}$$

Therefore from equation (6.5)

$$A = (1 - e_{21})/e_{12} \tag{6.7a}$$

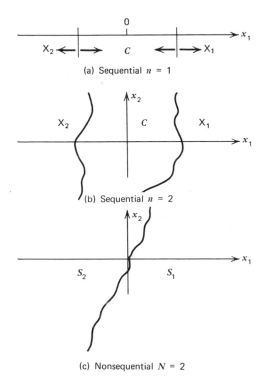

(a) Sequential $n = 1$

(b) Sequential $n = 2$

(c) Nonsequential $N = 2$

FIGURE 6.1.   Decision regions.

By a similar analysis for the lower stopping boundary, we obtain

$$B = e_{21}/(1 - e_{12}) \qquad (6.7b)$$

Thus the stopping boundaries for the SPRT are determined solely by the desired error rates for misclassifications of the first and second kind. Note also that the stopping boundaries are independent of n, the value of the number of samples observed thus far.

It is of interest to obtain some quantitative estimate of the expected number of features $\mathscr{E}(n)$ necessary before a boundary is crossed. Towards this end the log likelihood ratio becomes of interest.

$$L_n = \log \lambda_n \qquad (6.8)$$

There are two ways in which the process can terminate given that x is a member of Class S_1. We can therefore simply state that

$$\mathscr{E}(L_n \mid S_1) = (1 - e_{21}) \log A + e_{21} \log B \qquad (6.9a)$$

Similarly for x a member of class S_2

$$\mathscr{E}(L_n \mid S_2) = e_{12} \log A + (1 - e_{12}) \log B \qquad (6.9b)$$

If we assume independent samples and let

$$z_i = \log \frac{p(x_i \mid S_1)}{p(x_i \mid S_2)} \qquad (6.10)$$

then

$$L_n = \sum_{i=1}^{n} z_i \qquad (6.11a)$$

By defining a counter y_i which is zero or 1 depending on whether a decision has been made before stage $(i - 1)$ or not respectively, L_n then becomes

$$L_n = \sum_{i=1}^{\infty} y_i z_i \qquad (6.11b)$$

Note that by this definition y_i must necessarily be independent of z_i. The average value of the log likelihood ratio becomes

$$\mathscr{E}(L_n \mid S_1) = \mathscr{E}\left(\sum_{i=1}^{\infty} y_i z_i \mid S_1\right) \qquad (6.12)$$

Upon utilizing the independence of y_i and z_i as well as z_i and z_j, we obtain

$$\mathscr{E}(L_n \mid S_1) = \mathscr{E}\left(\sum_{i=1}^{\infty} y_i \mid S_1\right)\mathscr{E}(z \mid S_1) \qquad (6.13)$$

But the terminal value $n = \sum_{i=1}^{\infty} y_i$. Thus utilizing this fact and the results of equations (6.13) and (6.9a), one obtains

$$\mathscr{E}(n \mid S_1) = \frac{(1 - e_{21}) \log A + e_{21} \log B}{\mathscr{E}(z \mid S_1)} \qquad (6.14a)$$

By similar analysis

$$\mathscr{E}(n \mid S_2) = \frac{e_{12} \log A + (1 - e_{12}) \log B}{\mathscr{E}(z \mid S_2)} \qquad (6.14b)$$

This we conclude that for independent features the expected terminal number is proportional to a ratio whose numerator is a function of a priori defined error rates (e_{ij}) and whose denominator is the average log likelihood ratio.

The advantages of the SPRT are the fact that the procedure terminates with probability one for both S_1 and S_2 classes [1]. In addition the test minimizes both $\mathscr{E}(n \mid S_1)$ and $\mathscr{E}(n \mid S_2)$ for any set of given e_{12} and e_{21}. Thus there is no other procedure which will terminate (on the average) any sooner with the same or better error rates. The drawbacks of the SPRT are that the test may take too long due to stringent requirements on e_{12} and e_{21}. In other words, there is a finite probability that the test may take more than any fixed large number of features, and that probability increases as the error rates become smaller. In addition a particular pattern recognition problem may not be amenable to a truly sequential solution. For instance it may become prohibitively expensive to take more features beyond a certain point or additional features may simply be unavailable. Thus while the SPRT provides quite an appealing method for pattern classification, its applicability may be in question. Consequently, it becomes useful to modify the SPRT in such a way that pattern recognition solutions are more readily available; and while the modified SPRT will necessarily be suboptimal to the Wald SPRT, it may provide a useful alternative to the pattern classification problem. Perhaps the simplest modification that comes to mind is that of truncation. Thus, after N steps of a SPRT procedure, a decision will be forced (assuming a decision has not already been made) such that

$$\mathbf{x} \in S_1 \quad \text{if } \lambda_n \geq 1$$
$$\mathbf{x} \in S_2 \quad \text{if } \lambda_n < 1$$

and $\mathbf{x} = (x_1, x_2, \ldots, x_N)$. Thus truncation provides a compromise between the pure SPRT and the fixed sample size problem. Fu [4] has investigated other truncation and modification methods some of which we discuss below.

6.2 Modified Sequential Probability Ratio Test [4]

While the abrupt truncation of the SPRT at stage N was suggested in the above section it is not an optimal solution to the sequential but finite feature availability problem. Fu [4] has suggested an alternative modification in which the upper and lower stopping boundaries (A and B in SPRT) are time-varying or number-of-feature varying such that at feature N the boundaries collapse to force a terminal decision if one has not already occurred. The boundaries suggested are those given by

$$A(n) = \exp\left\{a\left(1 - \frac{n}{N}\right)^{r_1}\right\} \tag{6.15a}$$

$$B(n) = \exp\left\{-b\left(1 - \frac{n}{N}\right)^{r_2}\right\} \tag{6.15b}$$

where a and b are positive and r_1, r_2 are bounded by zero and one. The decision rule now becomes

$$\lambda_n \geq \exp\left\{a\left(1 - \frac{n}{N}\right)^{r_1}\right\} \qquad \text{choose } S_1$$

$$\exp\left\{-b\left(1 - \frac{n}{N}\right)^{r_2}\right\} < \lambda_n < \exp\left\{a\left(1 - \frac{n}{N}\right)^{r_1}\right\}$$

$$\text{select another feature}$$

$$\lambda_n \leq \exp\left\{-b\left(1 - \frac{n}{N}\right)^{r_2}\right\} \qquad \text{choose } S_2$$

Because the boundaries are a function of n, the terminal value, N, can be determined in advance. Figure 6.2 illustrates the stopping boundaries for both the SPRT and the modified version suggested by the boundaries of equation (6.15). Note that as $N \to \infty$ the modified SPRT approaches that of the Wald SPRT with $A = \exp(a)$ and $B = \exp(-b)$.

It is of value to be able to compare the performance of the test with the family of stopping boundaries of equation (6.15) with that of the constant stopping boundary SPRT. Denoting by a prime the modified test and utilizing the earlier derived results, we can define $\mathscr{E}'(n \mid S_1)$ to be the expected termination value when $\mathbf{x}$ is a member of class S_1. If we let $\mathscr{E}'(n \mid S_1, A)$ be the expected number of features for upper boundary (A) stopping given class S_1 and if $\mathscr{E}'(n \mid S_1, B)$

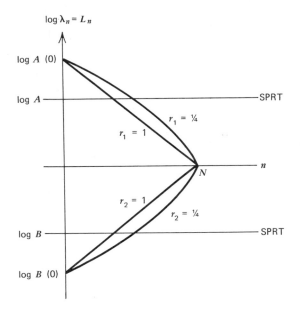

FIGURE 6.2.   Sequential stopping boundaries.

is the expected number of features for lower boundary stopping, then

$$\mathscr{E}'(n \mid S_1) = e'_{21}\mathscr{E}'(n \mid S_1, B) + (1 - e'_{21})\mathscr{E}'(n \mid S_1, A) \quad (6.16)$$

where e'_{21} is the error rate for the modified SPRT due to classifying $\mathbf{x}$ to be a member of class S_2 when it is actually a member of class S_1. This equation simply states that the average terminal value of n for class S_1 is the error rate of misclassification times the average number of misclassifications plus the probability of correct classification times the average number of correct classifications. To pursue the derivation it becomes necessary to make the assumption that we require e'_{21} to be quite small. Thus $1 - e'_{21}$ is approximately unity and

$$\mathscr{E}'(n \mid S_1) \cong \mathscr{E}'(n \mid S_1, A) \quad (6.17)$$

Again under the independent feature assumption we have

$$\mathscr{E}'(L_n \mid S_1) = \mathscr{E}'\left(\sum_{i=1}^{n} z_i \mid S_1\right) \quad (6.18)$$

which, by analogy to earlier results gives

$$\mathcal{E}'(L_n \mid S_1) = \mathcal{E}'(n \mid S_1)\mathcal{E}(z \mid S_1) \tag{6.19a}$$

where the prime is not present on $\mathcal{E}(z \mid S_1)$ due to the fact that this statistic is independent of the testing procedure and is only a function of the inherent statistics of the data. By the results of equation (6.17) we then obtain

$$\mathcal{E}'(L_n \mid S_1) \simeq \mathcal{E}'(n \mid S_1, A)\mathcal{E}(z \mid S_1) \tag{6.19b}$$

However the expected value of the log likelihood ratio, L_n, must simply be the average of the boundaries weighted by the probability of hitting a given boundary. Thus in analogy to equation (6.9a) we have

$$\mathcal{E}'(L_n \mid S_1) = e'_{21}\mathcal{E}'\left(\log\left(\exp\left(-b\left(1 - \frac{n}{N}\right)^{r_2}\right)\right) \mid S_1, B\right) + (1 - e'_{21})$$
$$\times \mathcal{E}'\left(\log\left(\exp\left(a\left(1 - \frac{n}{N}\right)^{r_1}\right)\right) \mid S_1, A\right) \tag{6.20a}$$

Using the small assumption of e'_{21}

$$\mathcal{E}'(L_n \mid S_1) \simeq a\mathcal{E}'\left(\left(1 - \frac{n}{N}\right)^{r_1} \mid S_1, A\right) \tag{6.20b}$$

By taking a binomial expansion in n/N and neglecting second and higher order terms we obtain

$$\mathcal{E}'(L_n \mid S_1) \simeq a - \frac{r_1}{N}a\mathcal{E}'(n \mid S_1, A) \tag{6.21}$$

Simply equating the results of equations (6.19b) and (6.21) and solving for $\mathcal{E}'(n \mid S_1, A)$ we conclude that

$$\mathcal{E}'(n \mid S_1, A) = a\left(\mathcal{E}(z \mid S_1) + \frac{r_1 a}{N}\right)^{-1} \tag{6.22}$$

In order to compare with the Wald SPRT assume that the starting points of the modified test are the same as the Wald boundaries. Under such assumptions Fu [4] has shown that

$$\mathcal{E}'(n \mid S_1) \simeq \mathcal{E}(n \mid S_1)\left(1 + \frac{r_1}{N}\mathcal{E}(n \mid S_1)\right)^{-1} \tag{6.23a}$$

thus

$$\frac{\mathscr{E}(n \mid S_1)}{1 + r_1} < \mathscr{E}'(n \mid S_1) \leq \mathscr{E}(n \mid S_1) \qquad (6.23b)$$

Consequently we can conclude that the convergent property of time-varying stopping boundaries provides, on the average, less number of feature measurements than the Wald test and this number is controlled by r_1. Therefore by properly constructing the time-varying stopping boundaries, we can terminate classification by a prespecified maximum number of features and the expected terminal value can be made less than the SPRT value. The error rates e'_{ij} can be found such that (see Fu [4])

$$e'_{12} \cong e^{-a}\left(1 + \frac{r_1 a^2}{N\mathscr{E}(z \mid S_1) + r_1 a}\right) \qquad (6.24a)$$

and

$$e'_{21} \approx e^{b}\left(1 + \frac{r_2 b^2}{N\mathscr{E}(z \mid S_2) - r_2 b}\right) \qquad (6.24b)$$

thus indicating that, as before in the SPRT, the error rates can be expressly related to the (a priori) stopping boundaries.

6.3 A Gaussian Example

At this point it is useful to develop an illustrative example comparing both the Wald and modified sequential probability ratio tests. Specifically let the features $x_1, x_2, \ldots$ be independent Gaussian random variables selected from either class S_1 with mean m_1 or class S_2 with mean $m_2 < m_1$, each with the same variance. After the first sample the log likelihood ratio becomes

$$L_1 = \log \frac{p(x_1 \mid S_1)}{p(x_1 \mid S_2)} \qquad (6.25a)$$

or

$$L_1 = \log\left(\frac{(\sigma\sqrt{2\pi})^{-1} \exp\{-(2\sigma^2)^{-1}(x_1 - m_1)^2\}}{(\sigma\sqrt{2\pi})^{-1} \exp\{-(2\sigma^2)^{-1}(x_1 - m_2)^2\}}\right) \qquad (6.25b$$

and finally

$$L_1 = \frac{1}{\sigma^2}\left[x_1\left(m_1 - m_2\right) - \tfrac{1}{2}\left(m_1^2 - m_2^2\right)\right] \qquad (6.25c)$$

The decision process for the SPRT compares L_1 with either $\log A$ or $\log B$. Solving for x_1, we have

$$x_1 \geq \frac{\sigma^2}{m_1 - m_2}\log A + \tfrac{1}{2}(m_1 + m_2) \quad : \text{choose } S_1$$

$$\frac{\sigma^2}{m_1 - m_2}\log B + \tfrac{1}{2}(m_1 + m_2) < x_1$$

$$< \frac{\sigma^2}{m_1 - m_2}\log A + \tfrac{1}{2}(m_1 + m_2)$$

$$: \text{take another feature}$$

$$x_1 \leq \frac{\sigma^2}{m_1 - m_2}\log B + \tfrac{1}{2}(m_1 + m_2) \quad : \text{choose } S_2$$

The decision process for the modified SPRT becomes

$$x_1 \geq \frac{\sigma^2}{m_1 - m_2}a\left(1 - \frac{n}{N}\right)^{r_1} + \tfrac{1}{2}(m_1 + m_2) \quad : \text{choose } S_1$$

$$\frac{-\sigma^2}{m_1 - m_2}b\left(1 - \frac{n}{N}\right)^{r_2} + \tfrac{1}{2}(m_1 + m_2) < x_1$$

$$< \frac{\sigma^2}{m_1 - m_2}a\left(1 - \frac{n}{N}\right)^{r_1}$$

$$+ \tfrac{1}{2}(m_1 + m_2)$$

$$: \text{take another feature}$$

$$x_1 \leq \frac{-\sigma^2 b}{m_1 - m_2}\left(1 - \frac{n}{N}\right)^{r_2} + \tfrac{1}{2}(m_1 + m_2) \quad : \text{choose } S_2$$

If the decision is made to take a second sample the log likelihood ratio becomes

$$L_2 = \log\frac{p(x_1 \mid S_1)}{p(x_1 \mid S_2)} + \log\frac{p(x_2 \mid S_1)}{p(x_2 \mid S_2)} \qquad (6.26)$$

and a corresponding set of decision rules results. In general at the nth stage of the process

$$L_n = \sum_{i=1}^{n} \log \frac{p(x_i \mid S_1)}{p(x_i \mid S_2)} \tag{6.27}$$

For the SPRT the decision mechanism becomes

$$\sum_{i=1}^{n} x_i \geq \frac{\sigma^2 \log A}{m_1 - m_2} + \frac{n}{2}(m_1 + m_2) \qquad : \text{choose } S_1$$

$$\frac{\sigma^2 \log B}{m_1 - m_2} + \frac{n}{2}(m_1 + m_2) < \sum_{i=1}^{n} x_i < \frac{\sigma^2 \log A}{m_1 - m_2} + \frac{n}{2}(m_1 + m_2)$$

$$\qquad\qquad : \text{take another feature}$$

$$\sum_{i=1}^{n} x_i \leq \frac{\sigma^2 \log B}{m_1 - m_2} + \frac{n}{2}(m_1 + m_2) \qquad : \text{choose } S_2$$

and for the modified SPRT the $\log A$ and $\log B$ terms are replaced by $a[1 - (n/N)]^{r_1}$ and $-b[1 - (n/N)]^{r_2}$ respectively. Note that in the former case the decision boundaries become parallel linear discriminant functions with an indecision zone width given by

$$\frac{\sigma^2}{m_1 - m_2} \log A/B.$$

For the latter test the indecision region width becomes

$$\frac{\sigma^2}{m_1 - m_2}\left(a\left(1 - \frac{n}{N}\right)^{r_1} + b\left(1 - \frac{n}{N}\right)^{r_2}\right)$$

Thus for the SPRT the boundaries are separated by a distance independent of n while for the modified SPRT, the separation is clearly a function of n. Also this separation clearly goes to zero as $n \to N$. In addition as $N \to \infty$ the modified SPRT boundaries become constant thus equaling a Wald SPRT with different error rates unless $\log A = a$ and $\log B = -b$. Thus we see that a terminal decision must be reached as $n \to N$ but by increasing N a test more similar to the Wald is implemented.

6.4 Dynamic Programming Techniques

The modification to the SPRT described in the above section simply forced the termination of the test by the Nth feature by varying the stopping boundaries in a monotonic fashion. No criterion of optimality was developed, resulting in an efficient computational algorithm with little knowledge as to the quality of the test. At the other end of the spectrum, it is possible to modify the SPRT in an optimal fashion, resulting in a computational algorithm somewhat more difficult to implement. Towards this end the use of dynamic programming becomes quite useful as a means of implementing a backwards procedure for solution of the modified SPRT pattern recognition problem. Dynamic programming will provide an optimal policy such that at each stage of the sequential test, the remaining decisions will also form an optimal policy recursively up to the terminal point, N, of the test [5]. The philosophy behind the dynamic programming viewpoint is probably best illustrated by Figure 6.3 in which the tracking and correction of a trajectory problem are performed according to an error correction criterion and a dynamic programming criterion. In the former case a radar tracks the missile and causes a correction back to the a priori trajectory. In the latter case, the radar tracks the missile and adjusts it to a new trajectory which is optimal for the missile's position at that particular observation time. Applying the same philosophy to the modified SPRT we note that at each stage, n, two alternatives exist. The first is to terminate taking samples and the second is to continue taking samples. An optimal decision at each stage is to minimize the associated risks between the two alternatives. Such a procedure requires knowledge of "future" risks or costs of taking more data. Using the following notation a statistical formulation of the problem can be developed for which the dynamic programming technique will provide a solution. (This notation is borrowed directly from Fu [4].) Let $\rho_n(x_1, \ldots, x_n)$ be the average risk of the modified SPRT process given $x_1, \ldots, x_n$ and let $C(x_1, \ldots, x_n)$ be the cost of obtaining the $n + 1$st feature, x_{n+1}, given $x_1, \ldots, x_n$. Finally, let $R(x_1, \ldots, x_n; S_k)$ be the risk associated with making a terminal decision at the nth stage as to membership in class S_k given

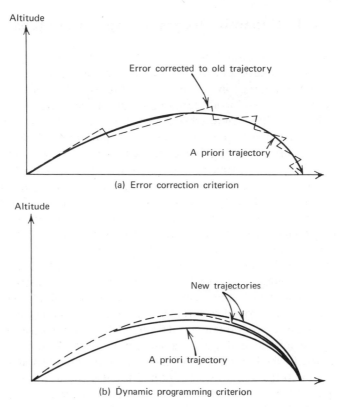

FIGURE 6.3.   A trajectory tracing example.

knowledge of $x_1, \ldots, x_n$. Note that we are not restricted to a two-class problem but a general k class situation can be handled by this notation. At the nth stage if the process is terminated, the average risk will be

$$\min_{1 \le k \le K} R(x_1, \ldots, x_n; S_k)$$

for an optimal decision rule. On the other hand, if at the nth stage, the process continues, then the average risk will be

$$C(x_1, \ldots, x_n) + \int_{X_{n+1}} \rho_{n+1}(x_1, \ldots, x_{n+1}) \, dP(x_{n+1} \mid x_1, \ldots, x_n)$$

This is the cost of taking the next feature plus the average risk associated with the remaining stages in the SPRT. Note that knowledge of $P(x_{n+1} \mid x_1, \ldots, x_n)$ is assumed available. Finally an optimal choice at the nth stage must be to minimize the two average risks described above. However, this then beomes the risk of the decision process for stage n until termination. Thus

$$\rho_n(x_1, \ldots, x_n) = \min\Big\{C(x_1, \ldots, x_n)$$

$$+ \int_{X_{n+1}} \rho_{n+1}(x_1, \ldots, x_n) \, dP(x_{n+1} \mid x_1, \ldots, x_n),$$

$$\min_{1 \leq k \leq K} \{R(x_1, \ldots, x_n; S_k)\}\Big\} \quad (6.28)$$

where the first argument is the expense of continuing and the second argument is that of terminating. This equation defines a recursive relationship between $\rho_n(x_1, \ldots, x_n)$ and $\rho_{n+1}(x_1, \ldots, x_{n+1})$ which can be solved by boundary conditions. One known boundary condition is that termination is forced at stage N. Thus

$$\rho_N(x_1, \ldots, x_N) = \min_{1 \leq k \leq K} \{R(x_1, \ldots, x_N; S_k)\} \quad (6.29)$$

$\rho_{N-1}(x_1, \ldots, x_{N-1})$ can now be related to $\rho_N(x_1, \ldots, x_N)$ according to equation (6.28) and working backwards to the first sample we find

$$\rho_1(x_1) = \min\{C(x_1) + \int_{X_2} \rho_2(x_1, x_2) \, dP(x_2 \mid x_1),$$

$$\min_{1 \leq k \leq K} \{R(x_1, x_2; S_k)\}\} \quad (6.30)$$

Mathematically, the generalized relationship of equation (6.28) and the boundary condition of equation (6.29) define an optimal process for requiring that the sequential process be terminated at the Nth stage. The stopping boundaries for such a process no longer are deterministically defined and therefore cannot be related to those of Figure 6.2. However, although we have mathematically defined an optimal solution to the terminated sequential process, computationally we have defined an impossible task. The "curse of dimensionality"* indeed takes its toll as illustrated by the following computation. Let each sample feature be quantized to q levels. Then assuming $\rho_n(x_1, \ldots, x_n)$, $R(x_1, \ldots, x_n; S_k)$, $C(x_1, \ldots, x_n)$ and $P(x_n \mid x_1, \ldots, x_{n-1})$ are all known and must be stored in a computer, then memory requirements alone are on the order of $\sum_{n=1}^{N} q^n$. For a moderate problem q might equal 10 and N might equal 100. The requirement of greater than 10^{100} storage locations is indeed grandiose. Because of the dimensionality requirements, assumptions and simplications must be made in order to apply the dynamic programming results described above. Fu [4] has shown that by assuming a first order Markov dependence, the storage-need behaves as $\sum_{n=1}^{N-1} \binom{q^2 + n - 1}{n}$; and by assuming independent features and multinomial distributions, the storage requirement drops to the order of $\sum_{n=1}^{N} \binom{n + q - 1}{q - 1}$. However, a limitation is still imposed by the need for statistical distribution knowledge where, in fact that knowledge may simply be unavailable or nonstationary in nature. In analogy to the justification for nonparametric techniques in Chapter 4, we will resort to a similar procedure here.

6.5 Nonparametric Techniques

One of the nonlinear transformations which was investigated in nonsequential clustering (Chapter 5) made use of ranking of data according to some similarity or metric as opposed to using the actual absolute data value. This technique is particularly appealing when the pattern space is not a metric space or when the features are of sufficiently variable units (feet, pounds, etc). A similar approach will be developed here utilizing certain properties of rank order statistics to aid in the nonparametric sequential process. We will not work toward a nonlinear transformation as before defined on rank orders, but here we will develop sequential ranks for terminal decision procedures. In the sequential environment we are observing samples or features of the vector $\mathbf{x}$ in time. At the nth stage we will

---

* A term attributed to Dr. Richard Bellman.

have knowledge of $\mathbf{x} = (x_1, x_2, \ldots, x_n)$ where each sample, x_i, might correspond to a dimension in pattern or feature space with an underlying distribution $P(x_i)$. We can define a sequential rank vector $\mathbf{R}$ which corresponds to $\mathbf{x}$ and which has, as its ith entry, the rank of the x_i sample with respect to all previous samples. Thus r_i can take on integer values from one to i. The examples in Table 6.1 illustrate some typical data values and their respective sequential rank vectors. The values of r_i imply that x_i is the r_ith smallest sample of the i previous samples. Note that at the nth stage of the sequential process, there are a total of $n!$ different possible sequential rank vectors corresponding to the $n!$ possible different orderings of n features.

Table 6.1 Sequential rank vectors

Actual data vector at nth stage	Sequential rank vector
$\mathbf{x} = (1.3, 2.9, 4.6, 2.3, 1.0)$	$\mathbf{R} = (1, 2, 3, 2, 1)$
$\mathbf{x} = (5.9, 4.8, 5.0, 1.2, 2.8, 9.0)$	$\mathbf{R} = (1, 1, 2, 1, 2, 6)$

It is of interest to investigate the probability distribution of an arbitrary feature ordering in terms of knowledge of the sequential rank vectors. Under certain assumptions, independence and Lehmann alternatives, [6], this relationship can be established. Towards this end it becomes necessary to briefly investigate the implication of the Lehmann alternative in the context of sequential processes. If we assume that the x's are independent and if we are interested in the distribution of the maximum of r of the x's, then let

$$Z = \max_{1 \le i \le r} \{x_i\} \qquad (6.31)$$

Then the distribution of Z, $P(Z)$, can be related to the distributions on the x's as

$$P(Z) = P(Z < z) \qquad (6.32a)$$

$$= P\left(\max_{1 \le i \le r} \{x_i\} < z \right) \qquad (6.32b)$$

$$= P(x_1 < z, x_2 < z, \ldots, x_r < z) \qquad (6.32c)$$

$$= P(x_1 < z)P(x_2 < z) \cdots P(x_r < z) \qquad (6.32d)$$

$$= P(x)^r \qquad (6.32e)$$

Thus $P(Z) = P(x)^r$ implies that the random variable Z is the maximum of r of the random variables x. Equation (6.32e) is often referred to as the Lehmann alternative and Figure 6.4 illustrates the densities of the $P(Z)$ distributions for a variety of $P(x)$ distributions and values of r. The significant implication from the figure is that there is an obvious tendency to drift toward the right as a function of increasing r. This is of course reasonable considering the maximum of a set of numbers is larger than the average of the set.

Returning to the question of the distribution of a particular ranking of samples, let

$$P(x_1 \leq x_2 \leq \cdots \leq x_n)$$

$$= \int_{-\infty}^{x_2} dP_1(x_1) \int_{-\infty}^{x_3} dP_2(x_2) \cdots \int_{-\infty}^{x_n} dP_{n-1}(x_{n-1}) \int_{-\infty}^{\infty} dP_n(x_n) \quad (6.33)$$

where $P_i(x_i)$ is the distribution of the ith sample occurring in the particular ranking as indicated. If we now assume the Lehmann alternative

$$P_i(x_i) = P(x_i)^{r_i} \quad (6.34)$$

we have implied that the distribution of the ith sample occurring in the ith position is equal to the distribution of the maximum of r_i of x_i samples (independent of position). This seems somewhat reasonable considering that for any ordering the x_ith sample is the maximum of r_i previous samples. Making a change of variable $q_i = P(x_i)$ and substituting into equation (6.33) utilizing the Lehmann alternative we obtain,

$$P(x_1 \leq x_2 \leq \cdots \leq x_n)$$

$$= \int_0^{q_2} dq_1^{r_1} \int_0^{q_3} dq_2^{r_2} \cdots \int_0^{q_n} dq_{n-1}^{r_{n-1}} \int_0^1 dq_n^{r_n} \quad (6.35)$$

Note that the limits of integration have changed due to the change in notation. Thus the ith integral ranges from 0 to $P(x_{i+1})$ corresponding to a range in the x_i dimension of $(-\infty, x_{i+1})$. Noting that

$$dq_i^{r_i} = r_i q_i^{r_i-1} dq_i \quad (6.36)$$

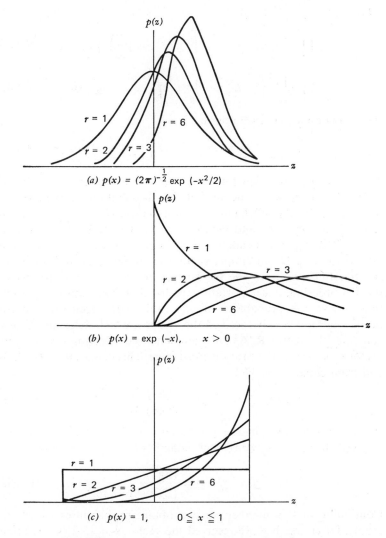

(a) $p(x) = (2\pi)^{-\frac{1}{2}} \exp(-x^2/2)$

(b) $p(x) = \exp(-x)$, $x > 0$

(c) $p(x) = 1$, $0 \leqq x \leqq 1$

FIGURE 6.4. Lehmann alternative distributions.

it is possible to integrate out the terms q_1 within its integral as below

$$P(x_1 \leq x_2 \leq \cdots \leq x_n)$$

$$= \prod_{i=1}^{n} r_i \left\{ \int_0^1 q_n^{r-1} \, dq_n \cdots \int_0^{q_3} q_2^{r_2-1} \, dq_2 \left(\frac{1}{r_1} \right)^{r_1} q_1 \Big|_0^{q_2} \right\} \qquad (6.37a)$$

$$= \prod_{i=1}^{n} r_i \left\{ \int_0^1 q_n^{r-1} \, dq_n \cdots \int_0^{q_3} \left(\frac{1}{r_1} \right)^{r_1+r_2-1} q_2 \, dq_2 \right\} \qquad (6.37b)$$

Repeating on q_2, etc., we obtain

$$P(x_1 \leq x_2 \leq \cdots \leq x_n) = \prod_{i=1}^{n} r_i \left(\sum_{j=1}^{i} r_j \right)^{-1} \qquad (6.37c)$$

This equation states that for independent nonidentically distributed features with rank r_i, the probability distribution of the specific order given by the left hand part of equation (6.37c) is a function only of the ranks, r_i, and independent of the specific distributions $P(x_i)$ of the features or samples. For orderings other than that given by equation (6.37c) a simple relabeling of features and their respective ranks will provide the correct probability of occurrence of the new ordering. It is important to realize that the results of equation (6.37c) give the probability of any rank order occurring *trained* on having sequentially received the vector **x** which deterministically generates the vector **R**. As an example consider having received the vector $\mathbf{x} = (1.2, 5.3, 4.8)$ at the third stage. This defines $\mathbf{R} = (1, 2, 2)$ and from equation (6.37c)

$$P(x_1 \leq x_2 \leq x_3) = \frac{(1)(2)(2)}{(1)(3)(5)} = \frac{4}{15} \qquad (6.38a)$$

If we are interested in the probability that $x_3 \leq x_1 \leq x_2$ having received the vector **x**, we relabel obtaining

$$P(x_3 \leq x_1 \leq x_2) = \frac{(2)(1)(2)}{(2)(3)(5)} = \frac{2}{15} \qquad (6.38b)$$

Continuing in this manner we can obtain probabilities for all $n!$ events. Of course had we received the vector $\mathbf{x} = (5.3, 1.2, 4.8)$ an entire different set of probabilities would have resulted. Problem 8 explores this question in greater depth. The significance of the result of equation (6.37c) is that by sequentially observing the ranks of incoming data we can determine the probabilities of any ordering of interest independent of the underlying probability distributions on the features themselves. Note that for identically distributed features the Lehmann alternative of equation (6.34) becomes

$$P_i(x_i) = P(x)^r \qquad r > 0 \qquad (6.39)$$

Substituting into our result of equation (6.37c) we see that the probability of any rank ordering

$$P(\mathbf{R}) = \frac{r^n}{\prod\limits_{i=1}^{n} ri} \qquad (6.40a)$$

$$= \frac{1}{n!} \qquad (6.40b)$$

as would be expected. In other words given equal distributions for each feature it is as likely to get one rank ordering as any other. Using this fact we can now couch the pattern recognition problem in a sequential probability ratio test environment based on Lehmann alternatives [7].

The procedure to be followed will be one of alternating known features with unknown ones in a sequential observation fashion. Thus let the prototype $\mathbf{y}$ be known and let the vector $\mathbf{x}$ be an unknown in which it is desired to determine if $\mathbf{x}$ comes from the distribution $P(y)$ or $P(y)^r$ corresponding to class S_1 or S_2 respectively. Let the unknown samples x_i be intermixed with known features y_i such that the vector of observation at the nth stage becomes

$$\mathbf{z} = (y_1, x_1, y_2, x_2, \ldots, y_n, x_n) \qquad (6.41)$$

Utilizing the SPRT we are interested in the reciprocal likelihood ratio

$$\lambda_n = \frac{P_n(\mathbf{R} \mid S_2)}{P_n(\mathbf{R} \mid S_1)} \qquad (6.42)$$

Assuming independent statistics and Lehmann alternatives we obtain

$$P(\mathbf{R} \mid S_1) = \frac{1}{n!} \qquad (6.43a)$$

$$P(\mathbf{R} \mid S_2) = \frac{r^{n/2}}{\prod\limits_{i=1}^{n} \sum\limits_{j=1}^{i} a_j} \qquad (6.43b)$$

where

$$a_j = 1 \qquad \text{if } z_i \text{ is a } y \qquad (6.43c)$$
$$= r \qquad \text{if } z_i \text{ is an } x$$

and n is even. The appropriate likelihood ratios for n even and odd respectively become

$$\lambda_n = \frac{n! \, r^{n/2}}{\prod\limits_{i=1}^{n} \sum\limits_{j=1}^{i} a_j} \qquad (6.44a)$$

$$\lambda_n = \frac{n! \, r^{(n-1)/2}}{\prod\limits_{i=1}^{n} \sum\limits_{j=1}^{i} a_j} \qquad (6.45a)$$

It now remains to specify the stopping boundaries A and B according to tolerable error rates, equations (6.7a) and (6.7b); and simply test λ_n against these boundaries. Figure 6.5 illustrates the technique for the data vectors

$\mathbf{y} = (10.47, 10.51, 9.78, 12.17, 9.95, 11.22, 9.31, 9.75, 8.56, 9.57)$
$\mathbf{x} = (12.5, 11.50, 13.50, 12.10, 13.55, 13.10,$

$$11.55, 11.45, 11.90, 13.45)$$

and $e_{12} = e_{21} = .05$. Fu [4] extends the Lehmann alternative concept to investigate the effect of the power, r, on the classification error as well as applicability to many-class problems.

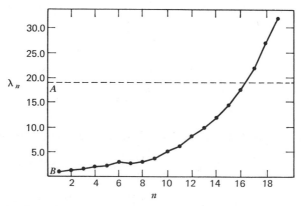

FIGURE 6.5. A Lehmann alternative experiment.

6.6 Supervised Sequential Bayesian Learning

The previous sections in this chapter have been concerned with developing sequential decision techniques such that classification becomes an end result to the processes. Closely allied to these objectives is that of sequentially learning some parameter which may be necessary to describe a statistic in order that a classification boundary may be better defined. Bayesian learning is one technique in which estimates of parameters may be made sequentially as prototype data arrives. Notice that we are talking about sequential prototypes rather than dimensions within a prototype. The analysis is of course similar in both cases. Specifically it will be assumed that the functional form of the statistic $p(\mathbf{x} \mid S_k)$ is known but it remains to define some parameter in order to completely describe $p(\mathbf{x}/S_k)$. Let the parameters necessary for complete description be given by the vector $\boldsymbol{\theta}$ where $\boldsymbol{\theta}$ may include means, covariances, and higher order statistical parameters. In the Bayesian learning technique it will be necessary to assume an a priori statistic on $\boldsymbol{\theta}$, $p(\boldsymbol{\theta}/S_k)$, which need only bound the true value of $\boldsymbol{\theta}$ and not exclude it. The objective is to modify the a priori distribution on $\boldsymbol{\theta}$ with sequential knowledge obtained from $\mathbf{x}_n$ such that $p(\boldsymbol{\theta}/\mathbf{x}_1, \ldots, \mathbf{x}_m, S_k)$ approaches a delta function at the true value of $\boldsymbol{\theta}$ [8]. Thus after receiving the first known prototype, $\mathbf{x}_1$

$$p(\boldsymbol{\theta}/\mathbf{x}_1, S_k) = \frac{p(\mathbf{x}_1/\boldsymbol{\theta}, S_k)p(\boldsymbol{\theta}/S_k)}{p(\mathbf{x}_1/S_k)} \tag{6.46a}$$

After the second prototype, $\mathbf{x}_2$

$$p(\boldsymbol{\theta}/\mathbf{x}_2, \mathbf{x}_1, S_k) = \frac{p(\mathbf{x}_2/\mathbf{x}_1, \boldsymbol{\theta}, S_k)p(\boldsymbol{\theta}/\mathbf{x}_1, S_k)}{p(\mathbf{x}_2/\mathbf{x}_1, S_k)} \tag{6.46b}$$

and in general after the mth stage, $\mathbf{x}_m$, we have

$$p(\boldsymbol{\theta}/\mathbf{x}_m, \ldots, \mathbf{x}_1, S_k)$$

$$= \frac{p(\mathbf{x}_m/\mathbf{x}_{m-1}, \ldots, \mathbf{x}_1, \boldsymbol{\theta}, S_k)p(\boldsymbol{\theta}/\mathbf{x}_{m-1}, \ldots, \mathbf{x}_1, S_k)}{p(\mathbf{x}_m/\mathbf{x}_{m-1}, \ldots, \mathbf{x}_1, S_k)} \tag{6.46c}$$

Investigating the above equation we see that $p(\mathbf{x}_m/\mathbf{x}_{m-1}, \ldots, \mathbf{x}_1, \boldsymbol{\theta}, S_k)$ is known if the prototypes themselves are independent and identically distributed. In other words

$$p(\mathbf{x}_m/\mathbf{x}_{m-1}, \ldots, \mathbf{x}_1, S_k) = p(\mathbf{x}_m/\boldsymbol{\theta}, S_k) = p(\mathbf{x}/\boldsymbol{\theta}, S_k) \quad (6.47)$$

which is known as to functional form a priori and as to exact form conditional on $\boldsymbol{\theta}$. Returning to equation (6.46c) the second term in the numerator is our last revision of $p(\boldsymbol{\theta})$ given previous knowledge and is determined recursively at the previous stage. It remains only to calculate the denominator $p(\mathbf{x}_m/\mathbf{x}_{m-1}, \ldots, \mathbf{x}_1, S_k)$ which can be done by a multidimensional integration of the form

$$p(\mathbf{x}_m/\mathbf{x}_{m-1}, \ldots, \mathbf{x}_1, S_k) = \int p(\mathbf{x}_m/\mathbf{x}_{m-1}, \ldots, \mathbf{x}_1, \boldsymbol{\theta}, S_k)$$
$$\times p(\boldsymbol{\theta}/\mathbf{x}_{m-1}, \ldots, \mathbf{x}_1, S_k) \, d\boldsymbol{\theta} \quad (6.48)$$

Thus we have defined all terms in equation (6.46c) and a recursive relationship results for determining all necessary distributions at the mth stage. The process can be repeated producing better and better estimates of $\boldsymbol{\theta}$ on the average assuming the true value of $\boldsymbol{\theta}$ was not a priori excluded.

One of the major drawbacks of the above procedure is computational complexity. It would indeed be convenient if we had a fixed computational algorithm for the iterative procedure described above. This will become possible if care is taken in selecting the a priori distribution $p(\boldsymbol{\theta}/S_k)$ to be a reproducing distribution when coupled with $p(\mathbf{x}/\boldsymbol{\theta}, S_k)$ in the Bayesian learning procedure. Thus if the a priori density function can be selected such that the a posteriori density function assumes the same functional form, then the computational task is greatly simplified. Fu [4] presents examples in which such reproducing densities are known for a variety of statistical assumptions. Perhaps the most common example is that afforded by the estimation of the mean vector, $\boldsymbol{\mu}$, of a Gaussian process with known covariance $[\Phi_x]$. In such a case

$$p(\mathbf{x}/\boldsymbol{\theta}, S_k) = N(\boldsymbol{\mu}, [\Phi_x]) \quad (6.49a)$$

and a reproducing distribution for $\boldsymbol{\theta}$ is also Gaussian

$$p(\boldsymbol{\theta}/S_k) = N(\boldsymbol{\mu}_0, [\Phi_0]) \quad (6.49b)$$

where $\boldsymbol{\mu}_0$ and $[\Phi_0]$ are initial guesses of the mean vector and covariance of $\boldsymbol{\theta}$ respectively. One of the problems at the end of the chapter is designed to verify that indeed $p(\theta/\mathbf{x}_m, \ldots, \mathbf{x}_1, S_k)$ is also Gaussian in form. It then simply becomes necessary to calculate the new means and covariance matrices at each stage of the iteration. These values become

$$\boldsymbol{\mu}_m = \frac{1}{m}[\Phi_x]\left[[\Phi_0] + \frac{1}{m}[\Phi_x]\right]^{-1}\boldsymbol{\mu}_0$$

$$+ [\Phi_0]\left[[\Phi_0] + \frac{1}{m}[\Phi_x]\right]^{-1}\langle x\rangle \qquad (6.50a)$$

and

$$[\Phi_m] = \frac{1}{m}[\Phi_x]\left[[\Phi_0] + \frac{1}{m}[\Phi_x]\right]^{-1}[\Phi_0] \qquad (6.50b)$$

where

$$\langle x\rangle = \frac{1}{m}\sum_{i=1}^{m}\mathbf{x}_i \qquad (6.50c)$$

is the sample mean. Note that for large m the estimated mean approaches the same mean and less and less dependence is based on the initial guesses $\boldsymbol{\mu}_0$ and $[\Phi_0]$.

6.7 Nonsupervised Sequential Bayesian Learning

In Chapter 5 we investigated a few nonsupervised learning techniques in which a priori knowledge of prototype classification was not available and consequently mixture distributions were utilized. One of the major drawbacks of nonsupervised Bayesian learning is that implementation often requires an exponentially growing machine. For instance, if we have K classes, S_k, from which the mth sample vector $\mathbf{x}_m$ can be generated, then there exists a mutually exclusive partition for the $\{\mathbf{x}_1, \ldots, \mathbf{x}_m\}$ set totaling K^m different events. Because the $\mathbf{x}_m$ are unknown as to their correct classification the mixture distribution at the mth stage becomes

$$p(\mathbf{x}/\mathbf{x}_m \cdots \mathbf{x}_1) = \sum_{\alpha=1}^{K^m} P(\mathbf{x}/\mathbf{x}_m, \ldots, \mathbf{x}_1, \mathcal{W}_\alpha)P(\mathcal{W}_\alpha/\mathbf{x}_m \cdots \mathbf{x}_1) \quad (6.51)$$

where $\mathcal{W}_\alpha$ is the αth partition. For a two-class problem $K = 2$, and the upper limit becomes 2^m. Note that $P(\mathcal{W}_\alpha/\mathbf{x}_1, \ldots, \mathbf{x}_m)$ must also be known and represents the probability that the αth partition occurred given the first m sample vectors. Fu [4] summarizes the work of Fralick [9] and others in showing how the exponentially increasing machine can be made finite by appropriate independence assumptions. Returning now to the Bayesian learning model for the parametric case, we have

$$p(\theta/\mathbf{x}_m, \ldots, \mathbf{x}_1)$$
$$= \sum_{\alpha=1}^{K^m} p(\theta/\mathbf{x}_m, \ldots, \mathbf{x}_1, \mathscr{W}_\alpha) p(\mathscr{W}_\alpha/\mathbf{x}_m, \ldots, \mathbf{x}_1) \quad (6.52)$$

Utilizing the results of Bayes theorem, equation (6.46c), and assuming conditional independence

$$p(\mathbf{x}_m/\theta, \mathbf{x}_{m-1}, \ldots, \mathbf{x}_1) = p(\mathbf{x}_m/\theta) \qquad (6.53a)$$

then

$$p(\mathbf{x}_m/\mathbf{x}_{m-1}, \ldots, \mathbf{x}_1, \theta)$$
$$= P(S_1)P(\mathbf{x}_m/\theta, S_1) + P(\bar{S}_1)P(\mathbf{x}_m/\theta, \bar{S}_1) \quad (6.53b)$$

where $\bar{S}_1$ means "not class S_1." This assumption allows a finite machine solution

$$p(\theta/\mathbf{x}_m, \ldots, \mathbf{x}_1) = p(\theta/\mathbf{x}_{m-1} \cdots \mathbf{x}_1)$$
$$\times \left[\frac{P(S_1)P(\mathbf{x}_m/\theta, S_1) + P(\bar{S}_1)P(\mathbf{x}_m/\theta, \bar{S}_1)}{P(\mathbf{x}_m/\mathbf{x}_{m-1}, \ldots, \mathbf{x}_1)} \right]$$
$$(6.53c)$$

Thus if $P(S_1)$, $P(\mathbf{x}_m/\theta, S_1)$ and $P(\mathbf{x}_m/\theta, \bar{S}_1)$ are known, $p(\theta/\mathbf{x}_m \cdots \mathbf{x}_1)$ can be recursively calculated as before. Hilborn and Lainiotis [10] have generalized the Bayesian nonsupervised learning approach to the case of a finite order Markov dependence model as opposed to the traditional statistically independent sample assumption. Their work has also resulted in a fixed size memory and machine for optimal implementation of the Bayes nonsupervised classifier.

6.8   Problems

1. Consider the problem of SPRT and determine whether the mean of an independent sample normal variable with unity

variance has the value $m_1 = 10$ or $m_2 = 9.5$. Decide with probability of error $e_{21} = .10$ and $e_{12} = .05$.

(a) Describe the test in terms of mathematical inequalities, i.e., what are the decisions and corresponding boundaries?

(b) The following data is provided for you in sequential order
$$x = 10.47, 10.51, 9.78, 12.17, 9.95, 11.22, 9.31, 9.75, 8.56,$$
$$9.52, 11.65, 10.35, 11.01, 10.52$$
What class is the data taken from?

(c) What is the value of n upon making a decision?

(d) Calculate $\mathscr{E}(n/S_1)$ and $\mathscr{E}(n/S_2)$. Compare your results with that of part (c).

2. Using the problem setup as in problem 1, apply the modified sequential probability ratio test. Terminate the test after 8 features, and let the modified SPRT starting boundaries be the same as the Wald SPRT constant boundaries. Let the time-varying boundaries be triangular ($r_1 = r_2 = 1$).

(a) Form a table with entries for each stage of the process such as:

n	Lower boundary	Upper boundary	Test data	Decision?
1				
2				
.				
.				
.				
8				

(b) How many samples were necessary before a decision was made?

3. Choosing $e_{12} = e_{21} = .1$, construct a sequential test for testing $S_1 : \sigma = 8$ against $S_2 : \sigma = 10$ for a normal variable with zero mean.

(a) The solution will require your deriving a general solution based on independent samples.

(b) Apply your results of part (a) to the numeric data specified in this problem.

4. Consider the problem of determining whether the SPRT and Bayes combination provides a better or worse error of misrecognition compared to that of the modified SPRT. To step through this problem, use the following notational standards.

n_i = Expected number of features before a SPRT decision is made, given that the features are obtained from class S_i.

N = Total allowable features before termination.

e_{ij}^S = SPRT error probability of deciding class i given true decision is class S_j.

e_{ij}^B = Bayes error probability of deciding class i given true decision is class S_j.

P_i = Probability that n_i is less than N given class S_i.

Assume equal a priori class probabilities and a symmetric loss function.

(a) Form an N dimensional integral expression for e_{ij}^B.

(b) Form an n_i dimensional integral expression for e_{ij}^S; be sure to specify the regions of integration in part (a) and part (b).

(c) Find the total misrecognition error properly combining the results of parts (a) and (b) and using P_i. Note that the two error events are mutually exclusive.

(d) Assume independent identically distributed features, i.e.,

$$p(x/S_j) = \prod_{l=1}^{n_i} p(x_l/S_j)$$

and solve for part (c) letting

$$\int_{\bar{X}_l} p(x_l/S_j)\, dx = E \qquad \bar{X}_l = \text{SPRT regions}$$

$$\int_{\bar{Y}_l} p(x_l/S_j)\, dx = F \qquad \bar{X}_l + \bar{Y}_l = \text{Bayes regions}$$

5. Using the results of equations (6.14a) and (6.14b), investigate the limit as $e_{21} \to 0$ and $e_{12} \to 0$ for $\mathscr{E}(n/s_1)$ and $\mathscr{E}(n/s_2)$.

6. Derive the decision rule for the nth stage of the "Gaussian example" for the SPRT and the modified SPRT as illustrated below equation (6.27).

7. Equation (6.37c) is the result of applying rank statistics and

Lehmann alternatives to a sequential recognition problem for nonidentically distributed samples conditioned upon having received a specific rank ordering.

(a) Prove that this result is bounded in $[0, 1]$ for $r_i > 0$.

(b) Show that the probabilities of all possible orderings conditioned upon having received a specific rank ordering sums to unity.

(c) What specific received rank ordering guarantees all orderings are equally likely?

(d) Is this ordering unique?

8. Equation (6.37c) is the probability distribution of the event $P(x_1 \leq x_2 \leq \cdots \leq x_n)$, but this event also implies that as data is presented in a sequential manner that each successive sample is the maximum of all previous samples—thus the relation between ranks, r_i, and Lehmann alternatives.

(a) To further understand this concept determine the $n! = 6$ different probabilities for the $n!$ rank statistics (sequential rank vector) having trained upon the first three data samples of $\mathbf{x} = 5, 9, 1$.

(b) Do these probabilities sum to unity?

(c) Repeat part (a) for each possible training sequence.

(d) Given the sequence 5, 9, 1 and the sequence 1, 9, 5 which sequence implies the greatest probability of occurrence of the event $x_1 \leq x_2 \leq x_3$?

(e) Which sequence of all of them implies the greatest probability of occurrence of the event $x_1 \leq x_2 \leq x_3$?

(f) Repeat part (e) for the event $x_3 \leq x_2 \leq x_1$.

(g) Can you conjecture an inequality from parts (e) and (f) and what is it?

9. You have the following data from a prototype of known classification.

$\mathbf{y} = 10.47, 10.51, 9.78, 12.17, 9.95, 11.22, 9.31, 9.75,$
$$8.56, 9.52, 11.65, 10.35, 11.01, 10.52.$$

and you wish to test whether $\mathbf{x}$ comes from the same or Lehmann alternative $(r = 2)$ distribution with a SPRT with error rates $e_{12} = e_{21} = 0.10$.

$\mathbf{x} = 11.50, 10.50, 12.50, 11.10, 12.55, 12.10, 10.55, 10.45,$
$$10.90, 12.45, 11.90, 11.50, 11.30, 11.70.$$

(a) Complete a table as a function of n with entries λ_n, **R**, "decision."

(b) What class does **x** belong to, S_y or Lehmann alternative?

(c) What is the value of n at your decision?

(d) Repeat parts (a), (b), (c) for the modified SPRT with $N = 14$ and triangular stopping boundaries ($r_1 = r_2 = 1$, equations (6.15a) and (6.15b) and use the Wald boundaries as initial conditions).

10. Your love for the course has increased to the point where you can hardly wait to finish the semester. Therefore you decide to tackle this problem with tremendous vigor. The problem smacks of a Bayesian learning technique applied to sequential recognition. You are presented with the following sequence of data

$$\mathbf{x} = 10.47, 10.51, 9.78, 12.17, 9.95, 11.22, 9.31, 9.75,$$
$$8.56, 9.52, 11.65, 10.35$$

and your inherent "artificial" intelligence indicates that the data is Gaussian, independent unity variance and the only problem is to determine the mean. Using Bayesian learning techniques applied to sequential data and a unity variance on the estimator:

(a) Solve for μ_n assuming independent vector valued statistics.

(b) What does your solution approach when $n \to \infty$?

(c) What can you say about μ_0 based on part (b)?

(d) Determine the mean of the above data at each stage with $\mu_0 = 9$. Note that this is actually a scalar problem.

11. It is suggested that the Gaussian distribution function is adequate as an a priori assumption in a Bayes "mean" learning procedure because the distribution is self-reproducing in developing the a posteriori density function statistics. Let

$$p(\theta) = \frac{1}{(2\pi)^{N/2} |[\Phi_0]|^{1/2}} \exp\{-\tfrac{1}{2}(\theta - \mu_0)'[\Phi_0]^{-1}(\theta - \mu_0)\}$$

and solve for $p(\mu/\mathbf{x}_1, \mathbf{x}_2, \ldots, \mathbf{x}_m)$ by successive application of Bayes formula, thus verifying that the distribution is indeed self-reproducing in this case.

12. Consider the two-class problem and the method of sequential probability ratio testing. Let λ_n be the likelihood ratio at the

nth observation sample. Let A and B be the decision boundaries.
(a) Describe the test procedure.
(b) Can you be guaranteed of making a decision in less than 10^6 observations?
(c) Fu modified the SPRT method. Using the modified SPRT method can you be guaranteed of making a decision in a finite number of observations?
(d) Describe the time-varying nature of the boundaries in the modified SPRT.
(e) Relate the modified SPRT technique to a Bayes classifier and state the difference between the Bayes machine and the modified SPRT if a decision has not been made by the final observation.
(f) Does the backward procedure for finite sequential recognition using dynamic programming imply time-varying boundaries?
(g) What is the Lehmann alternative?
(h) Are independent statistics assumed in the Lehmann alternative?

13. It is desired to learn a parameter, θ, of a density function in a sequential pattern recognition system.
(a) Using the concepts of Bayesian learning derive the recursive equation for the distribution $p(\theta/x_1, \ldots, x_n)$.
(b) Why are reproducing density functions useful in Bayesian learning?
(c) Can nonreproducing distributions be used in Bayesian learning?

6.9 References

1. Wald, A., *Sequential Analysis*, Wiley, New York, 1947.

2. Neyman, T. and E. S. Pearson, "On the Use and Interpretation of Certain Test Criteria for Purpose of Statistical Inference," *Biometrika* Pt. II, pp. 263–294, 1928.

3. Wald, A. and J. Wolfowitz, "Optimum Character of the Sequential Probability Ratio Test," *Ann. Math. Statistics*, vol. 19, pp. 326–339, 1948.

4. Fu, K. S, *Sequential Methods in Pattern Recognition and Machine Learning*, Academic Press, New York, 1968.

5 Bellman, R., *Dynamic Programming*, Princeton University Press, Princeton, N.J., 1957.

6 Lehmann, E. L., "The Power of Rank Tests," *Ann. Math. Statistics*, vol. 24, pp. 23–43, 1953.

7. Savage, I. R. and J. Sethuraman, "Stopping Time of a Rank-Order Sequential Probability Ratio Test Based on Lehmann Alternatives," *Ann. Math. Statistics*, vol. 37, no. 5, 11. 1154–1160, 1966.

8. Anderson, T. W., *An Introduction to Multivariate Statistical Analysis*, Wiley, New York, 1958.

9. Fralick, S. C., "Learning to Recognize Patterns Without a Teacher," *IEEE Trans. Information Theory*, vol. 13, pp. 57–64, 1967.

10. Hilborn, C. G., Jr. and D. G. Lainoitis, "Optimal Unsupervised Learning Multicategory Dependent Hypotheses Pattern Recognition," *IEEE Trans. Information Theory*, vol. IT-14, pp. 468–470, May 1968.

6.10   Related Bibliography

Cardillo, G. P. and K. S. Fu, "On Suboptimal Sequential Pattern Recognition," *IEEE Trans. on Computers*, vol. C-17, no. 8, pp. 789–792 (August 1968).

Chen, Chi-Han, "A Note on Sequential Decision Approach to Pattern Recognition and Machine Learning," *Info. and Control*, vol. 9, pp. 549–563 (1966).

Chien, Y. T., "A Sequential Decision Model for Selecting Feature Subsets in Pattern Recognition." *IEEE Trans. Comp.*, vol. C-20, no. 3, pp. 282–290 (March 1971).

Cooper, D. B. and J. H. Freeman, "On the Asymptotic Improvement in the Outcome of Supervised Learning Provided by Additional Nonsupervised Learning," *IEEE Trans. Computers*, vol. C-19, pp. 1055–1063 (November 1970).

Davisson, L. D., E. A. Feustel and G. W. Modestino, "The Effects of Dependence on Nonparametric Detection," *IEEE Trans. on Information Theory*, vol. IT-16, no. 1, pp. 32–41 (1970).

Fu, K. S., Y. T. Chien and G. P. Cardillo, "A Dynamic Programming Approach to Sequential Pattern Recognition, "*IEEE Trans. on Computers*, vol. EC-16, no. 6, pp. 790–803 (December 1967).

Kovalevsky, V., "Sequential Optimization in Pattern Recognition and Pattern Description," *Proc. IFIP Congress 68*, Edinburgh, Scotland (1968).

Pitt, M., and B. F. Womak, "A Sequentialization of the Patterson Classifier," *Proc. IEEE* (corres.) vol. 54, no. 12, pp. 1987 (December 1966).

Roberts, R. A. and C. T. Mullis, "A Bayes Sequential Test of *m* Hypotheses," *IEEE Trans. Information Theory*, vol. IT-16, no. 1, pp. 91–94 (January 1970).

Sage, A. P. and J. R. McLendon, "Discrete Sequential Detection and Likelihood Ratio Computation for Non-Gaussian Signals in Gaussian Noise," Symp. on Information Processing, Purdue, pp. 589 (April 28–30, 1969).

APPENDIX A

MULTIDIMENSIONAL ROTATIONS IN FEATURE SELECTION*

A.0 Introduction

This appendix presents a mathematical feature selection technique in the framework of finite dimensional vector spaces. The technique of interest utilizes rotational transformations as a means of feature selection. Significant feature selection must capitalize on interclass measures in order to define a low error rate pattern recognition system [1, 2], and rotational transformations are suggested for obtaining a few but significant number of features for classification purposes. The Karhunen-Loève transform provides a feature space in which the largest variance (eigenvalue) and energy dimensions can be selected for classification purposes. Unfortunately, the transformation requires considerable computation to form and diagonalize the covariance matrices. Thus other rotations are suggested which provide feature spaces for selection purposes and which are readily

---

* This appendix has been published elsewhere in modified form and is listed in reference [19].

implementable in a digital environment. The rotations which immediately come to mind are the Fast Fourier transform and Fast Hadamard or Walsh transform. In addition, an entire new class of fast transformations has been developed, each of which lends itself to the orthogonal rotation of pattern spaces for efficient feature selection [3, 4]. The Fourier, Hadamard or Walsh, Generalized Walsh, Kronecker, Haar, and Generalized Haar transforms are all subsets of the class of rapidly implementable rotations and therefore are particularly appealing to the feature selection task.

There have been earlier efforts utilizing certain of the above mentioned transforms for feature selection. Fu has emphasized the use of the mean square optimum Karhunen-Loève transform [5, 6]. The Fourier transform has been used in the specific problem of character recognition by a variety of independent researchers [7, 8]. The Hadamard transform, providing a multidimensional 45° rotation, also has been used for feature selection in the character recognition task [9, 10]. The Haar transform has been suggested as a possible feature selector in voice recognition [11] and is particularly appealing because it contains both local and global information. From a bandwidth reduction viewpoint the Fourier, Karhunen-Loève, Hadamard, and Haar transforms have all been investigated in two-variable formats for digital image processing with successful results [12–14]. Therefore it seems reasonable to extend the work to the dimensionality reduction portion of feature selection.

A.I Transformations

Let the pattern recognition problem be couched in the following notation. There will be K classes, S_k, indexed by $k = 1, 2, \ldots, K$. Let the dimensionality of the pattern space be equal to R. Let the pattern space be designated by the subscript x and the rotated space by subscript A. Then assuming a second order statistic (a covariance function) can be measured or modeled for each class, S_k, let it be designated $[\Phi_x^{(k)}]$. Then a generalized covariance matrix descriptive of the pattern recognition problem becomes

$$[\Phi_x] = \sum_{k=1}^{K} P(S_k)[\Phi_x^{(k)}] \qquad (A.1)$$

where the $P(S_k)$ are the a priori class distributions.

A linear transformation provided by a unitary operator $[A]$, will map the pattern space into a rotated space whose basis vectors are the orthogonal columns of the matrix $[A]$. The features in the new space are linear combinations of the original axes according to the structure of $[A]$. The second order statistics in the rotated space become

$$[\Phi_A] = [A]^t[\Phi_x][A] \qquad (A.2)$$

The objective now is to find dimensions in the rotated space which provide greater discriminatory powers for classification than in the original space. The following transforms are discussed with respect to correlation and computer implementation considerations.

KARHUNEN-LOÈVE TRANSFORM. This expansion is optimum in a variety of criterion [5, 15] of which mean square truncation error and entropy interpretation are just two. The transformation results in a covariance function which is diagonal with entries equal to the eigenvalues of $[\Phi_x]$:

$$[E_x]^t[\Phi_x][E_x] = [\lambda] \qquad (A.3)$$

The coefficients in the rotated space become statistically uncorrelated and for Gaussian statistics become statistically independent. Appendix B attempts to justify the need for independent features. Consequently, each coordinate in the new space lends itself to independent processing and interpretation. One of the major drawbacks of the Karhunen-Loève transform is the need to diagonalize a usually large covariance matrix. Once the eigenvectors are obtained, the actual transformation implementation will require R^2 computer operations.

FOURIER TRANSFORM. With the advent of the Fast Fourier Transform [16] the Fourier transform has found considerable application in digital processing. The transformation is unitary and

$$[A_F] = \left[\exp\left(\frac{2\pi iux}{R}\right)\right] \qquad (A.4)$$

It can be shown by the symmetric Toeplitz distribution theorem [17] that the Fourier transform is asymptotically equivalent to the Karhunen-Loève transform. Consequently, although it is sub-optimal in a mean square error sense, it is "close" to the optimum while simultaneously affording efficient computer implementation in $R \log_2 R$ computer operations.

WALSH/HADAMARD TRANSFORM.   This transformation is particularly appealing for a variety of reasons. First it is implementable in $R \log_2 R$ additions (or subtractions), i.e., no multiplications [3 , 4]. It is binary in nature making it quite appealing for semi-conductor special purpose computer implementation. It has an analogy between sequency [19] and frequency where sequency is proportional to the number of zero crossings of a Walsh wave and frequency is proportional to the number or zero crossings of a complex trigonometric wave. The transformation matrix can be described in the following notation

$$[A_W] = [(-1)^{\sum\limits_{i=0}^{n-1} u_i x_i}] \tag{A.5}$$

where u_i and x_i are the binary bits representing the row and column indices.

HAAR TRANSFORM.   The Haar transform provides a domain which is both locally sensitive as well as globally sensitive. In the Fourier and Walsh cases each transform coefficient is a function of all coordinates in the original pattern space (global), whereas this is only true for the first two coefficients in the Haar case. In fact $R/2$ coefficients in the Haar domain measure the adjacent correlation of coordinates in the original space taken two at a time, $R/4$ measure coordinates taken four at a time, etc., up to R/R coefficients measuring R coordinates of the pattern space. The transformation is implementable in $2(R - 1)$ additions (or subtractions) [4]. Figure A.1 displays the three transforms: Fourier, Walsh, and Haar for the $R = 8$ case.

It is possible to interpret the rotated spaces in terms of the remaining amount of correlation in the off-diagonal entries of their respective covariance matrices $[\Phi_A]$. For highly correlated pattern space prototype data it appears that the Karhunen-Loève, Fourier, Walsh, Haar, and pattern space domains provide increasingly correlated features respectively. Therefore, if the degree of correlation remaining amongst feature dimensions can be an indication of potentially useful features, the above transform domains can be so utilized. See Appendix B.

$$[A_F] = \frac{1}{2\sqrt{2}} \begin{bmatrix} w^0 & w^0 & w^0 & w^0 & w^0 & w^0 & w^0 & w^0 \\ w^0 & w^1 & w^2 & w^3 & w^4 & w^5 & w^6 & w^7 \\ w^0 & w^2 & w^4 & w^6 & w^0 & w^2 & w^4 & w^6 \\ w^0 & w^3 & w^6 & w^1 & w^4 & w^7 & w^2 & w^5 \\ w^0 & w^4 & w^0 & w^4 & w^0 & w^4 & w^0 & w^4 \\ w^0 & w^5 & w^2 & w^7 & w^4 & w^1 & w^6 & w^3 \\ w^0 & w^6 & w^4 & w^2 & w^0 & w^6 & w^4 & w^2 \\ w^0 & w^7 & w^6 & w^5 & w^4 & w^3 & w^2 & w^1 \end{bmatrix} \quad w = \exp\left(\frac{2\pi i}{8}\right)$$

(a) Fourier Transform

$$[A_W] = \frac{1}{2\sqrt{2}} \begin{bmatrix} 1 & 1 & 1 & 1 & 1 & 1 & 1 & 1 \\ 1 & -1 & 1 & -1 & 1 & -1 & 1 & -1 \\ 1 & 1 & -1 & -1 & 1 & 1 & -1 & -1 \\ 1 & -1 & -1 & 1 & 1 & -1 & -1 & 1 \\ 1 & 1 & 1 & 1 & -1 & -1 & -1 & -1 \\ 1 & -1 & 1 & -1 & -1 & 1 & -1 & 1 \\ 1 & 1 & -1 & -1 & -1 & -1 & 1 & 1 \\ 1 & -1 & -1 & 1 & -1 & 1 & 1 & -1 \end{bmatrix}$$

(b) Walsh/Hadamard Transform

$$[A_H] = \begin{bmatrix} 1 & 1 & 1 & 1 & 1 & 1 & 1 & 1 \\ 1 & 1 & 1 & 1 & -1 & -1 & -1 & -1 \\ \sqrt{2} & \sqrt{2} & -\sqrt{2} & -\sqrt{2} & 0 & 0 & 0 & 0 \\ 0 & 0 & 0 & 0 & \sqrt{2} & \sqrt{2} & -\sqrt{2} & -\sqrt{2} \\ 2 & -2 & 0 & 0 & 0 & 0 & 0 & 0 \\ 0 & 0 & 2 & -2 & 0 & 0 & 0 & 0 \\ 0 & 0 & 0 & 0 & 2 & -2 & 0 & 0 \\ 0 & 0 & 0 & 0 & 0 & 0 & 2 & -2 \end{bmatrix} \begin{matrix} \left.\right\}R/R \\ \left.\right\}R/R \\ \left.\right\}R/4 \\ \\ \left.\right\}R/2 \\ \\ \\ \end{matrix}$$

(c) Haar Transform

FIGURE A.I.

A.2   A Pattern Recognition Experiment

PATTERN SPACE. The pattern recognition experiment consists of the traditional numeral character recognition where the number of classes is ten ($K = 10$). This particular problem was selected because of both the historical significance (this problem has been variously attacked from the heuristic, linguistic, and mathematical approaches) and because of the inherently large amount of correlation in the samples in the pattern space. The characters were hand-written and digitized according to a 12×16 ($R = 192$) raster scan of eight levels of gray for each sample or dimension in the pattern space. Figure A.2 presents typical prototypes for 3 of the 10 classes both in gray scale rendition and in computer printout form.

ROTATED SPACES. The rotated spaces used in this experiment include the Fourier, Walsh, and Haar. The Karhunen-Loève space was not computed due to the need to diagonalize a 192×192 matrix. The three "typical" prototypes are displayed in their rotated form in the three different spaces in Figure A.3. The displays are normalized to 64 positive gray levels and represent magnitudes only. Due to the limitations of photography the large dynamic range in the transform domains cannot be maintained in the displays.

FEATURE SELECTION PROCESS. The criterion for selecting pertinent dimensions or features is one of simply maintaining those features which have the largest variance across the sample means of the classes. Thus by ordering the dimensions according to their largest variance it is possible to retain a few number of features and still maintain relatively good classification accuracy. In the rotated spaces it will be found that certain dimensions vary considerably more than others thus giving greater discriminating power in fewer features. An example of this phenomenon is presented in Figure A.4 where equal a priori class statistics are assumed ($P(S_k) = 1/10$). The four plots are experimentally determined and represent the variance values of the features when ordered in monotonically decreasing fashion. Because all transformations are unitary, second order properties are preserved. This means that the area under each curve is the same. Note that only the first 100 features are plotted. It is evident that the pattern space spreads its variance energy over

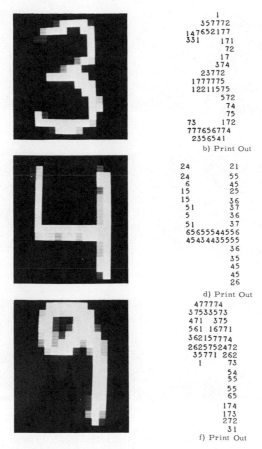

```
            1
         357772
     147652177
     331      171
              72
              17
             374
           23772
         1777775
         12211575
              572
              74
              75
     73       172
     777656774
     2356541
         b) Print Out


     24        21
     24        55
      6        45
     15        25
     15        36
     51        37
      5        36
     51        37
     65655544556
     45434435555
              36
              35
              45
              45
              26

         d) Print Out
     477774
     37533573
     471   375
     561  16771
     362157774
     2625752472
     35771  262
     1       73
             54
             55
             55
             65
            174
            173
            272
             31
         f) Print Out
```

FIGURE A.2. Typical prototypes for three classes.

many more features than the other domains, with the Haar space being next, as would be expected from the local-global structure of that transform. Both the Fourier and Walsh tend to compact the variance energy in a few number of features.

CLASSIFICATION ALGORITHM. A minimum distance classifier with respect to means is selected for illustration purposes. Such an algorithm results in linear discriminant functions (see Chapter 3). The classification procedure is to measure the distance of the unknown to each mean (in rotated space if appropriate) and select the

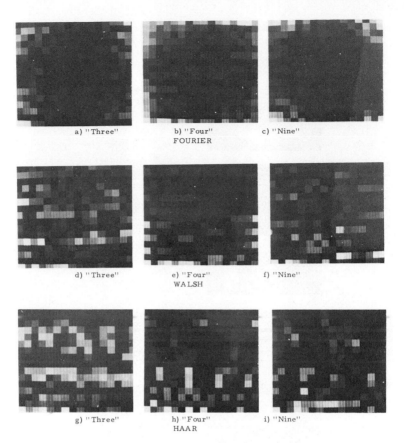

FIGURE A.3.   Typical rotated prototypes.

class to which the unknown is closest. When the distance is a Euclidean measure, the performance in all rotated spaces (unitary transforms) when retaining all features, must be identical. Again this is because such transformations preserve inner products.

COMPUTATIONAL RESULTS. The experimental results are exemplary of the fact that uncorrelated and largely varying features tend to be more efficient for classification purposes. Figure A.5 graphically displays the results of correct classification of 500 prototypes in the four spaces (pattern, Haar, Walsh, Fourier) as a function

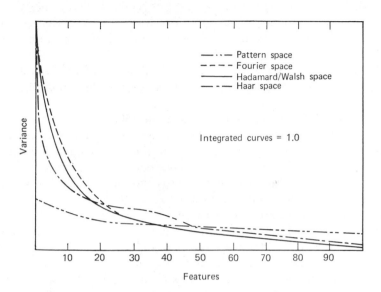

FIGURE A.4.   Variance versus features in four spaces.

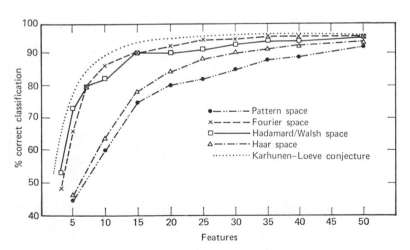

FIGURE A.5.   Correct classification versus features retained—prototypes.

of the number of largest varying features retained. This result is for testing on the training data only. The lower curve is the pattern space curve and the Haar, Walsh, and Fourier curves are all higher respectively. The Karhunen-Loève curve is conjectured to be as indicated in each space with associated misclassification error. It is evident that the Fourier space provides considerable improvement over the pattern space.

The above experiment was repeated with 500 unknowns in place of the 500 prototypes which defined the means of the classes. Again the features retained were selected according to maximum variance and again the ranking behaved somewhat similar to before. See Figure A.6. The classification error was typically 2% to 7% worse than the error on the prototypes which is as would be expected considering that the means were not defined by the unknowns. This increase in misclassification can be attributed to the classification algorithm which is admittedly rather unsophisticated. However the point to be made is one of feature selection and not classification. Each space provides 88% correct classification after 25, 35, 50, and 120 features retained for the Fourier, Walsh, Haar, and pattern spaces respectively.

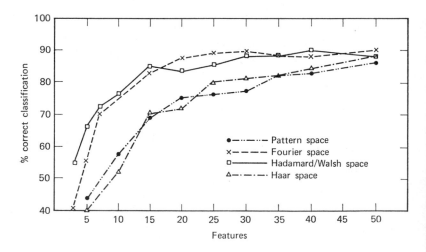

FIGURE A.6. Correct classification versus features retained—unknowns.

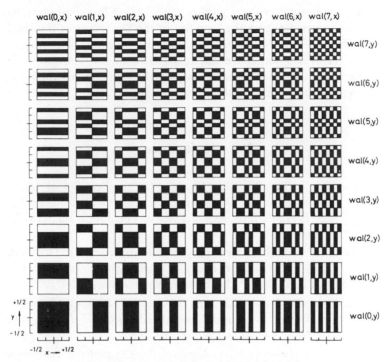

FIGURE A.7. The first 64 Walsh masks.

WALSH IMPLEMENTATION. While the Fourier space both theoretically and experimentally provides the most efficient features (of the rotations investigated here) the Walsh space is not too much poorer. Considering the number of computations saved over the FFT (only real additions versus complex arithmetic) the Walsh domain may become very appealing. Another advantage Walsh features may provide is in the use of binary masks. The Walsh basis vectors are graphically illustrated in Figure A.7.

A.3 Acknowledgments

The author is indebted to Mr. David Peasner, Group Manager of Recognition Equipment Corporation for providing the excellent set of data for this pattern recognition experiment. The computational effort was carried out on the facilities of the University of Southern California Electrical Engineering Image Processing Laboratory. Finally the Walsh masks are due to Dr. Henning F. Harmuth who so graciously provided these examples through the photographic facilities of the ITT-Electro Physics Laboratories.

A.3   References

1. Kadota, T. T., and L. A. Shepp, "On the Best Set of Linear Observables for Discriminating Two Gaussian Signals," *IEEE Trans. Information Theory*, Vol. IT-13, pp. 278–281 (April, 1967).

2. Tou, J. T., and R. P. Heydorn, "Some Approaches to Optimum Feature Extraction" *Computers and Information Sciences— II*, Ed. J. Tou, Academic Press, New York, 1967.

3. H. C. Andrews and J. Kane, "Kronecker Matrices, Computer Implementation, and Generalized Spectra," *JACM*, Vol. 17, No. 2 (April 1970), pp. 260–268.

4. H. C. Andrews and K. L. Caspari, "A Generalized Technique for Spectral Analysis," *IEEE Transactions on Computers*, Vol. C-19, No. 1 (January 1970), pp. 16–25.

5. K. S. Fu, *Sequential Methods in Pattern Recognition and Machine Learning*, Academic Press, New York, 1968, Chapter 2.

6. S. Tomita, S. Noguchi, and J. Oizumi, "On Evaluation of Handwritten Characters by Karhunen-Loève Orthonormal System," *Third Hawaii International Conference on Systems Science, Part I*, 1970, pp. 501–504.

7. G. Granlund, "Recognition of Letters with Fourier Methods," *IEEE Computer Group Repository*, R-70-98.

8. O. H. Tallman, II, Lt. Col. USAF, *The Classification of Visual Images by Spatial Filtering*, Air Force Institute of Technology, School of Engineering, dissertation, June 1969.

9. J. W. Carl, Capt., USAF, *Generalized Harmonic Analysis for Pattern Recognition: A Biologically Derived Method*, Air Force Institute of Technology, School of Engineering, thesis, August 1968.

10. P. I. P. Boulton, *Smearing Techniques in Pattern Identification*, Ph.D. dissertation, University of Toronto, 1966.

11. H. J. Bremermann, "Pattern Recognition Functionals, and Entropy," *IEEE Transactions on Bio-Medical Engineering*, July 1968, pp. 201–207.

12. W. K. Pratt, J. Kane, and H. C. Andrews, "Hadamard Transform Image Coding," *Proceedings IEEE*, Vol. 57, No. 1, January, 1969, pp. 58–68.

13. H. C. Andrews and W. K. Pratt, "Transform Data Coding," *PIB Symposium on Computer Processing in Communication*, April 1969.

14. H. C. Andrews and W. K. Pratt, "Digital Image Transform Processing," *Proceedings Symposium and Workshop Applications of Walsh Functions*, 1970.

15. W. B. Davenport, Jr., and W. L. Root, *An Introduction to the Theory of Random Signals and Noise*, McGraw-Hill, New York, 1958.

16. J. W. Cooley and J. W. Tukey, "An Algorithm for the Machine Calculation of Complex Fourier Series," *Mathematics of Computation*, Vol. 19, No. 90, pp. 297–301, 1956.

17. V. Grenander and G. Szego, *Toeplitz Forms and Their Applications*, University of California Press, Berkeley and Los Angeles, 1958.

18. H. F. Harmuth, *Transmission of Information by Orthogonal Functions*, Springer Verlag, New York, 1969.

19. H. C. Andrews, "Multidimensional Rotations in Feature Selection," *IEEE Transactions on Computers*, Vol. C-20, No. 9, pp. 1045–1051 (Sept. 1971).

APPENDIX B

A RATE DISTORTION CRITERION FOR FEATURE SELECTION

B.0 Introduction

The objective of this appendix is to outline a procedure, borrowed from Information Theoretic concepts, which effectively describes an optimal feature selection technique for subsequent classification purposes. The generality of the procedure provides optimality in concept, but specific implementation still remains to be developed. It will be necessary to divert our attention briefly to develop some information theoretic concepts which then will lead to the definition of the rate distortion function [1]. This function will then become a useful tool in evaluating feature selection techniques; and, in certain circumstances, will lead the direction in improving feature selection mechanisms.

A specific example utilizing the multidimensional rotations mentioned in Chapter 2 and developed in Appendix A will be used to illustrate the rate distortion concept. Unfortunately, for analytic reasons we will be restricted to a fidelity criterion and Gaussian statistics which are not necessarily applicable to all pattern recognition problems. However, coupled with the multidimensional rotations and Gaussian assumptions, various Gauss-Markov examples will be further investigated.

The advantage of the rate distortion approach can be simply stated as follows. Given a source of data it is desirable to encode the data as efficiently as possible and still minimize the distortion introduced by the encoding process. The fidelity criterion which describes the distortion measure is system definable, and the rate distortion function $R(D)$ provides a lower bound on the number of bits necessary to encode the source to within a distortion D. This means that one can do no better than the number of bits provided by the rate distortion function and still reconstruct the source to within the fidelity D. Traditionally, the fidelity criterion has been a mean square error estimate or other function estimating type of process typically useful for waveform analysis. However, in the context of the pattern recognition environment, if the fidelity criterion is misclassification error rate, then the rate distortion function will provide a lower bound on the dimensionality (bits) necessary to achieve a particular distortion (misclassification error). This then may provide a guide to the best feature selection possible for a given misclassification error in terms of dimensionality or bits of encoding (storage). Toward obtaining this bound, the following section investigates the rate distortion function.

B.1   The Rate Distortion Function

Probably the simplest definition of the rate distortion function is obtained from the discrete memoryless source which implies that a finite alphabet, W, is generated by the source, that successive letters of the alphabet are statistically independent, and identically distributed. Assume that there exists another finite alphabet, Z, which is used to describe what the receiver interprets the output of the source to be. A single letter fidelity criterion then becomes a matrix of non-negative entries which describe the distortion suffered, $d(w, z)$, when the receiver interprets the output of the source which is a w to be a z. The rate distortion function for such a source and fidelity criterion is defined to be the minimum mutual information taken over all conditional probability distributions such that the average distortion is less than or equal to D. Mathematically, let $p(w)$, $q(z/w)$ be the source distribution and receiver conditional distribution respectively. Then the average distortion becomes

$$d(q) = \sum_w \sum_z p(w)q(z/w) \, d(w, z) \tag{B.1}$$

Let

$$Q_D = \{q(z/w) : d(q) \leq D\} \tag{B.2}$$

and the mutual information that z gives about w with respect to the receiver statistics q is

$$I(q) = \sum_w \sum_z p(w)q(z/w) \log_2 \frac{q(z/w)}{p(z)} \tag{B.3}$$

The rate distortion function then becomes

$$R(D) = \min_{q \in Q_D} I(q) \tag{B.4}$$

and can be shown to be monotonic decreasing for increasing D, convex downward, continuous at $D = 0$, and upper bounded by the entropy of the source with equality only if $q(z/w) = \delta(z - w)$. This last property can be interpreted to mean that the entropy of the source is the rate of information production subject to zero distortion (distortionless information processing or perfect reproduction) and will always be larger (require more bits to describe) than the rate distortion function for the corresponding source.

In the light of the above definitions it seems appropriate that the source alphabet W could be descriptive of a set of prototypes $\mathbf{y}_m^{(k)}$ where each letter corresponded to a prototype of a given class. The receiver alphabet Z could represent the classification decisions S_k and the distortion measure could be related to a cost function on misclassified points. Then the rate distortion function would measure the minimum number of bits necessary to classify to within a misclassification error rate D.

The rate distortion concept has been generalized to time discrete memoryless sources [2] where

$$d(q) = \int_{-\infty}^{\infty} \int p(w)q(z/w) \, d(z, w) \, dw \, dz \tag{B.5}$$

Again let the set Q_D be defined as in equation (B.2) and the mutual information as a function of the conditional distribution q becomes

$$I(q) = \int_{-\infty}^{\infty} \int p(w)q(z/w) \log \frac{q(z/w)}{p(x)} \, dw \, dx \qquad (B.6)$$

The rate distortion function then becomes

$$R(D) = \inf_{q \in Q_D} I(q) \qquad (B.7)$$

and for the Gaussian case with a mean square error distortion measure

$$R(D) = \tfrac{1}{2}\max\left\{0, \log \frac{\sigma^2}{D}\right\} \qquad (B.8)$$

The more interesting sources are those which contain memory, and would be characteristic of vector sources describing prototypes in the pattern recognition context. Intuitively the most interesting sources which lend themselves to data compression and feature selection are those with memory because of the inherent correlation of dimensions in the transducer and pattern spaces respectively. Again restricting our attention to the single letter distortion criterion we have

$$d_n(\mathbf{w}, \mathbf{z}) = \frac{1}{n} \sum_{i=1}^{n} d(w_i, z_i) \qquad (B.9)$$

and in analogy with earlier work

$$d(q) = \int_{-\infty}^{\infty} \int p(\mathbf{w})q(\mathbf{z}/\mathbf{w}) \, d_n(\mathbf{w}, \mathbf{z}) \, d\mathbf{w} \, d\mathbf{z} \qquad (B.10)$$

Letting

$$Q_D = \{q(\mathbf{z}/\mathbf{w}) : d(q) \le D\} \qquad (B.11)$$

Then

$$I(q) = \int_{-\infty}^{\infty} \int p(\mathbf{w})q(\mathbf{z}/\mathbf{w}) \log \frac{q(\mathbf{z}/\mathbf{w})}{p(\mathbf{z})} \, d\mathbf{w} \, d\mathbf{z} \qquad (B.12)$$

and

$$R_n(D) = \frac{1}{n} \inf_{q \in Q_D} I(q) \qquad (B.13)$$

Finally the rate distortion function for such a source must be defined for all time (due to memory) and becomes

$$R(D) = \lim_{n \to \infty} R_n(D) \qquad (B.14)$$

which can be shown to always exist for stationary statistics. The exact $R(D)$ for memory sources is extremely difficult to calculate and is known for only a limited number of situations. Unfortunately most of these are related to mean square error and Gaussian distributions leaving much needed research to adapt the results to the pattern recognition field. However, in the light of the results of Appendix A it may be useful to interpret those results in the restricted Gaussian memory source mean square error context. An attempt in this direction is made in the following section.

B.2 Gaussian Statistics and Multidimensional Rotations

In the previous appendix second order statistics (covariance matrices) were rotated to new spaces defined by basis vectors comprising the rows of orthogonal matrices. Feature selection was then performed in rotated space and it was determined that considerable improvement in classification for the same number of retained features was experienced in certain spaces over others. Thus the results of that experiment indicated that the Fourier, Walsh, Haar, and original spaces provided decreasingly efficient features for classification purposes, respectively. A possible explanation for this ordering lies in a rate distortion interpretation of a basis restricted system suggested by Pearl [3]. Such a system simply requires the assumption that the features in rotated space be statistically independent even though the off-diagonal elements in the rotated covariance matrices are clearly nonzero except for the Karhunen-Loève case. The motivation for such an assumption is in the desire to use suboptimal rotations in a mean square error sense which may provide other computational or implementation advantages for feature selection. It is desired to measure how badly we suffer from the optimum by utilization of the rate distortion function as a yardstick. Under the assumption of Gaussian statistics and mean square error fidelity D, the rate distortion function for a single Gaussian source with variance σ^2 was given by equation (B.8).

For an N-vector source with correlated components, the optimum rate is obtained by first decorrelating the source using the Karhunen-Loève transform and obtaining the eigenvalues $\lambda_k^{(w)}$, and then distributing a total distortion D among the N independent sources in such a way that the total rate per sample

$$R_w(D) = \frac{1}{2N}\sum_{k=1}^{N}\max\left\{0, \log\frac{\lambda_k^{(w)}}{D_k}\right\} \tag{B.15a}$$

be minimized, subject to

$$D = \frac{1}{N}\sum_{k=1}^{N}D_k \qquad D_k \geq 0 \tag{B.15b}$$

The solution to this minimization problem is given parametrically and yields the rate

$$R_w(D) = \frac{1}{2N}\sum_{k=1}^{N}\max\left\{0, \log\frac{\lambda_k^{(w)}}{\theta}\right\} \tag{B.16a}$$

where θ is a parameter satisfying

$$D(\theta) = \frac{1}{N}\sum_{k=1}^{N}\min(\theta, \lambda_k^{(w)}) \tag{B.16b}$$

In attempting to employ the rate distortion function for assessing the feature selection efficiency of the process $z = [A]w$ where $[A]$ is unitary, one faces the problem that since

$$\lambda_k^{(z)} = \lambda_k^{(w)} \qquad k = 1, 2, \ldots \tag{B.17}$$

the processes w and z possess the same rate-distortion function. Equations (B.16), therefore, provide no information on the degree of correlation reduction caused by the transform $[A]$. To extract such information one must resort to the basis-restricted structure of Pearl which forces the a priori assumption that only the diagonal elements of $[\Phi_A]$ are available as features. We are again faced with the problem of optimally distributing the distortion components D_k among the N correlated sources z_k in such a way that the total rate per sample be minimized, subject to fixed total distortion D. Due to a priori restrictions no cross-terms appear in the distortion measure, and therefore, there is no way one can utilize knowledge of correlation among the z_k's to reduce D. Thus the optimal encoder is constructed by regarding each z_k as independent, and applying the "water-filling" procedure of equation (B.16) to the set $\{\phi_A(k, k)\}$. Consequently, the optimal Basis-Restricted rate distortion function for the process z is given by

$$R_z(D) = \frac{1}{2N}\sum_{k=1}^{N} \max\left\{0, \log \frac{\phi_A(k, k)}{\theta}\right\} \qquad \text{(B.18a)}$$

$$D(\theta) = \frac{1}{N}\sum_{k=1}^{N}\min[\theta, \phi_A(k, k)] \qquad \text{(B.18b)}$$

which provides the desired performance measure on the coding efficiency of the transform A. It is important to mention that for equation (B.18) to be a true rate distortion measure, consecutive blocks of N vectors must be considered to be independent. Possibly the significance of the results of equation (B.18) is the algebraic similarity to the known rate for the Gaussian source given by equation (B.16).

It is conjectured that Basis-Restricted encoding of stationary sources for feature selection would result in rates which behave as

$$R_{K\text{-}L}(D) < R_F(D) < R_W(D) < R_H(D) < R_I(D) \qquad \text{(B.19)}$$

where the subscripts imply the domain in which feature selection actually occurs (K-L = Karhunen-Loève; F = Fourier; W = Walsh/Hadamard; H = Haar; I = Identify.) However it is emphasized that these rates are interpretable as lower bounds to the feature selection coding if indeed feature selection is based on a Gaussian distribution mean square error distortion. It is interesting that the conjecture of equation (B.19) and the experimental results of the following section both tend to substantiate the results of Appendix A in the effectiveness of various transforms for the feature selection process. The above conjecture is based upon the intuitive feel that the remaining correlation in the off-diagonal elements of the rotated covariance matrices is increasingly important in going from left to right in equation (B.19). Stated differently the more uncorrelated the coefficients, the more effective the feature for selection purposes.

B.3   A Gauss-Markov Example

To further substantiate the suggestions made in the previous section a computer calculation of the rates given by equation (B.18) for a first order Gaussian-Markov source was performed. Such a source has memory or correlation and covariance matrix given by

$$[\Phi_G] = [\rho^{|r-s|}] \qquad 0 < \rho < 1 \qquad (B.20)$$

where r and s index the rows and columns. Figure B.1 shows the experimental case for $\rho = .95$ and the dimension of the covariance matrix, $N = 256$. For all distortions calculated, the conjectured inequalities hold with the Fourier and Karhunen-Loève being very close. The Walsh and Haar rates are identical to within the second decimal point, both requiring additional coding bits over the Fourier for all distortions. While the increase in rate necessary using the Fourier, Walsh, and Haar transforms appears minor, the identity transform (or no transform) gives a markedly poorer performance. Qualitatively, this phenomenon can be interpreted in the

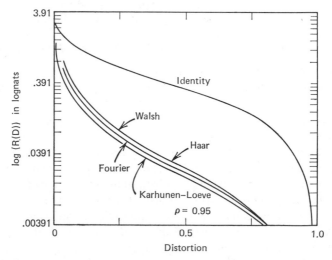

FIGURE B.1.   Rate distortion for various transforms for first order Gauss-Markov process ($\rho = .95$, $N = 256$).

following way: the identity transform leaves all correlation remaining in the process. The other transforms, while not totally uncorrelating the data, tend in that direction, resulting in much smaller rates than simply coding the original process as if it were comprised of statistically uncorrelated samples.

A brief comment on the results of the figure warrant stating. From these results it appears that the Haar and Walsh transforms are equivalent in their effect at uncorrelating first order Gauss-Markov data. This is indeed the case because such a process is defined by adjacent correlation which is what the Haar transform concentrates $N/2$ coefficients measuring. Possibly the choice of example was poor in illustrating the conjecture of equation (B.19). A second order Gaussian-Markov process with adjacent correlation zero provides a somewhat better example. Its covariance matrix is given by

$$[\Phi_G] = \left[\frac{1 + (-1)^{|r-s|}}{2} \rho^{|r-s|/2}\right] \qquad 0 < \rho < 1 \qquad (B.21)$$

where again r and s index the rows and columns. This matrix is similar to that of equation (B.20) except every other diagonal row

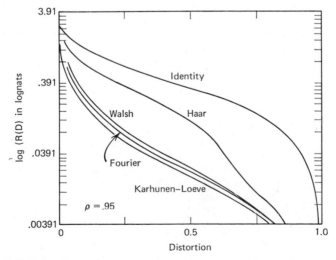

FIGURE B.2.   Rate distortion for various transforms for a second order Gauss-Markov process ($\rho = .95$, $N = 256$).

is zero. The results of the previous simulation on this process are presented in Figure B.2 in which it becomes quite obvious that the Walsh transform tends to uncorrelate the process much more than does the Haar transform. These results are in close agreement with the experimental results of the previous appendix.

B.4 References

1. Andrews, H. C., "Bibliography on Rate Distortion Theory," *IEEE Trans. on Information Theory*, vol. IT-17, no. 2, pp. 198–199 (March, 1971).

2. Berger, T., *Rate Distortion Theory: A Mathematical Basis for Data Compression*, Prentice-Hall, Englewood Cliffs, N.J., 1971.

3. Pearl, J., "Basis Restricted Transformations and Performance Measures for Spectral Representations," *Proc. of the Fourth Hawaii International Conference on System Sciences*, pp. 321–323 (January, 1971).

AUTHOR INDEX

SUBJECT INDEX